# How to Run a Magazine in this Digital Age

# How to Launch a Magazine in this Digital Age

**MARY HOGARTH, EDITED BY JOHN JENKINS**

BLOOMSBURY

NEW YORK · LONDON · NEW DELHI · SYDNEY

**Bloomsbury Academic**

An imprint of Bloomsbury Publishing Inc

1385 Broadway
New York
NY 10018
USA

50 Bedford Square
London
WC1B 3DP
UK

**www.bloomsbury.com**

**Bloomsbury is a registered trade mark of Bloomsbury Publishing Plc**

First published 2014

**Library of Congress Cataloging-in-Publication Data**

A catalog record for this book is available from the Library of Congress

ISBN: HB: 978-1-4411-6190-1
PB: 978-1-4411-7799-5
ePDF: 978-1-4411-4859-9
ePub: 978-1-4411-1109-8

Typeset by RefineCatch Limited, Bungay, Suffolk, UK
Printed and bound in the United States of America

# Contents

# Acknowledgements

My thanks to all the extremely busy people who have generously shared their experience and knowledge of the magazine industry.

There are many things in this book I wish I had known when I first started out, the most important lesson is perhaps to listen.

A good mentor is priceless. Most of all I would like to thank my former boss John Jenkins, for his encouragement and editing.

Finally I would like to thank Katie Gallof at Bloomsbury for her continued support and patience.

# Introduction

This book is written for those of you who have a brilliant idea for a new magazine – whether it's a business venture, charity initiative, student project or an idea that evolved (as many do) at your kitchen table. Whatever your reason, this book has the inside knowledge and necessary tools to help you turn your idea into a reality, while guiding you through the highs and the lows. Publishing is a complex business with many facets to grasp along the way. Unfortunately, until now, finding a UK publication that covered the whole process, including magazine business plans, was virtually impossible.

As a former managing editor and now a magazine consultant I have been involved in the launch of four magazines – two have succeeded, one failed and the other didn't get past the development stage. However, all four provided valuable lessons. You can never do enough research and don't ignore feedback.

As a magazine tutor at Southampton Solent University I have also seen numerous ideas from students – some good, some bad and even a few ugly ones. Many are of course reflections of the current market such as the standard football and lifestyle titles. Many lack imagination and sustainability.

Occasionally students come up with rare innovative concepts, which have caught the attention of high profile industry figures. Such gems have been submitted to the annual Magazine Academy Awards organized by the Periodical Training Council – a training body that accredits magazine journalism courses at universities and colleges nationwide.

Good ideas are not restricted to students. There are many people who come up with brilliant products, but then fail because they do not have sufficient knowledge of their market or the necessary business acumen. Unless you have an understanding of the publishing business, know the pitfalls and costs involved at the start, it is likely your magazine will not be in print to mark its first birthday.

You will also have a considerable advantage if you are a specialist in one of the key areas: editorial, production, advertising sales or circulation. An aptitude for marketing and financial management, which is not difficult to acquire, is essential.

# Who is this book for?

It is for anyone. Whether you are a student developing a title for an assessment brief, an editor with a brilliant idea or if you have tried to start a magazine and failed, but want to start again – this book will help put you on the road to success.

With actual case studies – together with advice from top industry professionals, *How To Launch a Magazine in this Digital Age* seeks to guide you through the pitfalls of publishing. It will also give you the tools and inside knowledge to increase your chances of success.

# Do you have what it takes?

Some successful titles have been started from small beginnings and made their owners fortunes. Entrepreneur, publisher and poet, Felix Dennis, who was imprisoned in 1971 as co-editor of *OZ* magazine for conspiring to corrupt public morals (Greenstreet, 2010), went on to start his own magazine publishing company in 1973. Titles in the Felix Dennis Publishing portfolio now include *The Week*, *Auto Express*, *Maxim*, *Viz*, *Computer Shopper*, *Monkey* and *Evo*. The annual *Sunday Times Rich List* estimates that Felix Dennis is the 88th richest individual in the UK.

Why was he so successful? He knew what his audience wanted and built his titles around that focus. Of course he had business acumen too. Today there are so many resources for starting your own business. You must have a basic understanding of how to budget and know the difference between profit and loss.

A new title's potential to succeed is mostly dependent on the publisher's ability to identify a gap in the market. That means meticulous research of the target audience, then successfully applying that data to form a strong business plan. Also a sound business plan is vital as it provides a map for where you want to go and how to get there. Your publication won't survive without one. Sufficient start-up funds should not be under estimated whether partly self-funded, from private investors or bank loans, or, as in most cases, a combination of all three.

# What makes a magazine successful?

There are several factors. But initially it is a great idea that taps into a niche market. An idea for another lifestyle magazine is unlikely to work because the market is already saturated with such titles owned by large corporations with huge resources.

First work out how original your idea is before investing time and energy to take it forward. If there are no similar titles, check why – perhaps some have failed because it is an unsustainable market. Alternatively, if only one or two rivals are in circulation this can often indicate potential – can your magazine offer a unique selling point (USP) that the others can't? Whatever the case, research is essential. Not only must you know everything about your audience, but your rivals too. Neglect the latter at your peril!

## How to use this text

Use this book as a resource. It is set out in sequence to take you from the initial concept to launching your first issue. Resources include case studies and advice from industry experts to help you along the way. At the end of each chapter you will find an action plan designed to help you put into practice what you have learned. Tempting as it might be, do not skip these exercises because without them you may not get the full benefit.

At the end of the book there is a 'useful contacts' section to get you started.

## Online tools

Although the book contains everything you need to know about magazine publishing www.magazineexpert.org has been set up as an online learning interactive tool. You will be able to post questions, as well as have access to a variety of resources. There are also useful links to distributors, printers and other essential industry contacts.

The site also contains blogs from a variety of contributors looking at current magazine trends, the future of publishing and other related issues. But do remember the website is designed to work in conjunction with this book not in place of it.

# 1

# A gap in the market

**Y**ou have a great idea for a new magazine. Excited, you are eager to draft out the design. But before getting carried away on the fun part – content and design – it is crucial to do extensive research on competitors, the market and the sustainability of your idea, before developing an initial overview of your title. First, check out the direct and indirect competition; this will tell you if your concept is feasible. Are there are any publications in this genre? If so, how many?

If there are more than three, it is likely the market could become saturated with the introduction of another title. Fewer than three indicates there is room for an additional magazine. However, if no titles exist there is probably a good reason – the idea could prove unsustainable, in which case you need to proceed with caution. You must consider two aspects:

- What is your maximum and minimum market share for readers?

- How much is the total advertising press spend in terms of potential revenue gain, or do you have to create the demand?

According to the Professional Publisher's Association (PPA), the number of new titles launched hit a low spot in the first half of 2010. Just 24 new magazines emerged on the news-stands – a sharp contrast to 2008 when 143 publications were launched. Despite the downturn in trading, new title launches have slowly increased with the latest figures showing 69 new magazines in the second half of 2011 (PPA, 2013). Yet market growth is slow as these statistics demonstrate, therefore it is crucial to undertake substantial research before developing any media product. Audiences, distribution, potential revenue streams and long-term sustainability are crucial factors. Remember ideas need substance.

This chapter will take you through the stages to ascertain if your idea is achievable and sustainable, before moving on to the business of publishing. In-depth research is essential in the early stages as it can prevent a costly mistake. Producing a pilot issue – only to be told by the distributors that your magazine won't work so they won't be taking it on – is a waste of time and money.

Getting to the end of that first year with poor sales figures and the bank about to foreclose is also a scenario that can be avoided with diligent financial planning. Having an idea is one thing, but in business this must be backed up by sufficient data to prove your magazine will be financially viable. This is vital if you want to convince a bank, finance director or a business angel to back you.

# What's your idea?

Magazines are about information and entertainment. This formula has always been – and continues to be – the key to successful publishing. Early magazines such as *The Ladies Mercury* published in 1693 by John Dunton and *The Gentleman's Magazine* published by Edward Cave in 1731 captured their readers by focusing on content that mattered. Today, market leaders include celebrity gossip magazines and specialized publications. Thus two of the golden rules of publishing are: know your reader and be topical.

Why should a reader spend money and time on your magazine? The answer should be because he or she needs part or all of its content. Tap into a consumer need and it is likely the magazine will succeed.

---

## CASE STUDY

A group of third year degree students at Southampton Solent University, taking a unit on magazine publishing, came up with an idea for a swimming title. Their magazine, aptly named *Deep End*, was aimed at those who swam competitively or were working towards competing in the sport. It hit the right note. It was right on trend following the Olympics and a TV series about freshwater swimming. Moreover, their initial research revealed a gap in the UK market.

The group worked on a plan to develop *Deep End* as a specialist monthly title. Their unique selling point (USP) was to provide a detailed insight into what is fast becoming a popular worldwide sport. *Deep End*'s editorial pillars would focus on how to improve swimming ability with advice on nutrition and fitness, expert opinions and interviews with professional athletes. News from the swimming world would also feature to ensure that *Deep End* readers were always in the know. The aim was to make *Deep End* essential reading for swimmers.

Once developed, the group's concept package – which consisted of a business plan, pilot issue and media kit – was entered into the 2012 Periodical Training Council's Magazine Academy Awards, in the best new magazine concept category.

There are only two placements – the winner and highly commended. *Deep End* was highly commended, a considerable achievement considering the competition.

Jack Johnson, the group's project manager reveals how he, Greg Lott and Adam Flinn came up with the concept.

After extensive market research into various types of magazines, ranging from sport to business, we decided to use our strengths and focus on an area where we knew we could use our own knowledge to the best effect. This was in the area of exercise and sport, and having scanned the shelves of various newsagents, and searched publishing and magazine outlet websites, we discovered the lack of an off-the-shelf swimming magazine. Therefore, we decided to look into how we could make this magazine the most effective and how we could attract what is such a wide audience.

My colleague, Greg Lott, used to be an athlete and reads> *Runner's World,* whereas I play tennis at club level and read *Tennishead.* Both these titles provide advice on how to improve as a runner or a tennis player. After lengthy discussions, we decided that this was what we wanted *Deep End* to be – a magazine to provide swimmers with a range of topics that educate and entertain.

We undertook both rival analysis and reader surveys for our product research. While there was a lack of off-the-shelf swimming magazines in the UK, we researched online and subscription-based competitors. Therefore, we downloaded and bought *Swimming Times, Aqua Zone* and *H2Open,* carefully analysing each magazine to see what they offered and what we could do differently. The only off-the-shelf magazine out of these three was *H2Open,* but this was solely based around open water swimming, whereas we wanted to aim our publication at a wider audience – both open and pool.

Our audience research consisted of a reader survey. We asked 40 people, via social media and face-to-face, various questions, including: how much swimming experience they have, whether the proposed magazine concept would be something that interested them and whether they had ever bought a swimming magazine.

What made our magazine viable?

I believe it is viable for two reasons. First, The *Daily Telegraph* revealed in 2010 that 3.6 million people were regularly swimming, while The Leisure Database Company reported that 84 per cent of the UK's population lives within two miles of a swimming pool. This proves that swimming is popular, accessible and an enjoyable sport.

Secondly, I believe that our magazine is current. The London 2012 Olympic Games proved how popular swimming is in this country and the event was one of the first to sell out. Rebecca Adlington, Ellie Simmonds, Keri-Anne Payne and Liam Tancock have become household names who are now inspiring a nation to be active.

When people become active they strive to improve and our magazine helps people to do exactly that.

# Defining the sector

An idea must be defined in terms of where it might fit in the news-stands. The first step is to think about the genre – sport, lifestyle, specialists, travel and food for example, then consider where it will fit. What about positioning on the news-stands?

There are numerous categories with many crossovers. As the number of magazines increases, the market has segmented into sectors with mass circulation and numerous specialist or niche titles. It is crucial to identify a magazine's genre as well as the sector. The five core categories are:

- **Consumer:** Covers mainstream lifestyle magazines. This category can be confusing as it encompasses many titles, which can also be classed as specialist titles, such as health and fitness, interior home and food magazines. At present this sector is vast and oversubscribed. There is much competition, with many of the big publishing houses – Bauer Media and IPC, which have tremendous resources – competing against each other for readers.
  **Development potential:** Proceed with caution. It is difficult to create an original product when there are so few gaps.

- **B2B (business to business):** Specialist knowledge, specific to a business sector. This is a rapidly growing market. Business owners, professionals and graduates want – and will pay for – specialist knowledge to get ahead of their game, no matter what their profession – from tradesman, retailers and publicans to lawyers, architects and bankers.
  **Development potential:** A growing market, this category has considerable potential for development.

- **Specialist:** This section relates to hobbies, crafts, sports and any subject that requires specialist knowledge such as bee-keeping or family history. Again it has the potential for growth, but the danger for any niche title is the ability to attract a sufficient volume of readers to make it sustainable.
  **Development potential:** Could soon be saturated. If your idea falls into this category you must ensure you can obtain a sufficient market share.

- **Customer publishing:** This is an opportunity for businesses to reach out to customers by producing a magazine specifically for them. Also known as **B2C** (business to consumer) this sector has seen a rapid growth as major businesses and charities such as Virgin Media, M&S,

BMW, The RSPB, The Writers' Guild, Tesco and ASOS.com have developed strong titles. Key examples here are *Healthy* from Boots, *Dare* at Superdrug, *The National Trust Magazine* and *Money Sense* from NatWest.

**Development potential:** A growth area, with supermarket magazines currently achieving the highest circulation figures with Asda topping the chart at nearly two million per issue. Why opt for customer publishing? It has been proven to build brand loyalty and is another way for businesses to develop their client base. It also poses little financial risk to the publisher.

- **Localized:** These magazines are area specific – whether it is state, county or city/town. During the past few years, the UK publishing group, Archant, have taken on numerous county magazines as more readers want news that relates directly to them and where they live. Achieving a high volume of sales is difficult as there are so many free local titles.
  **Development potential:** With the emphasis on local communities this is another area of growth. A controlled, high volume of distribution to desirable selected postcodes are likely to attract a high volume of advertising sales.

Getting the genre right is essential. Defining the sector can be more difficult as some titles can fall between two areas. B2B often includes specialist titles. Ensure your concept has a clear identity, one that can be easily categorized enabling potential readers to find the title easily. However, there is inevitably some crossover and many subcategories. Your magazine must fit into one of the main sectors and its genre needs to be clearly defined.

# Testing sustainability

Crashing after a few weeks following research is much better than being rejected by a potential distributor, or worse – not selling once on the news-stands. This is why, before investing serious money into developing a magazine, it is essential to first prove the title will be sustainable in the long term. A good test used by some publishers is to answer three questions:

1 **Why this** – looks at the gap in the market. How wide is it? Are there already too many titles or is there room for expansion? This helps a publisher identify a target audience; then ask: what is different about this title?

2  **Why us** – is used to consider what experience a publisher can bring to the new title, such as specialist knowledge of the subject. Also whether there is a synergy with other titles in the publisher's stable. A publisher keeping to a particular sector can strengthen their business, as they become experts in their particular field. For example, William Reed Business Media concentrates on the B2B market, while Future PLC specializes in five categories – technology, entertainment and video games, sport and auto, music and creative titles.

One of the reasons for its success is that Future keeps to its core business strategy, even if this means culling titles. In November 2012, Future closed three titles *Xbox World*, *PSM3* and *PlayStation*. Future's head of entertainment, Clair Porteous, justified the closures, citing the company's digital strategy, stating: 'This decision has been taken as Future continues to focus on its strategy of accelerating digital growth across its international digitally-focussed brand business' (Press Gazette, 14 Nov 2012).

3  **Why now** – this aspect considers trends, timing of the launch and potential rivals. The first consideration is does the magazine fit with current or new trends? And if so, will it be sustainable? A new magazine on self-publishing might have more impact if launched during the literary festival season around October. Launching at this time, the publisher may be able to achieve extra publicity by collaborating with one of the festivals. Rival publications must also be taken into account. It is always prudent to anticipate a rival publisher's reaction to a new title.

Set out your three priorities carefully. This task requires research to pinpoint these accurately before further steps can be taken. Don't rush this process. Accuracy now will help with the title's development. Mistakes could be costly.

Once these have been determined, think about long-term viability. Consider how the publishing market has evolved in the past ten years. Publishers no longer just print their content in magazines. Today they produce content across several platforms – digital, online and in social media. Don't forget about TV magazines, where magazine content is broadcast as a series of slide show stills accompanied by a voiceover. They are often shown on screens in hairdressers or garage waiting rooms, while content is more of an advertising vehicle than serious editorial these still present a publishing option. This could be a brand extension if your magazine relates to a specialized subject where merchandize or skills are sold, such as a garage waiting room, doctor's surgery, or perhaps even a retail outlet.

This market has grown phenomenally – and as technology evolves, it continues to expand. A publisher needs to be ahead of the game. A new title must evolve. Thus, when developing a new concept, gauge the zeitgeist. Focusing on how a magazine will work in five years' time is crucial to its future.

# Checking out the competition

A lack of original ideas is usually is the first stumbling block of any would-be publisher. With more than 4,000 consumer titles currently on sale in the UK (BRAD, 2012), it is unlikely that your idea is unique. Odds are it will have been thought of – if not launched – by another publisher, and if so that title may or may not have been successful. If successful, similar magazines would have soon followed, as the first title would have established a market need. But if not, it is likely that the audience was insufficient to sustain it.

Bear in mind that a title insufficiently profitable for a major company could well be worthwhile for a small independent publisher. For example, some years ago IPC closed a magazine on Wild West culture (circulation 47,000) and *Companions* (circulation 200,000). Both would have delighted a smaller outfit.

When developing a magazine concept, compiling a detailed list of competitors is crucial. Include direct rivals as well as those on the periphery. Start with BRAD. If you don't have access to BRAD, search all magazine publishers, this should reveal publications which are either direct rivals or likely to produce some similar content. Also check the trade press, this can yield information on forthcoming titles. Are there any stories on a similar launch? Forewarned is forearmed. Finally, a morning spent searching the news-stand in a large newsagent will also be beneficial.

Once potential rivals have been identified, copies of the publications – both print and digital – must be purchased. Ideally obtain six months' worth of back issues to build an accurate picture of editorial and advertising content. Each rival must be costed to calculate potential spend and revenue, its content must also be closely studied.

Evaluate the following points:

- **Brand identity:** How does the title look – is it glossy, perfect bound or saddle-stitched?

- **Editorial content:** First look at the contents page(s). How are cover stories signposted? Can you identify the editorial pillars? How many regular slots does the magazine contain? Next, what about features? Look at the length, style and focus. Analyse how closely these fit with the title's online/digital copies. Are readers directed to additional content on other platforms?

- **Circulation/readership:** Evaluate the circulation figures for the past year. How do these compare? Is there an increase or decrease in sales? Can you identify any spikes in sales for specific issues? Who is the magazine targeting as its core readers?

- **Advertising sales:** Analysing adverts will give you an idea of the revenue. Rates can be found in a magazine's media pack or on BRAD. Identify the advertising/editorial ratio and consider how closely the advertisements align with the genre and content. Next, evaluate the advertisements. How many pages of adverts, including the covers, does the magazine contain? Are some big brand names? If you have a few issues of the magazine, look for regular advertisers and note how often they advertise. Is it obvious how may advertisers have booked a series, for example? Next, look at the smaller advertisements, and what about classifieds? Don't forget the digital issue – how interactive are the adverts? And – if so – how much more does this cost the advertiser?
  Always remember that page yield will be lower than rate card/media pack prices, sometimes less than half.

- **Publisher's promotion strategies:** How much in-house promotion does the magazine contain for brand extensions, future issues or subscription sales? Also, when buying the magazine – take note of its position on the news-stand. Was it in a PoS (point of sale) display? For digital editions, examine where the magazine falls in its category. Did it appear among the first five titles during a search?

- **Platforms:** Scrutinize how far the title extends. Does it have online radio and TV extensions, such as *Q Magazine* published by Bauer Media? What about apps and the title's website?

Do try to obtain an advertising media pack (aka rate card or, more recently, media kit) for each magazine. This will provide a wealth of information on readers, print, digital and online rates, advertisers, circulation and brand identity.

## The value of a brand eye

For those who haven't heard of a brand eye, it is a technique used by some publishing houses to assess the market as well as the positioning of potential rivals. It defines the category, parameters and market positioning. The example shown in Figure 1.1, denotes a monthly, UK writing magazine aimed at

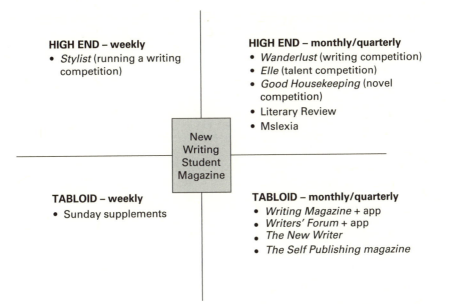

**HIGH END – weekly**
- *Stylist* (running a writing competition)

**HIGH END – monthly/quarterly**
- *Wanderlust* (writing competition)
- *Elle* (talent competition)
- *Good Housekeeping* (novel competition)
- Literary Review
- Mslexia

New Writing Student Magazine

**TABLOID – weekly**
- Sunday supplements

**TABLOID – monthly/quarterly**
- *Writing Magazine* + app
- *Writers' Forum* + app
- *The New Writer*
- *The Self Publishing magazine*

**Figure 1.1** *Sample Brand Eye*

students and young writers aged 18–30. The new concept sits on the axis while rival publications are plotted around it as shown in the example below, which features a new concept for a writing magazine.

This brand eye demonstrates the current market positioning, showing the nearest competitors (nearest to the concept) and those on the peripheral. In-depth market analysis is crucial. Do not be tempted to skimp on this research. Include all competitions such as subscription-only titles and apps. Also, any publications that feature sections or competitions on the genre must be plotted to produce a clear idea of how saturated the market is with titles on writing.

On the peripheries in this brand eye are *Stylist, Good Housekeeping, Wanderlust, Elle* and Sunday supplements. Further research revealed that *Stylist* and *Good Housekeeping* had a stronger connection to the genre than the other titles.

*Stylist* ran a major crime fiction competition with reciprocal partners Faber and Faber to find and publish a debut crime writer. While *Good Housekeeping* periodically runs a section on how to write along side a short story or novel writing competition. Further investigation showed that in January 2012 *Good Housekeeping* teamed up with Orion books for a novel writing competition offering a first prize of a publishing deal with an advance of £25,000.

This competition tactic taps into the readers' needs as more budding authors emerge following the rise of self-publishing. Both *Stylist* and *Good*

*Housekeeping* saw and acted upon an opportunity to tap into this market. This demonstrates that by extending their brand to cover this genre, the titles have the potential to increase their circulation and therefore revenue. Remember that supply equals demand.

Another growing consumer need is apps, which should be investigated with rigor. Study how many apps your competitors have and their content. Don't forget to check rivals in English speaking markets. Look at similar or identical titles in America, New Zealand and Australasia as they can often be a source of inspiration when it comes to readers and content.

# Developing an overview

Having gathered data on all potential rival titles, the next stage is to build an initial overview of the concept. Do this before investing or sourcing the funds needed to develop the product. This point marks the start of the process to turn a concept into a magazine. Think about:

- **Audiences:** who will read your magazine?
- **Circulation:** your initial print run.
- **Frequency**: how often you will publish – bimonthly, monthly, weekly.
- **Cover price:** cost to the reader.
- **Distribution methods:** subscription and news-stand, direct or targeted?

Who will read the magazine, how often and where will it be published? When considering distribution, do not forget to consider non-traditional outlets for sales.

Publication frequency has also evolved in this age of technology. Before the Internet many publishers would begin with a quarterly title with a view to increasing production to bimonthly, then monthly. Following the rapid advances in technology, audiences' expectations are high. Many of today's readers want 24-hour news, social media and digital media products for their phones or tablets. Many readers are no longer content to wait three months for the next issue. As a new publisher you should consider this.

Although monthly titles are popular, in recent years there has been a growth in weeklies with the emergence of gossip magazines such as *Hello, OK, Now, Reveal* and *Closer*. However, sales seem to have reached a plateau.

Interestingly, the *Press Gazette* revealed that in the first half of 2012 free supermarket magazines and TV listing titles dominated the top ten magazine sales. At the top was Asda, which achieved a circulation of nearly two million.

Number four on the list was *Take a Break*, which achieved a circulation of 786,849, although down 2.1 per cent on the previous year; while in at number five was *Saga* with a circulation of up to 632,217, an increase of 2.4 per cent, but not all paid for at the full rate.

However, one of the best performers of the year was *Style at Home*, which doubled its circulation, perhaps reflecting the trend of improving rather than moving. Among the worst performers of the year were *Pregnancy & Birth* –38.6 per cent, *More* –37.6 per cent, *Doctor Who Adventures Magazine* –36.2 per cent, *Reader's Digest* –35.5 per cent and *Women's Fitness* –25 per cent (Press Gazette, 16 Aug 2012).

Whether you choose to publish monthly, biweekly or weekly you must create a need in your readers. To keep pace with consumers, a publisher must also deliver fresh content online on a daily basis, as well as producing an interactive digital edition.

# Summary

While the basic framework for developing a magazine concept has been outlined in this chapter, key questions every publisher should ask at the concept stage have also been bought to the fore. We have also looked at the history of magazines, the volume of today's stock and how many new launches fail within the first two years.

Surviving in such a tough economic climate requires an outstanding concept. Any new concept must identify its market. All potential rivals must be methodically analysed and a gap in the market must be measured.

Fail to do this and the title is likely to be rejected as soon as it is presented to a market distributor or retail buyer. An expert eye will spot if a product is too similar in content to a rival publication.

Research should continue to be ongoing once the magazine is established. A publisher must keep track of the audience's buying, reading and browsing habits. Measuring digital usage, web and social media traffic can be time consuming. However, the technology now exists to make this a much easier and more economical task. Recent developments include Adobe's Marketing Cloud to make the task easier. Using the Marketing Cloud, data researchers can access a complete set of analytics – social, advertising, target and web experience management – from one place. It will help publishers use data on web and social media more effectively for their print, digital and online audience.

Having read the chapter, use the tools covered to identify a gap in the market. Decide on the title's market positioning by defining the sector and category, then make sense of the data gleaned from your research.

The action plan at the end of this chapter has been designed to guide you through the initial stages of developing an idea. Each stage must be completed to assess whether your idea has the potential to be developed: focusing on the three priorities (why this, why us, why now) will test the feasibility of your idea. But for your idea to work there must be a suitable gap in the market.

What should you do if the market is saturated? Abandon the concept altogether before investing a substantial amount of cash. Of course, there is an exception to every rule, but would you be willing to bet £60,000? Because that is the approximate cost of setting up and launching a small magazine on the news-stands.

Remember all of these stages are vital. Neglect these at your peril.

# INDUSTRY INPUT

**Bill Dunn, now editor-in-chief at Redwood Publishing, has worked for some of the biggest names in publishing including John Brown, Dennis Publishing, Condé Nast and The National Magazine Company. Having been involved in numerous launches, he shares his experiences – both good and bad – of the process.**

**Figure 1.2** *Bill Dunn*

*Developing any new title is about gaining experience and learning from that. One of my early ideas (an idea my wife, Katy, and I had) was a title that was to be comprised totally of lists, aimed at a sophisticated male/female audience. After showing it around a few companies, we settled on Dennis Publishing, who liked the idea and had the vision to let us explore it. We worked with Ash Gibson (ex-GQ and* Men's Health *designer) to produce a dummy.*

*Then we started trying to position it. We went to a newsagent off Oxford Street near Dennis's offices, and tried to figure out where it would sit, even putting the dummy on the shelves. This is a valuable exercise if you can find a big enough newsagent, and I really recommend it. Turned out it didn't really fit anywhere. So Dennis started trying to get us to turn it into a men's mag. We didn't want to do this (especially as I'd just spent nine years working in this segment) so we turned them down.*

*We really believed there was a market for an intelligent, listy, unisex title. They really believed it should be a lad's mag. And all the evidence shows that they were right – because a year later* Shortlist *was created (not by Dennis) and did fantastically well. Shows what we know! The lesson is, always work out your audience first. This is crucial. Next decide objectively if the idea is any good.*

*My advice is to undertake as much research as you can before you start to develop a magazine. It's a bit like painting a wall at home – the majority of work is in the preparation of the wall, and even when every part of your brain is crying out to start painting, you've still got to keep sanding away. With magazine launches, 70 per cent is the research (or sanding) – is there a market out there? Only 30 per cent is in the painting, i.e. actually developing the magazine.*

*Audience research can be difficult and vexing. I've been in focus groups where the audience is behind a glass wall reading your mag. It's usually a bit of an eye-opener. I remember one I sat on for GQ where they really believed the adverts were part of the editorial. And they were meant to be ABC1 readers (i.e. quite clever). I had to restrain myself from breaking the glass and ramming the things I'd written in their faces. I had an old editor who said that magazines were too important to be judged by amateurs (focus groups) and a bit of me is still arrogant enough to believe that.*

*Even if you can't afford organized focus groups, you can do all sorts – show it to friends, people in the street, anyone who might conceivably like this title. Obviously if you're doing a high fashion title there's probably no point in showing it to your plumber. But you never know – you might have a stylish plumber. The main thing, when you've been thinking about a magazine idea for seven days a week for a few months, is to get other people to look at it objectively. Because you may well have completely lost the plot.*

*Defining a new title's genre/category on the news-stand can be a problem, particularly if it appears to be between two sectors. If this happens, choose the bigger sector then stick with it. Avoid market saturation. Although there are no hard and fast rules to define if a genre or category is saturated, it's usually obvious. Anyone with an idea for a men's magazine up their sleeve right now had better look carefully at what makes it special. Even something unique has no guarantee of survival. The Word was a unique – and I think wonderful – title, and even that's died. It's tough out there. My most successful publication launch was Volvo Cars' customer magazine, which has now been rebranded as LIV.*

*What is my advice on developing a new magazine? You get a real tingle when you get a really good, innovative idea. Trust that tingle. It's probably right. But if the editor becomes bored with the concept then it's time to start again.*

---

## ACTION PLAN

1  Organize your research. Before proceeding you should compile the following:

- Your three whys.

- A complete analysis of rival publications.

- A brand eye.

2  From this, produce an outline of your concept; an example is given in Figure 1.3. This will give you an overview to see if the idea has the potential, before going on the next stage, which is likely to require a financial investment.

| Concept Title : | |
|---|---|
| Outline of your idea (100 words ) : | |
| Products UCP : | |
| Mission statement (30 words ) : | |
| Product Format : | • Platforms – <br> • Page size – <br> • Pagination – <br> • Frequency – |
| Initial profile of your potential target audience : | |
| Main rival publications : | |

**Figure 1.3**

3  Having completed this task, re-evaluate your concept. Market-proof it and strengthen weaknesses that could hinder success.

# 2

# Developing your magazine

**N**ow you have the concept, it is time to start building. Developing a magazine requires strategic planning. The early stages – studying competitors as described in the previous chapter – should have provided a wealth of research on your competitors and the market in general. Now the magazine needs to evolve from an idea into a product. That product must be based on research and analysis. The data you have gathered must be applied to test the viability of your idea. It is no good compiling research, then not analysing it sufficiently.

Like any new product, a magazine requires a solid base. This chapter will help you to come up with a strong title, define your unique selling point, map out the basic editorial framework plus format and decide on the right cover price. A new magazine requires a solid structure on which to build.

## Naming a title

Coming up with an original name is one of the hardest aspects of developing a concept. It needs to be informative, make a visual impact yet be sufficiently descriptive for users to find online. As the masthead on the cover, the name also needs to fit, be memorable and reflect the brand you are aiming to create. Spending time to get the name right is a sound investment.

Obviously the name must reflect the content, be distinctive and avoid confusion with competitors. Avoid abbreviations, as these are unlikely to show up on search engines.

For example, lifestyle publications are mostly about aspirational desires, therefore this should be reflected in the name. One such magazine that makes an impact is the American title, *All About You*, a lifestyle magazine targeted at women aged 25–40. Not only is the title eye-catching, but it also taps into that perceived 30-something need of 'me time'.

Another example of an apt title is, *Choice*, a UK magazine aimed at the retirement sector. Started up (by co-authors John Jenkins and John Kemp) in

1974, it is still going strong today. Its name is a key factor because it focuses on the positive side of retirement as opposed to the negative, which often used to be associated with mature readers. A name often can dictate success or failure no matter how much investment it attracts. Such is the story with *Heyday* – established in 2006 for Age Concern as a non-profit membership scheme. Despite receiving backing of £22 million (as reported in *Marketing Magazine*) it was not sustainable in the long-term as it failed to meet targets. By 2007 *Heyday* had not achieved the 500,000-membership target, gaining only 50,000 members. By 2009 it had closed. This was in marked contrast to *Saga Magazine* – edited by an editor who was headhunted for the job – which defied many rules to break the 1,000,000-circulation barrier. While there is no proof that its name was the reason *Heyday* closed, it is unlikely to have inspired the intended audience.

However, in the specialist sector – particularly among popular sports – names are not as distinctive and therefore are likely to have less impact. In the UK market, the running category has five titles containing the word 'Running' or 'Runner' – *Men's Running, Women's Running, Running Fitness, Running Trail, Great Marathon Runners* and *Runner's World*.

The safety first moral is . . . if there are several magazines using 'Running' in their title, choose another one. But do check that the name you choose hasn't been registered elsewhere, nor must you take a competitor's name and attempt to pass it off as original. Legally any publisher can trademark a logo. However, stopping a rival taking your name could prove difficult and costly. Unfortunately action can only be taken if it can be proved to cause confusion among consumers.

When you have chosen the name, protect it online. Don't forget about your web and social media profiles. Register the title with as many domain options as possible – .com, .org, .net, .uk, then set up your social media accounts.

It is best to come up with two or three potential names, then test each one to see which looks better on the page. See how it fits. Remember layout is about balance. If layout isn't in your skillset then it's advisable to get a designer or experienced magazine sub-editor involved. Most designers can develop a good masthead for a rudimentary title.

Below is my list of great titles. Take inspiration and remember the KIS technique – keep it simple.

- *Easy Living*
- *Car*
- *Country Living*
- *Esquire*

- *Glamour*
- *Good Housekeeping*
- *Men Only*
- *Mountain Bike Rider (MBR)*
- *Muckshifters Journal*
- *Playboy*
- *Smallerholder*
- *Time*
- *The Week*
- *Wanderlust*
- *Which*
- *Writer's Digest.*

# Defining the USP

The USP, aka unique selling point, is the key to marketing your magazine. *Entrepreneur.com* defines this as 'The factor or consideration presented by a seller as the reason that one product or service is different from and better than that of the competition' (*Entrepreneur.com*, 2012).

Pinpointing your title's USP requires creativity. One way to start is to look at how other companies define and use their USPs. Consider what they say they sell, not just their product or service characteristics; you can learn much about how companies distinguish themselves from competitors.

For example, Charles Revson, founder of Revlon, always used to say he sold hope, not make-up. Some airlines sell friendly, efficient service, while others sell on-time service. The John Lewis Partnership sells trust, Vodafone customer care and the Wal-Mart brand – aka Asda in the UK – trades on value for money. What has each brand got in common? They have all found a USP 'peg' on which to hang their marketing strategy.

According to *Entrepreneur*, a business can peg its USP on the four P's of marketing – product characteristics, price structure, placement strategy (location and distribution) or promotional strategy. Furthermore it identifies five key strategies to develop a successful USP. These are:

1  **Put yourself in your customer's shoes:** Entrepreneurs are too involved in their product or service and forget a crucial factor – it is the customer's needs, not their own, that they must satisfy.

**Action:** Think about what your reader needs and wants from your product.

2  **Remember, price is never the only reason people buy.** A rival may beat you on price, in which case other features, which can be offered instead, must be identified. The quality is remembered long after the price is forgotten rule applies not only to building.
   **Action:** Decide what strength will fit readers' needs and use as a selling point.

3  **Know what motivates your customers' behaviour and buying decisions.** Effective marketing means a publisher has to understand readers' behaviour and this involves looking beyond the traditional demographics, such as age, gender, race, income and geographic location.
   **Action:** Find out what drives and motivates your readers.

4  Cosmetics and liquor companies are great examples of industries that know the value of psychologically oriented promotion. They understand that customers buy these products based more on their desires than their needs.
   **Action:** Ascertain your readers' hopes and fears – these should shape your USP.

5  **Uncover the real reasons customers might buy your product instead of a competitor's product.** Keeping in touch with readers will provide a wealth of information on which to base your marketing strategy.
   **Action:** Survey your readers on a regular basis to identify changing trends and needs.

Don't forget the jackpot idea. This is where you create a demand. What might your readers need and how can you tap into that demand? Thoroughly researching the hopes and fears of potential readers may well highlight that potential jackpot idea.

Once identified, the point of a USP is to define your magazine in terms of identity, function and interest. Remember its purpose is to sell so it must make an impact on your reader as well as create the need to purchase the title. A USP must be a one-liner – short, effective and simple. For example on *Writers' Forum* our USP was: Britain's best magazine for writers. Simple yes, but effective and eye-catching. On *Vegetarian Living* it is HEALTHY*SUSTAINABLE*DELICIOUS. Again, simple but effective offering not only a synopsis, but also incorporating brand values and readers' needs. *Zest*, a health and fitness title published by Hearst, defines its USP as: To help women turn good intentions into great results.

Bottom line? A USP must represent brand values, reflect a publication's identity and be visible on every cover. Many publishers use it as the tag line and to maximize its sales value position it in a prominent place. The best position is above the masthead, it must be one of the first things readers see when browsing the news-stands.

# Developing the format

This is the fun part. Deciding on a basic format for your magazine is exciting, but needs to be handled with caution. Get the mix right and your magazine will reflect the brand identity and values, therefore attracting your target readers. Get it wrong, and sales will suffer, which in turn will impact on the core of your business. The framework must consist of:

- **Frequency:** how often will it be published?
- **Page size:** smaller than the standard A4 or larger?
- **Pagination:** number of pages per issue.
- **Production:** today it is essential to include a digital edition as well a print edition.

Deciding on frequency can be difficult. Previously, a small publisher would launch a new quarterly title then as it grew so did the frequency – moving to bimonthly, then monthly. However, in today's age of technology and 24-hour shopping, most consumers are hungry for content. Hence producing a quarterly title rarely works. Readers don't want to wait too long between issues and are likely to move to a competitor. Assess consumer demand and consider the market before deciding on frequency.

Today monthly titles are the norm, but these are backed up by online and social media content that is constantly updated, usually on a daily, sometimes hourly basis. You may decide to publish weekly, but be aware that this strategy will substantially raise your start-up costs.

Next consider the page size of your title. This should depend on consumption. The three most popular pages sizes are A4, American A4 (US letter) and A5 as illustrated in Figure 2.1. But don't forget about A3 for a quasi-tabloid neo-print format, like the *London Review of Books*.

When deciding on size, think about where and how readers will consume content. What is the magazine's purpose or *raison d'être*? Is it likely to be consumed on the move, read in the office, used for specialist knowledge as part of a hobby such as sewing, writing or cooking or kept on a coffee table?

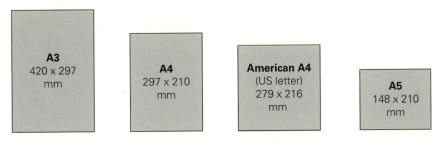

**Figure 2.1** *Magazine formats*

Also examine your main competitors' layout. Take a ruler and measure the dimensions of the closest rival publication.

Also take into account market trends. *Glamour Magazine* already a success in America, selling more than two million copies an issue launched a pocket-sized edition in the UK in 2001. So successful was the first issue that according to InPublishing.com 'the first issue found its way into 581,337 handbags' (Marshall, 2003). Why was it so successful? Because the publisher, Condé Nast, carried out extensive research prior to the launch, testing the idea for a smaller format on 1,000 potential readers. Out of those surveyed, 90 per cent said they would buy the magazine. Also the marketing budget was reportedly in excess of £5 million.

Today how a title is consumed again depends on the readership, but in this digital age flexibility is the key. If tablets are the preferred method, then an A5 format is probably the best choice as it is likely to fit (unaltered) the average tablet screen, sparing users the bother of adjusting the magnification. This also works better if your digital user consumes the magazine on a smart phone. If the plan is to have a small print circulation, but high tablet distribution then the page size should be kept to A4 or perhaps smaller.

When setting the pagination, a new publisher needs to be familiar with industry practices. For print purposes, standard A4 magazines are usually printed in sections of eight pages. The four covers (front, inside front, inside back and outside back) are printed separately because the choice of paper will be different, generally heavier with a gloss or matt finish. Pages can also be printed in sections of 16 and 32, depending on your printer. Whether the printer uses sections of 8, 16 or 32, ensure that the magazine's inside pages are divisible by eight. For example a magazine's pagination might be 72 + 4, but not 75 + 4.

For digital publishing, there are no such constraints as these are published as PDFs. But in order to be in the correct format – to view as a double page – pagination must end on an even number, a left-hand page. This is the same as compiling the print issue.

However, the pagination should be balance. Consider the following:

- What's the ratio of advertising to editorial pages?
- The optimum number of articles?
- How many pages do you want to produce?
- And how many are you capable of producing?

As with most aspects of business, your answers should be about achievability. If you have a small editorial team, it might be prudent to start with a modest 64 + 4 page issue, which is packed with quality editorial, rather than an 80 + 4 page that includes lots of filler content as because the team were overstretched.

An increase in pagination should be made once the readership grows. A larger circulation will generate more advertising revenue in terms of higher rates and more space sales, which will enable the publication to expand and hire more staff. With *Writer's Forum* we started with a 64 + 4 page issue launching on the news-stands with an initial circulation of 20,000. The pagination was then increased to 80 + 4 as the magazine grew.

In contrast *Golf World* limped along for years relying on generic advertising for revenue. Thanks to the flair and initiative of advertising manager Bob Brand it broke through to carry advertising for luxury items such as wines, spirits, executive cars and expensive watches. Brand was so successful that the publisher found after a while that pagination exceeded the optimum profit level before the advertising rate could be raised. This followed a record issue, in terms of pagination, which came close to losing money.

# Paper and pricing

Once decisions on pricing and frequency have been made, consider how the magazine will look and feel. Choosing the right paper stock and finish is crucial. Your choices must reflect the magazine's identity in order to appeal to readers. If producing an eco-magazine, then the readership is likely to expect the publisher to use paper from a sustainable stock and carbon-neutral printing.

Other factors such as audience engagement are also important. For example producing a quality magazine for an audience whose priority is budget purchases is unlikely to achieve news-stand high sales. Why? Two reasons. The first is the cost to produce such a magazine would have to be reflected in the cover price, which may make it unaffordable to your readership. Another reason is that your potential readers seeing a high-end finish may not realize the magazine is for them and will revert to a product that reflects their comfort zone. For example, printing on heavy top quality paper would be out of character for a title like *Which,* of the Consumers' Association.

Paper choices should be divided into covers and inside pages. Magazine covers are generally a heavier weight. Cover paper starts about 100 gms upwards. While the inside pages tend to be between 60 and 90 gms. Covers are often ultra violet (UV) varnished or laminated to achieve that professional, polished look. The weight of paper can increase mail-out costs, while the coating can increase your printing bill.

Types of paper coating:

- **Gloss:** These have a high reflection and high ink lift, which gives vibrant colour and intensity to printed images.

- **Matt:** has no surface reflection, it feels smooth and dull to the touch, but somewhat rougher than a gloss paper. The ink lift is not as pronounced as gloss paper so images appear slightly flatter in appearance. However, readability is improved.

- **Silk:** Like matt paper, but this has no surface reflection, it also feels smooth to touch. This is a good compromise between gloss and matt, with high readability and quality reproduction. However, your print should use a seal to prevent ink rub when the magazine is handled, as ink does not dry as effectively as it would on gloss paper.

- **Uncoated:** This is on-trend particularly with those magazines trying to achieve a scrapbook feel. Previously quality was compromised using this type of paper, but due to developments in technology, superior image reproduction is achievable.

Magazine paper types are separated into four categories as follows:

- **Super-calendered (SC):** An economical choice, used for large volume print quantities on lightweight paper, usually weighs between 39 gsm and 60 gsm.

- **Lightweight coated (LWC):** Gives a better range of brightness on heavier weights. It is reasonably priced and single-coated. The paper weighs between 35 gsm and 70 gsm.

- **Medium weight coated (MWC):** A good choice as it handles full colour reproduction exceptionally well, while maintaining good opacity, bulk and reasonable longevity. Most grades are double-coated. The paper weighs between 60 gsm and 100 gsm.

- **Woodfree coated (WFC):** A practical choice for covers. Weighs between 80 gsm and 400 gsm. This paper is strong, bright, high in bulk, has longevity and opacity giving high quality reproduction. It is also available in double and triple-coated options.

Many papers are imported from Scandinavia and Canada so it pays to check currency fluctuations.

Magazine covers need durable finishes to cope with wear and tear. Another option is embossing or foil blocking the magazine title to make the cover more appealing. Some publications use this only for special issues, like bumper Christmas or summer editions.

Today almost any combination is possible, so it is worth talking to paper manufacturers and your printer. Take time to choose the right paper and finish, which will reflect your brand identity and appeal to readers. But don't bust the budget.

# Deciding on editorial focus

Getting the size, look, and feel of the publication right is crucial and should be prioritized before you start planning your editorial focus. Once decided, content can then be outlined.

The first stage is to define your editorial pillars. These are the themes on which a publication's content is built. The pillars for *Writer's Forum* were: novel writing, short fiction, self-publishing, eBooks, freelance writing, poetry, author profiles, how-to pieces, and writing courses. In *Vegetarian Living* they included seasonal food, healthy heating, eco-living, and meal planners. Each set of pillars reflected the voice and ethos of the their title, thus defining the identity.

But how do you define editorial pillars? Freelance writer and former chief sub-editor, Kate Pettifer describes these as a core value or objective on which you build your brand.

It could be a mission statement, an aspiration for the impact your content will have, or a point of difference that sets your title apart from its competitors.

Put another way, editorial pillars define your title's underlying purpose and are the drivers or filters for how you build/select your content. Editorial pillars become the benchmarks you refer back to when you want to measure content against your brand values – does the content deliver on the editorial pillars that underpin your brand? The answer should always be yes; if not, scrap or rework your content.

When developing pillars for a new magazine, Kate advises doing lots of research.

> Editorial pillars come from two starting points – firstly, the reason you've been inspired to create a new publication, such as a gap in the market, points of difference from competitor titles, or a simply brilliant idea. Secondly, pillars come from sharply targeting specific readers. Who exactly are your readers and how are you reaching them? Plot your title against its rivals on graphs and know exactly where you sit in your market. Advertisers will want to know all of this too.
>
> Take a title such as *Grazia*. A couple of pillars spring to mind. Firstly, it took a traditionally mass-market subject area – weekly magazines trading in celebrities and gossip – and applied the gloss of a monthly plus a more intelligent treatment. This truly set it apart. To deliver on this pillar, they would have, I imagine, spent a lot of time asking, is this glamorous enough? Is it smart enough? Secondly, it married high fashion (a subject traditionally delivered with gravitas/sincerity) with irreverent fun – the tone was knowing and its captions humorous without compromising its commitment to high-end brands and trailblazing new labels.

How much consideration if any, should be given to potential advertisers? Kate advises proceeding with caution.

> Focus too much on advertisers and you risk jeopardizing the strength of your idea for a publication. If you have a strong idea and a well-defined readership, this will naturally attract advertisers. That said, it's unrealistic to think you can ignore advertising in this economic climate. Advertising remains the key income stream for magazines – there's so little if any, net profit in the actual cover price of a print glossy.
>
> *Eve* launched in 2000 as a monthly glossy for thirty-somethings, akin to *Red*, with the aim of broadening the interest areas covered by women's magazines beyond the usual fashion/beauty/health, was truly ground-breaking in its design and scope of content (the first issue had a graphic feature about colonic irrigation at a Thai health spa, for example).

According to Kate, 'the upshot of such a radical proposition was that its readership was inevitably quite niche and its glossy/glamour factor somewhat compromised. Both of which are off-putting to mainstream advertisers, who are drawn to glamorously presented content and big readership figures.'

*Eve* went on to reinvent itself in a more glamorous, mainstream format under its second editor, Jane Bruton, followed by Sara Cremer under whose editorship it achieved phenomenal success. When Sara moved to Redwood in

2007, Nic McCarthy took the reins. Sadly despite a redesign, the publication folded in 2008 following stiff competition from titles such as *Red* and *Easy Living*.

'Also, bear in mind that some titles are born out of advertising demand,' says Kate. 'Condé Nast *Traveller* grew out of *Vogue, Coast* grew out of *Country Living*. Sometimes stream-lining a title and creating a niche, sister publication, will strengthen its commercial appeal.'

When building pillars, points to consider are:

- **Your title's voice:** what should be the main focus?

- **The genre:** where are the boundaries?

- **Competitors:** where are the gaps, what aspects do they neglect or not cover?

- **Advertisers:** how can you expand the subject to maximize advertising?

Once pillars have been defined, think about including regular slots in every issue. These are features or content containing the same theme but with different content. These are unique to every title. For example for a national women's lifestyle magazine aimed at professionals aged 25–40 these might include: 'Top tweets of the month', 'My home office', 'Relationships' and 'On the couch with a lifestyle coach'.

Kate Pettifer defines good content as features that are strongly angled to meet the readership's interests.

> It is relevant, topical, informative and entertaining, in an ideal world. It should be fresh and insightful in the way it's presented, and also reflects the brand in the way the content is delivered. If you can meet all of the above, you'll not only keep your readers, but also reinforce your brand – which, more than ever, is what a magazine must be.

Should content be changed for digital editions, and if so, how much? According to Kate, content for online needs to be pithy, scaled down, distilled into a much smaller word count and possibly reformatted into bite-size chunks.

> Online readers skim-read heavily, so draw them in with interesting paragraph headers, first words and subheads, etc. You also need to think about search engine optimization (SEO) – how will surfers find your page, what keywords can you bring in to lure a bigger audience? Introducing a little repetition – although a no-no in print – is actually advisable online, for search-engine purposes.

Thirdly, consider how interactive your content is for apps, online and digital: can readers respond to it, share it using social tools, get involved and give an opinion? Can you make the content work harder, by linking it to other pages online or by using it to generate activity in other digital media such as Instagram, Facebook, Twitter or Pinterest? Online content needs to be more than a straightforward, passive reading experience.

What advice would Kate give to a new editor tasked with developing a style guide for layout and content? 'Don't try this alone: if you're from a words background, your creative director and/or photography director are your wingmen in establishing a strong visual branding.'

Don't underestimate the power of detail: tone of voice, words used and banned, caption styles – all of these minutiae help build a brand. Let your editorial pillars be your filters for deciding what's in and what's out. Just as you can recognize a good logo by looking at a fraction of it, you should be able to recognize a magazine by its caption style, tone of voice and style of photography.

## Deadlines and editorial calendars

Planning in any editorial office is crucial. Once a magazine concept moves towards development, schedules will need to be drawn up. First, production schedules need to be determined to set deadlines. This should then be followed by setting out an editorial calendar – a plan giving the basic outline of each issue noting specific events/dates relevant to the genre.

Production deadlines are decided by liaising with your distributor and printer. The distributor will give you the magazine's on-sale dates for the following 12 months – this is the date that your magazine goes on sale in your assigned retail outlets. When you have these dates, work out a printing schedule with your printing representative. He or she will then give you the date that each issue must be submitted in order to be delivered in time to meet the distribution deadline.

Production dates are worked backwards from the printer deadline – otherwise known as going to press. This remains the same for digital issues, which originate from PDFs. You must calculate sufficient time to gather, proofread and layout all your content including advertising copy.

For *Writers' Forum,* we followed a four-week cycle; here is a rough outline of our production schedule:

- **Week 4 (deadline):** All content must be laid out, subbed and proofread plus all advertisements must be client approved before the deadline. Pages turned into PDFs by midday of the deadline.

- **Week 3:** Deadline set for advert submissions as well as advertorials and promotions. Adverts sent to advertisers for copy approval. All editorial copy must be laid out ready to be subbed and approved.

- **Week 2:** Deadline for all content and pictures. These must now be ready to be paged-up.

- **Week 1:** Copy tasting from freelance submissions, main feature selected, cover picture and story obtained, plus competitions and miscellaneous items such as puzzles or crosswords etc. selected.

The majority of content must be planned well in advance. When the title is in the latter development stages, the editor and staff should have a conference to plan the next 12 month's content. This is known also as the editorial calendar – and is a must for any publication.

A calendar will not only benefit editorial staff who need to work to a plan, but also your advertising sales team who need to know each issue's focus and key features in order to maximize potential sales. Advertisers also benefit as they can then choose their insertions to maximize their potential gain. Advertising deadlines for each issue can also be included in the rate card or media pack alongside the rates to ensure clients have all the information they need.

Of course the plan isn't set in stone, things will change during the year, but the basic framework will remain in place. Remember you must hold regular editorial conferences. Good planning underpins any publication be it digital, print or online.

# Summary

In this chapter we have covered how to develop those factors that – with in-depth research – will turn your idea into a magazine. Industry experts have provided their input into what makes a title successful in terms of content, image, paper and pricing. But remember, every title is unique and this must be reflected in all aspects of the publication.

There are three questions you should ask at this stage of development. These are:

- How do I want the magazine to look and feel?

- Editorial pillars that will enhance this title are?

- What do my readers want to read about?

Work out these basics and the rest will fall into place. How the magazine looks and feels plus its core content will mostly depend on the genre, audience and your budget – in that order. High-end magazines must invest in quality production, while business and specialist title should invest in recruiting specialist, well-known writers.

Don't follow your competitors too closely. The key to success is remaining unique – the same content repackaged in similar magazines quickly becomes boring. Therefore set your own pillars. Take risks with content, layout and style. The market and the title's revenue potential should be key factors for deciding how much money to invest in production. Remember that all costs need to be recouped. Magazines must – like every business – produce a profit.

When it comes to planning content and the production schedule, build in more time than you think you need. There are always unforeseen problems before a magazine goes to press. A freelance may not deliver copy on time, an interview may be cancelled and advertisers may pull out. Plans need to be flexible in order to accommodate the unexpected. They should also be continually updated and amended. As they say 'change happens'.

# INDUSTRY INPUT

**Figure 2.2** *Mark Payton*

**Mark Payton, editorial director at Haymarket Consumer Media, who has been involved in many magazine launches and relaunches, including *Stuff*, shares his experiences.**

*What makes a new title viable? Either a defined space in the market that fulfils an audience need, or a poorly-served sector. With the newsstand as tough an environment as it is right now, I would also guide any new publisher into considering something that has serious subscriptions potential.*

*A good magazine proposition is remarkably close in discipline to the skills of a good marketer – is the proposition fundamentally saleable? Take WhatCar?: it has taken years to establish its status as the buyers guide for British car buyers . . . but it came from a publisher's sense that nobody was answering a simple question in a booming market – namely, which car do I buy?*

*Remember that today's audiences are extremely sensitive to value. To not take that into account when deciding on format and pagination would be foolhardy. Yet balance is crucial – I know of colleagues in the industry that have studied the design of others to the point where they lose interest and faith in their own original idea.*

*Focus groups and research are vital to a new launch, although I try to treat them as a guide to be interpreted, not a line-by-line rulebook. I would also suggest showing your research subjects real extremes. I've sat in sessions where groups of quite similar propositions all score highly – then the scores collapse when you show them a stark contrast.*

*With any new title the three most important factors to consider are:*

- ***Simplicity:** can you describe the job the title does for its target audience in one sentence?*

- ***Talent:** the best idea in the world can flounder if the creative team is unable to deliver it.*

- ***Quality:** can you demonstrate, page for page, that it is better than rival publications?*

*A publisher must have an intimate knowledge of the editorial strengths and weaknesses of rivals. In the same breath, they shouldn't be overwhelmed –*

*chances are, the strong rival became that strong from focusing on doing the job well. So if you have an approach that you passionately believe in, concentrate on making that the best it can be. I can think of scenarios where a team became so fixated on the rival that they forgot about their own knitting.*

*I have two magazine launches that I'm proud of – The Net and Stuff, although the latter was more relaunch than launch. The Net was a mass-market monthly launched into the peak of the first dotcom boom, and did very well for several years. When the bubble burst, the advertisers vanished – but the title was still selling well, and was a very good magazine. Its success came from focus – we concentrated on reviewing the best new sites in a really entertaining way.*

*Stuff was more relaunch than launch, although it felt like we were producing a brand new magazine. I was given the job of rejuvenating the title when we bought it from Dennis Publishing. It's now the world's best-selling technology monthly. The success came from single-mindedness: concentrate on doing one thing very well, in Stuff's case showcasing new hardware.*

*With regards to disastrous launches, I have been lucky. There's nothing that I could call a disaster in terms of sales, although I've had a fair share that could have done better. Lessons? Never be afraid to ask for improvements – it's amazing how a group of talented people can be uncomfortable with a proposition, but nobody says anything. If it's wrong, or not good enough, speak up.*

*My advice to any new publisher/editor with a great idea for a magazine is – do your research. There are more cost-effective ways to gauge a market now than ever – all of the research tools are there, and usually free. Dummying is equally cost-effective, and a great way of testing reactions.*

*Don't underestimate the competition: do not ignore a rival's strengths. And although the new idea is your baby, ask yourself – would you buy it?*

---

## ACTION PLAN

It is crucial to define your USP, before developing an outline of your new title. Once you have this then answer the following questions:

- How do I want the magazine look and feel?

- Editorial pillars that will enhance this title are?

- What do my readers want to read about?

Explore all options thoroughly. Approach printers for quotes on producing print and digital versions of your title. Don't be afraid to ask for samples of paper and if confused by any terms used in the quote, then clarify the meaning.

---

# 3

# Target audiences

**G**etting your audience profile right is paramount. One of the first rules is to remember that the magazine is for the reader, not just for you (the publisher) or the editor. There is a contract between you and the reader. In return for their money and time you are undertaking to inform or entertain them, preferably both. Content should be tailored to their needs, but not necessarily dictated by them. To survive and evolve a new publication needs a diverse readership – with an essential core group who will remain loyal, supporting the publication as it grows. But a magazine must also be able to acquire new readers along the way.

This chapter will demonstrate how to identify potential readers using a variety of tools to gather data and build an accurate audience profile. Spending time gathering this data is an investment. Audience profiling is valuable information as it is used in media packs (advertising sales brochures) to attract advertisers and thus generate a good income stream through a high volume of advertising sales. Initial research although consuming and costly, is part of a solid foundation for your title.

Your research must be ongoing as the magazine evolves. Continue to find out if and how your readers have changed and what they think about content, advertising and design. However, some publishers make the mistake of gathering data, but not analysing it sufficiently. Carefully study the data you generate – be it audience research or circulation figures. Such diligence will ensure your audience data remains current and that you have an accurate picture, which will help identify any problems as well as predict future trends. Demographic maps and data charts can identify areas of success and failure, which you can address.

## Identifying potential readers

The first step is to build what some publishers refer to as a pen profile. This determines the sex, age and audience classification group of core readers.

Determining a pen profile will provide a basic framework to build a detailed outline of your core audience. Gauging potential readers by their interests will also provide an indication of the number of copies you expect to sell.

To build the pen profile, decide the ratio of male/female readers, their age group and social classification. Although a class system no longer exists, social – and audience – classification is now segregated by knowledge derived from education, which in turn generates a higher income level.

Most publishing houses still use the ABC audience classification, a social grading system defined by the occupation of the Chief Income Earner (CIE) outlined in Table 3.1 below. It was developed more than 50 years ago for use in the National Readership Survey and is seen as an industry standard for segregating audiences.

Once a pen profile is in place, in-depth research can begin. You need to build a detailed picture to ensure that your magazine's content will be deemed useful to the target audience. Matching content to a readership is an essential formula for success.

For example, when working on the launch of *Vegetarian Living* the team had to decide whether to restrict the publication solely to vegetarians and perhaps vegans. By doing this, other groups such as meat reducers or those thinking about embarking on a meat-free diet, would be seemingly excluded. It seemed that tailoring content only for these two groups would significantly define the title and subsequently limit circulation potential. However, if the magazine's content wasn't sufficiently defined it could fail to entice its target audiences.

Research revealed a wide audience potential. The Vegetarian Society had around 20,000 members, while the Vegan Society website in the Media, Key Facts section claimed: 'there are at least 150,000 vegans in the UK', with 'the UK meat-free foods market in 2008 was valued at £739 million' (The Vegan

## Table 3.1

| Social grade | CIE's occupation |
|---|---|
| A | Higher managerial, administrative and professional |
| B | Intermediate managerial, administrative and professional |
| C1 | Supervisory, clerical and junior managerial, administrative and professional |
| C2 | Skilled manual workers |
| D | Semi-skilled and unskilled manual workers |
| E | State pensioners, casual and lowest grade workers, unemployed with state benefits only |

Society, 2013). Added to this were the numerous meat eaters interested in introducing vegetarian aspects to their diet, those who had concerns about their health, wellbeing and the environment. Taking these into consideration significantly increases circulation potential, giving the magazine a greater chance of success.

To gain such significant data, audience research needs to be carefully planned. Two key questions at this stage are:

- How will you reach your target survey group(s)?
- What incentive can you provide them to participate in your research?

If you are setting up a specialist magazine or B2B, then your target group may well be easier to identify. When developing *Vegetarian Living,* the team found that there are numerous vegetarian and vegan groups in the UK. All of these could be approached to take part in a target audience survey. But with those titles that fall under a more general concept or lifestyle sector it is more difficult to find a sample group.

It is also wise to consider how to encourage people to take part in a focus group. Most need an incentive, so you may need to set aside a budget for a prize draw – be it cash or goods, otherwise your response rate is likely to be low. A poor response will not provide a clear indication of your potential readers. As a result, you may not be able to prove that your magazine concept is viable.

## Researching your audience

Getting to know your potential audience, their hobbies, habits, spending patterns, likes and dislikes will enable you to build a detailed profile of your readers. As any professional writer will tell you, it is impossible to write a successful magazine article, book or novel without knowledge of the reader. Audience demographics are an invaluable asset to any media kit. According to the National Readership Survey, which measures readership data for more than 300 publications, there are five principles to gaining accurate data (NRS, 2013). These are:

1  Create a level playing field, so that all publications are measured on a like-for-like basis.

2  Move respondents efficiently through the long list of titles surveyed, so that they can identify the titles that they do read. This is done by the Extended Media List (EML) technique, which presents titles initially in groups of six, so that the respondent can decide which groups of six include titles that they have read and discard the rest.

3 Make respondent recognition the key principle when deciding how to prompt titles and allocate them to the EML screens.

4 Minimize title confusion by prompting titles that may be prone to confusion alongside one another.

5 Rotate the order in which publications are presented to respondents to avoid bias and offset any fatigue effects. Not only is the overall order rotated, but also the position in which each title is shown in its group of six.

Getting to know your potential audience can only be achieved by undertaking detailed research methods using surveys, polls and also – once established – monitoring your title's circulation pattern to see where spikes or dips occur. Gathering such data will increase your appeal to advertisers and can be used to enhance the publication.

So how do you compile a survey that will prompt the answers you seek? Try one of the many online survey tools: these collate and format data into reports and charts. Although some of these are free, those which enable significant responses and unlimited questions are the best option. Mostly their prices are reasonable. For example a basic free survey package would limit your monthly responses to around 50 and only allow users ten questions.

Only enabling 50 respondents to complete a survey is not going to provide sufficient data. Paying for these tools should be considered an investment. However, do your homework by comparing the options available before choosing your survey tool. Here are two options well worth considering.

1 **Smart survey** (http://www.smart-survey.co.uk) offer a professional package for around £23 a month, for this users get a storage allowance of 1,500 responses per month, unlimited questions and question types.

2 **Free online surveys** (http://freeonlinesurveys.com/) is an American-based programme that works with all social platforms including Twitter, WordPress, Facebook and Google+. Its basic student package is for $9.99 per month. With this option, the user gets a storage allowance of 1,000 responses per month and unlimited questions. There are two other packages: $19.99 per month and $180 per year.

Online survey tools offer the most flexibility with data capture and storage. As well as collating and formatting responses, survey tools will into turn data into graphs to provide a clear picture.

When compiling a questionnaire think carefully about the type and style of questions, as these factors will determine the quality of responses you are like to get. Most questions should be multiple-choice – particularly when it comes to age and incomes, which should be in bandings. For example a question such as 'what is your annual household income?' should have about five banding options to choose from – '£10,000–£19,999', '£20,000–£24,999' for example. Respondents tend to react positively to this style of questioning because it is less invasive with fewer negative connotations. Use open style questions to avoid a plain 'yes' or 'no' answer.

Before writing the survey, identify your key objectives. What do you need to find out about your potential readers? Once you have clarified this, start compiling the survey.

Data gathering such as this is likely to concern a person's age group, income (to clarify audience classification), marital status, occupation, what he or she spends money on, interests, hopes and fears, plus plans for the future. Finding out their hopes and fears will also prompt key editorial pillars. Remember editorial content is a commodity. If readers feel their lives will be enhanced by your title's content – either emotionally, physically or financially – then they are more likely to buy the magazine or subscribe. This particularly applies to lifestyle, B2B and specialist publications.

Beware of questions that concern ethnicity. These are always included in government surveys and their mere inclusion can be classified as racist.

Reaching a potential audience can be difficult. A publisher should use several methods to ensure a survey is widely distributed, thus maximizing the response ratio. This can be done using several methods, which include:

- **Special interest groups** – identifying ones to whom your title will appeal and getting the chair person/organizer to circulate your survey.

- **Email listings** – distributing a survey link via email to a database of contacts bought from a third party or acquired as part of a reciprocal deal.

- **Social media sites** – such as Facebook or Twitter to target potential readers (for B2B magazines, sites such as LinkedIn should be utilized).

- **A direct mail** – sending out a postal survey. Best avoided unless targeting your specific market as you are unlikely to get a high response.

- **A personal approach** – sending a team out to the high street or conference venues can also work well.

## A word of warning on data protection

When using email or direct mail databases do ensure that the owners of every email/postal address have given their permission to be contacted in respect of marketing initiatives. In order to combat the numerous complaints on privacy intrusion by researchers and telesales operatives, the Market Research Society has set out a Code of Conduct for members.

The ten principles of the code are (2010, p.5):

1  Researchers shall ensure that participation in their activities is based on voluntary informed consent.

2  Researchers shall be straightforward and honest in all their professional and business relationships.

3  Researchers shall be transparent as to the subject and purpose of data collection.

4  Researchers shall respect the confidentiality of information collected in their professional activities.

5  Researchers shall respect the rights and well-being of all individuals.

6  Researchers shall ensure that respondents are not harmed or adversely affected by their professional activities.

7  Researchers shall balance the needs of individuals, clients and their professional activities.

8  Researchers shall exercise independent professional judgment in the design, conduct and reporting of their professional activities.

9  Researchers shall ensure that their professional activities are conducted by persons with appropriate training, qualifications and experience.

10  Researchers shall protect the reputation and integrity of the profession.

Reputation management is essential so you must keep within these boundaries to avoid negative publicity, as these factors could impact on the success of your magazine. From good survey data, you can build a detailed audience demographic to determine what your readers want, and for inclusion in your media kit, thus highlighting the potential reach for advertisers.

---

## CASE STUDY – *WRITERS' FORUM*

When Writers International Ltd first took over *Writers' Forum* it was a quarterly magazine only available on subscription resulting in low circulation and a limited audience. The new publisher realized that the audience potential was not being maximized so decided the only way forward was to relaunch on the news-stand. The editorial team decided to research both the existing and potential readers to ascertain more data to make sure that *Writers' Forum* contained solid content to inspire, entertain and inform its audience.

In 2000, the age of technology had gathered pace after initial changes in the Seventies, which revolutionized the media. Although broadband was a few years from making its debut, the power of the internet and email was emerging as was the era of desktop computers and laptops. It was these factors that increased an interest in writing, thus from demand sprang a range of opportunities in this genre, from writing courses and holidays to conferences, competitions and self-publishing companies. As a result, the need for writing magazines increased, revealing a potentially large market of amateur and professional writers desperate for information, platforms and ideas. Soon writing would be a major source of second incomes around the world.

Tapping into this development was essential if *Writers' Forum* was to succeed, so the next step was to source and measure the number of potential readers to gauge circulation potential. An initial study revealed there were more than 1,000 writing groups in the UK and around ten major annual conferences – such groups had the potential to provide a wealth of information. To reach this potential audience, the team compiled a survey and sent it to organizers of writing circles and conferences.

Our survey consisted of questions relating principally to writing, others of a more general nature to ascertain income, peripheral interests and lifestyle choices. The results revealed that the majority wanted to earn money from their writing, receive recognition and see their work in print. It also showed that many would-be writers not only sought inspiration, but practical information on a range of related topics – from how to get published to choosing a good course and setting up a home office. Findings revealed there a growing market, as well as a wide potential for advertising revenue within this genre.

This need developed alongside a huge increase in people's interest in genealogy on both sides of the Atlantic. Thus readers wanted to know how to document and publish their family history.

Gaining a realistic picture of audience demographics ensured that not only did *Writers' Forum* grow into a successful national magazine, but that it was sustainable. A decade later the title is still going strong, despite several new rivals emerging.

---

# Building audience profiles

Having gained a huge amount of data from audience surveys, a publisher should then focus on building profiles. Many publishing houses, particularly those with lifestyle titles in their stable, categorize demographics into audience and reader profiles. The former gives a general overall picture of audience demographics, while the latter provides an in-depth summary of an average reader encompassing their lifestyle, habits and use of technology as well as hopes and fears.

Such data not only provides valuable information for content direction, it also helps to predict future trends. For example in 2010, when surveyed, many readers would have put laptops as their main source of access to the Internet. Two years later – with the development of tablets, smart phones and internet TVs – that same group would demonstrate a different behaviour and usage pattern in the way they consume news, entertainment and content. Thus from this a publisher might surmise that an investment in app development would meet readers changing needs.

Initially when working on the development of *Vegetarian Living* early audience research concluded that readers would be in the ABC1 category, aged between 25 and 50, with a higher ratio of female readers (approximately 66 per cent female to 34 per cent male). The initial audience profile identified *Vegetarian Living* readers as:

- Passionate reformers who have, or are in the process of, adopting a vegan lifestyle.

- Believing a healthy diet without meat is crucial to their – and the planet's – well-being.

- Being passionate about vegan food – always looking for new recipes and ideas.

- Having a household income of £42,000+.

- Married or living with a partner.

- Being a parent to at least one child.

- Owning a pet.

- Taking two holidays a year as well as couple of mini breaks, but always try to offset their carbon footprint.

- Looking for ways to save energy in their home.

- Thinking about growing their own vegetables.

- Shopping in Tesco or Morrisons, but sometimes go to M&S or Waitrose for a treat.

- Willing to pay a premium for quality, ethical and environmentally friendly products.

- Having tried alternative therapy treatments for an illness or injury.

From the initial research, the team then compiled an in-depth reader profile defining the typical *Vegetarian Living* reader as likely to be:

A 32-year-old female, who is living with a partner and has one child. She works part-time as a teacher, is adventurous when it comes to food and likes to try out different recipes on a regular basis.

She prefers to cook from scratch, often experimenting at the weekend when she has more time. Our reader wants quality products and doesn't mind paying a premium for them. She is concerned about the environment, avoids foods with additives, likes to use natural cleaning products and is currently trying out green beauty treats. Although the family takes at least one holiday abroad every year, she tries to balances this by offsetting their carbon footprint.

Her aspirations include a hope to adopt a more healthy/ethical lifestyle and she is looking for information and products to help her achieve this. While fears consist of becoming susceptible to disease as a result of a poor diet and worrying about the sustainability of the environment.

A second survey was implemented a few months following the launch, this time targeting those who had read *Vegetarian Living*. This survey was sponsored by an advertiser and included a competition prize in the package to further incentivize audience participation. To further encourage audience participation the survey was published online and inside the magazine.

The questions differed from the launch survey, as the objective was now to ascertain which elements of the content the readers liked and those they didn't. General questions about *Vegetarian Living* probed on how long each issue was kept in a household, favourite reads, as well as why and where they purchased the publication. The 'about you' section looked at demographics, lifestyle, habits and internet usage.

Findings revealed that readers valued the magazine's content and brand values. Moreover, it gave the publisher a clear indication of how many people read each copy. Results revealed that for every copy sold 2.6 people read the magazine. Therefore on a distribution of 40,000 copies the total readership could be set at 100,000 – nearly three times the circulation. Including readership data as well as circulation figures will make an impact on your media kit as it can more than double the potential reach of the magazine.

## Sustaining a core readership

The key to having a loyal readership is being able to keep up-to-date with your readers' ever changing needs, ensuring that the magazine continues to evolve in the way it delivers content. As the above example demonstrated, finding out how your magazine is read and its content consumed is vital to achieving sustainability in the long term. Rather like a relationship – do not take readers for granted. A publisher must continue to get to know existing readers, while seeking to build the circulation.

Stagnation is dangerous as familiarity tends to breed contempt. Relying on existing readers will not allow your magazine to grow and eventually the circulation will drop as the core group move on to other titles, have a change in circumstances, or simply stop buying your magazine. Circulation seldom stands still. It grows or it declines.

Thus a relationship must be built and nurtured. Today's magazine readers – be they print, digital or online – want a conversation, a magazine must now be deemed to be interactive. Editorial is no longer a one-way, top down distribution channel. With so much interactive technology at their figure tips, readers now want input into the publication and they want a channel for their views. Thus the more a publisher knows about his or her readers, the more successful a publication is likely to be.

That said, your magazine must develop its own personality; therefore should not be designed solely to adhere to the research drawn from your survey results. It needs to develop its own voice to evolve and establish – by alchemy – a soul.

# Attracting subscribers

Subscribers must be considered an asset. Having a strong subscription list for both print and digital editions will ensure that cash flow is maximized, while also providing a database of consumer details.

A list of names and addresses enables you to contact readers with news, information, special offers and events. In addition (as long as you have obtained their permission) you can also share the data with related partners such as advertisers – and for this you can charge a fee. From a cash flow perspective, it is good to have readers paying for their magazine up front – be it for a year or six months. As funds from most revenue streams take time to filter through obtaining money in advance will significantly improve a publication's cash flow and provide a cushion against unexpected events.

There are three key factors that will turn readers into subscribers, these are:

1  The product (title) must have quality content that has a perceived value to the consumer.

2  Secondly readers must have trust in the publication. Trust to be sure it is sustainable so they won't lose money and also that the content is bona fide.

3  Lastly the content must be needed to inform, empower or entertain. If a reader loves the magazine they will be more inclined to subscribe, but

if they only like it then it is more likely to become an occasional buy, while browsing the news-stands.

Special offer incentives such as free gifts or money off the cover price can also help turn a reader into a subscriber. Free gifts should always reflect the identity of the publication. For example, on *Vegetarian Living* free subscriber gifts must be vegetarian and vegan friendly to reflect the ethos of the magazine. But *Writers' Forum* giving a supply of cereal bars or organic hand cream is unlikely to incentivize a purchase, as it doesn't relate to the product. But including a free guide on how to publish your first novel or a list of relevant websites could motivate a reader to subscribe. Always factor in costings when offering free gifts. Subscribers' gifts also provide an opportunity for sponsorship either by a corporate partner or advertiser in return for free promotion in the magazine or online.

Larger publishing houses can afford to offer a bigger discount on subscriptions due to the volume, but for the average publisher the range is likely to be between 10 and 20 per cent off the cover price. When working out how much to charge for a 6- or 12-month subscription a publisher must include the cost of postage, which is rapidly rising. Discount too much and the magazine will lose money, but too little discount will not incentivize your reader to pay up front. However, with subscriptions to digital editions facilitated via apps, the cost is significantly less.

Once incentives are in place and the price is set, it is essential to publicize the offer and measure responses. Ways to publicize subscription offers include a page advert or loose insert in your magazine. You should also use social media. There also may be opportunities to collaborate with a reciprocal partner to reach their members or clients by offering an exclusive deal.

For example, with *Vegetarian Living* the team approached the Vegetarian Society and secured editorial in their newsletter by offering an exclusive subscription discount to society members. The newsletter went out to 20,000 members – all of whom fell within our target audience profile. Subsequently the collaboration was a success resulting in many new subscribers. The cost to the publisher for this deal was minimal because outlay was limited to fees for paying the PR consultant to organize this deal plus the additional 5 per cent discount added on each subscription fee.

If you are setting up a specialist or B2B publication, try to secure a strategic partnership by approaching groups, societies or organizations within the genre. Reaching your target audience using this method is far cheaper and more effective than a direct mailshot, which may be too wide in terms of your audience constraints and thus involve unacceptable wastage.

However, in some cases direct mail can be effective, but a publisher must first evaluate a control group. Always aim directly at your target market and ensure that the cost of such a marketing initiative can be recouped. For example *Writers' Forum* sent out a mailshot to members of writing circles nationwide and gained a good response rate, which more than covered the costs of the exercise.

Also don't forget about existing subscribers who might have friends or relatives who would like to subscribe. Savvy publishers often include a leaflet in subscribers' copies or an extra page in digital editions, with special offers on gift subscriptions or recommending a friend. A member get member campaign is a cheap, but effective marketing tactic.

# Summary

Throughout this chapter we have covered not only how to define your initial audience, but how to build an in-depth reader profile to develop a sustainable title. Thus when defining your audience:

- Identify your potential readers.

- Build a pen profile summarizing the group.

- Compile a survey to confirm your initial ideas. Results will also produce the necessary data to develop profiles for your media kit.

- Pinpoint potential groups of people who can help with your research.

- Think about the long-term – how can you build a solid subscription base?

Bill Dunn of Redwood Publishing has developed numerous titles and knows the importance of a two-sided conversation between an editor and the reader; he says: 'If you're having a conversation it always helps to know who you're talking to. That's good advice.'

But while taking into consideration your audiences' needs, it is crucial that your publication has its own voice, which needs to be strong and independent. Quality content should be unique and not unduly influenced by rival publications or trends.

# INDUSTRY INPUT

**Figure 3.1** *James Pembroke*

**James Pembroke of James Pembroke Publishing has a wealth of experience and insight. Here he offers an insight into *The Oldie* and an antidote to some current industry practices.**

The Oldie *began in November 1991 when founder Richard Ingrams had the idea for a humorous magazine, which was directed at a generation who felt disenfranchized and disenchanted with the formulaic nature of the national press. By February 1992 he had launched the magazine without doing any research.*

*Unlike many consumer magazines where audiences are specifically targeted and profiled* The Oldie *team are totally against targeting an audience using traditional demographic models of age, class or sex. The magazine is for anyone who appreciates good writing. In fact 'Bugger the readers' is Ingrams' motto.*

*Readership is only evaluated for advertising sales purposes using a reader survey every four years. How do we get* The Oldie *readers to respond to surveys? Prizes, but they need to feel a sense of belonging. The response rate to a survey is highly indicative of the magazine's popularity.*

*Although research may help content when developing a magazine concept, the all-important tone is instinctive. A good editor is the leader of a gang who sets the agenda and drives fashions rather than follows them. Magazines are there to make people think they are ahead of the game in every way. Given the high cost of getting a title on the news-stand (£30,000– £50,000), I think showing a dummy to focus groups can only help to fine-tune, but readers don't really know what they want until you give it to them. Too many publishers are dictated to by readers.*

*Building subscriptions is also important. The best way to do this we have found is to put inserts in the subscription copies of like-minded titles.*

*Despite the digital revolution, technology has had little impact on our readers. They like to think of themselves as digital deniers – 25 per cent don't have the internet. Will developments affect how magazine content is consumed in the next 10 years? Perhaps. I think a lot of magazines will be forced to go digital, but ink on paper will always be the medium for luxury and highly photographic content.*

*That said, it is essential that publishing houses keep pace with advances in technology, but at present they are all blowing a lot of cash going down blind alleys for fear of being dubbed 'luddites' instead of holding back to gauge the market. Media companies want to be seen to be cutting edge but have drawn no firm conclusions and are still shooting in the dark. The take up of iPad versions is risible. However, at The Oldie no action is being taken to keep pace with technology given that a quarter of the readership doesn't use the internet.*

*What do our readers like most about The Oldie? The cartoons.*

## ACTION PLAN

Research your audience. Compile a survey using one of the online survey tools to determine your audience and reader profile.

The survey should include the basic questions outlined in this chapter, which must be clear and concise. Remember to ensure about three-quarters of the questions are multiple-choice and phrase awkward enquiries carefully so as not to upset respondents. Sensitive issues are usually, age, marital status, income and home.

Aim for at least 1,000 responses. Do analyse the data carefully before compiling your audience profile. When you have done this, think about organizing a focus group to gain further insight.

# 4

# Publishing strategies: Print, digital and online

**W**hen magazines first evolved there was only one method of production – print. *The Ladies Mercury*, published monthly in 1693 was the first recorded magazine. Today publishers have many forms of output – print, digital, and ePublishing where material can be downloaded in PDF format as well as websites and blogs. With the onset of smart phones, iPads and tablets now dominating the market, magazines are also produced as digital editions along with apps.

The one-method production (print) model is seldom viable for most magazines. Audiences and advertisers expect titles to have multi-platform presence. How much content that goes on to a publication's website depends on the magazine's stance, its audience and the publisher's long-term vision. Hence when developing a new concept or relaunching an existing publication, it is crucial to think about your publishing strategies as a whole.

This chapter will examine which and how many platforms a title should use. It will look at formats that are essential, ones that are advisable and the content needed in each to build a viable title – thus keeping readers and advertisers happy. Is pandering to advertisers vital? No, but if they are going to spend money on advertising space then they will want a quality product that attracts a targeted market. Always consider potential advertisers alongside readers as both contribute to the revenue stream and can therefore make or break it.

## How many platforms?

During the past decade the publishing model was likely to include a print edition, and website with support from social media. But with smart phones and tablets now capturing a significant market share, consumers' needs are changing. Therefore the model must adapt, as with change comes demand. Today, as readers' lives become more mobile they want portable content available across a range of devices.

To keep pace with this demand more publishing houses are adding apps and digital editions to sit alongside the traditional print edition and website. According to Apple's financial report, it has sold more than 17 million iPads in the third quarter of 2012 and 26 million iPhones (Apple, 2012). In 2012 IPC announced that it would make 30 of its magazine brands available internationally on Apple Newsstand, after recent news that its parent Time Inc. is to place all its US brands on the platform (Batten, 2012a).

The rise in digital magazine editions suggests that by 2016 it is likely that a high percentage of publications will be in digital or online formats only. At the Inspiration & Innovation: Publishing 2011 conference organized by the Professional Publishers' Association, there were many examples of innovative uses of multi-platform content. Among the speakers was Giles Barrie, editor of *Property Week*, who has created TV shows linked to the magazine including a spin-off from the TV series *Come Dine With Me* entitled *Property Come Dine With Me*. He advised publishers to gain expert knowledge and concentrate on building audiences. Using data gained from readers to tailor content – by looking at who reads what – in a funnel effect, he said was also important.

Moreover digital versions must have a variety of content such as podcasts and video clips to explore your reader's experience. The aim is to build reader loyalty to ensure that your magazine is their first port of call. That is why digital magazines should have that added extra content as well as:

- Strong visual images.

- Consistent layouts to maintain brand identity.

- Fast download speeds, particularly important for creating and selling archives.

- Have embedded content that isn't elsewhere on the site.

## What do your readers want?

A publisher must know their audience well to build a sustainable product, looking at their needs, lifestyle, desires, then consider how they will engage with the magazine. It is crucial to consider how a reader consumes a magazine as well as analysing how that consumption may change in the future. For example, are the majority media savvy, consuming the title on a digital device during a coffee break at work or on the train as part of their daily commute? If so, a digital publication is essential.

But if it's part of a relaxation ritual – say on a Friday night with a glass of wine – then your reader may prefer the print version. Other considerations include the publishing sector it falls in. A digital version of a B2B or specialist title could include interactive links and adverts revenue. It would also give the magazine a more interactive, immediate quality and therefore the perceived value is likely to be higher.

Readers' age groups, social bracketing and technical abilities are also factors to consider. Although technology is developing rapidly, your readers may not be moving at the same pace. For example, some of your readers might not yet have an iPad or tablet equivalent so opting to produce a digital-only version might exclude this group. Other potential readers will prefer the feel, smell and layout of the traditional magazine.

The only way to decide on your initial production output is to include such questions in your audience surveys and ask focus groups. Only then will you be able to make a balanced decision as to the best formats and whether equal digital and print production would be advantageous as an added extra.

Remember every title should be unique, what suits one may not be right for a similar publication. Only thorough research will enable you to determine the best method.

As with any business, publishing continues to evolve, which is why publishers must also look at the long term when developing a magazine. Questions such as *what your readers will want in five years' time* are crucial. Next, consider how technology might evolve and plan accordingly.

## Print strategies

Although print publications face an uncertain future, some niche titles are flourishing. Certainly the mainstream lifestyle market appears to be currently saturated, but there is room for new magazines in the specialist areas and contract publishing. In today's global society, the term local is becoming more valued. Here, the term 'local' is defined as being part of a small community, though not necessarily within the same area. The community can be a small group of people with a common interest such as a hobby, business or beliefs, as well as those who share a village/neighbourhood or town.

Setting out strategies at the beginning for a print publication is essential. Defining three key strategies for success could make the difference between a magazine that sells and one that doesn't. Hence at the development stage decide on:

- **USP (unique selling point):** Each publication must have one that defines it. This will keep a magazine on track and ensure that everyone associated with it – readers, advertisers and partners – are clear on the title's purpose. For example the USP for *Vegetarian Living* magazine was defined as: Vegetarians, vegans and meat reducers looking to lead a more ethical and healthy lifestyle. It is crucial that the content must reflect the USP and not deviate from it once the publication is established.

- **Distribution – how will the title reach readers:** This strategy must reflect your target readership and their needs. Decide whether you will use a combination of subscription and wholesale through retail outlets, subscription only or free localized distribution. Whatever your strategy, it must be efficient and profitable.

- **Revenue streams – how will it make a profit:** Don't rely on advertising and circulation alone to generate sufficient income to produce a healthy profit. Today publications need multiple revenue streams to build a secure future and ensure cash flow. Think of creative strategies, which while generating revenue could also help to build reader loyalty and brand awareness. Reader events work well, as do selling affiliated goods or services.

Remember whatever strategies you decide on with print, in order to make a profit you must keep costs low. Creating strong revenue streams will sustain the publication for the long term. About 80 per cent of new magazines fail in the first two years. According to the Professional Publishers' Association, 209 new magazines were launched between 2009 and 2010 – statistically 167 of these are likely to have failed.

To test out the market, *Vegetarian Living Magazine* launched with a print run of 20,000. This had sufficient volume to both attract advertisers and to get a good price on the printing quote. By 2012, circulation has doubled. The publisher's strategy was to start low to secure the circulation volume and avoid having lots of leftover copies, which would have wasted money and could impact on cash flow jeopardizing the title's future. However, every title is different. Starting with a large circulation – particularly if you have the security of a large publishing house supporting the new launch, would work just as well, providing the target market is carefully researched and can sustain the volume.

# Print vs digital

As previously established, a publisher must embrace print and digital. However, some argue that print is too expensive to produce and distribute, and therefore could soon be obsolete. Yet while digital content in the form of PDF versions for apps is more cost effective, print should not be discounted. To produce a print edition the following costs would need to be factored into your business plan:

- Editorial
- Printing
- Distribution to retail outlets
- Subscription mail-outs
- In-store promotions
- Marketing.

Printers often require the cost of the paper to be paid for upfront, before printing a magazine. Distribution charges equate to 50 per cent of the cover price on every copy sold. This is divided between the distributor, wholesaler and retailer.

So what advantages does print have? First a print edition is accessible to everyone. The reader does not need to rely on computers, internet access or smart phone applications to read it. Print media has the power to excite people who are in relaxation mode, those who come in from work and want to forget about their laptop or phone for an hour. Some advertisers are returning to print editions because of its retention value and reference purposes or it's passed on to friends – thus extending the life and penetration of the adverts inside. This is particularly true of niche titles.

'From an advertiser's point of view print editions are making a comeback because clients want a medium that readers retain and also pass on to their colleagues, friends and relatives. Despite an uncertain financial climate, *Writers' Forum* print advertising sales have remained consistent because they are now starting to value the print medium,' says Wendy O'Brien, advertising manager of *Writers' Forum* magazine.

Readership figures can far outweigh the circulation. For example, a magazine with a circulation of 20,000 might have a readership of 60,000 if every copy is passed on to friends or colleagues and read by at least three people. At its height, *Reader's Digest* claimed 17 readers for each copy.

On the negative side, print editions cannot be updated and are expensive to distribute, whereas digital editions place fewer demands on the retail price so costs would be:

- Editorial

- Production

- Virtual distribution, i.e. online distribution via an app store.

On balance digital editions appear to have a financial edge in today's market. Not only are they cost-effective, but they can also be frequently updated, as well as adding an interactive element to their content. That said it is advisable to use both formats. The key question is: what will readers want in five years' time? Being able to anticipate the market will always put you a step ahead of competitors.

Long term, the result is likely to be a high growth of digital editions and a reduction in print. While digital distribution charges will be substantially lower than hard copy issues, production and content costs may increase as technology advances to further expand the boundaries.

## CASE STUDY – *VEGETARIAN LIVING*

## Table 4.1

| | |
|---|---|
| Launched | August 2010 by Select Publisher Services. |
| Platforms | Print, followed by online. Digital edition launched in 2011. |
| USP | Vegetarians, vegans and meat reducers looking to lead a more ethical and healthy lifestyle. |
| Objective | To be the best vegetarian magazine in the UK. |
| Strategy | Mostly print orientated, distributed in the UK through retail outlets and subscription sales. |
| Key Revenue Streams | Distribution and subscription sales, advertising plus sponsorship deals. |
| Circulation | 20,000 when launched. By August 2011 it had reached 40,000 with a readership of approximate 80,000. |
| Readership | ABC1 group with the majority being females aged 25–55. Approximately 60% of the readership is vegetarian, 24% vegan and 16% occasional meat-eaters. |

**Table 4.1** (Continued)

| | |
|---|---|
| Key readership facts (based on survey results): | • 80% of readers keep each issue for more than one month, of which more than half share their copy with at least one friend.<br>• More than 50% have purchased a product after reading a review or advert within the magazine.<br>• Almost 50% occasionally buy products online, with 33% buying products online all the time.<br>• 95% of readers trust the advice that *Vegetarian Living* gives its readers about products, with over 95% recommending the magazine to a friend. |
| Strengths | The magazine's strength is the relationship it has with readers by listening and responding to their issues – that strategy sells copies. |
| Weaknesses | The team should be wary of familiarity. This can result in stagnation where the magazine does not continue to evolve in order to keep ahead of rivals and the readership informed and entertained. |

# Freemium magazines

Founded by Mike Soutar, publishing house ShortList Media launched a series of free, weekly lifestyle titles such as *Shortlist, Stylist* and now *MODE,* a biannual men's fashion magazine. Subsequently a new trend has emerged. Previously giveaway titles were frowned upon as having little content or quality – free meant cheap. Remember that magazine that came through your door, which probably went straight in the recycling? ShortList Media's stable of high-end content mixed with mainstream style has changed the concept, proving that readers will value a free magazine if the content is good.

So how does the company's model work? For a start, these titles are weekly, readers don't have to wait three more weeks to get the next issue. The content doesn't have time to be past its sell-by date. Also this publisher has targeted the high-end market. Their magazines are aimed at readers who are professionals with a good disposable income or have future income expectations as their career advances.

Advertisers want to exploit into a mass market that spends and are looking for a product with a large ABC1 audience. In a tough economic climate like this, advertisers need to get maximum return for their advertising budget. This strategy has steered them away from small circulations, instead opting for maximum reach using online platforms, and now, free magazines. Currently *Shortlist* has a circulation in excess of 500,000 distributing to banks, universities, gyms, airlines, Eurostar and the BBC. Its sister publication, *Stylist*, achieved similar figures. Get the product and the distribution right, and free magazines can compete among the top players.

However, there are potential flaws for small publishers. First, high distribution means large start-up fees to cover production and printing. Secondly, large resources are necessary to produce a weekly magazine. Both aspects can be financially prohibitive as the magazine is likely to run at a loss for at least the first year while building up advertising clientele.

As a result, a business model that produces a quality free magazine on a limited budget and has a small to medium circulation of between 20,000 to 50,000 copies is unlikely to work. So what are your options? Additional revenue streams which bring in sufficient funds to finance the title or an affiliation partnership where costs are shared would make this model more viable. Also you could develop a pay wall on the website – but you would need to provide a suitable incentive for the reader to pay – such as must-have content or a product which is affiliated with the magazine.

Using the growth of the *Metro* and *Evening Standard,* it appears that even free daily newspapers have the potential to succeed. The key here is frequency and content – quality, accuracy and reader involvement. But you must do your research. Are local advertisers willing to pay for such a medium? If you decide to develop a national free magazine, caution is urged, as the financial costs could prove prohibitive unless you can put together a solid distribution plan and secure lots of advertising sales prior to the launch. It will also need a solid business plan to prove it is a sufficiently viable concept to raise start-up capital.

## Magazine websites

Today almost every publication has a website. However, when *Writers' Forum* launched on to the news-stands in 2000, few magazines were online. By 2006 many titles and newspapers had at least a basic online provision – usually just a duplication of the issue and updated on a monthly or weekly basis depending on the publication's frequency (also known as shovelware). Now it is the norm to have a website updated on a weekly, if not daily basis. The bigger players such as IPC, Bauer Media and NatMags, now Hearst UK, have dedicated content editors constantly updating material.

Any new title entering the market must start life with a strong online presence. Don't wait until after the launch, build in the website along with a digital platform at the start so you launch the magazine and online content together. At the planning stage you must develop a clear online strategy, which ties in with the magazine, but doesn't duplicate the majority of your content. It must complement the title, not detract readers from buying issues. When developing a site for your publication, consider the following aspects:

- **Content:** How many pages, sections and adverts?

- **Revenue:** Will your site be pay per view, free or have a pay wall to generate additional income?

- **Adverts:** What ratio per page?

- **Interactivity:** The site should be about having a conversation with your readers. How will you get readers involved? Can they provide some of the copy?

- **Sales opportunities:** Archive and sell back issues, but do describe back issues in terms of themes to maximize sales.

It is also essential to set an online style guide, which reflects the publication's identity. Websites need meticulous planning and organization of content. Remember the aim is to generate maximum traffic as well as a site that is easy to navigate. A site that has lots of pages, gimmicks and pop-up ads often takes ages to download, which will be off-putting. Keep it simple, but be consistent.

Consider the best way to structure content. It must be logical and easily accessible. Like magazines, every site must have a style guide that reflects its brand. Decide on visual imagery, tone, style and format. How long will the taster copy be? What about longer articles? There isn't a definitive answer, as each publication will have different online requirements. Research similar publications and sites, but as a general guideline don't include articles of more than 750 words. Generally online features/copy tends to be short and to the point, while headlines must be kept simple to maximize tagline opportunities.

What about extra content? Copy from each issue should not be regurgitated for the website. For example if you are running an exclusive interview in the magazine, online content should be repurposed (not regurgitated) with fresh material plus either a short video clip or podcast. Readers need to see a clear difference between the printed edition and online content.

Poor content online is off-putting to users so avoid text that is repetitive, too long or not relevant. Don't produce lengthy copy that requires too much scrolling as a site has less than a minute to convince the viewer that it is worth investigating. Remember your audience can make or break your site with a click of their mouse.

## A social media presence

A publisher's use of social media can make the difference between success and failure. It can:

- Boost circulation.

- Increase competition entries.

- Create a feeling of community among your readership.

Social media has revolutionized the way businesses operate. Most products – from fashion to food – have a presence on social media. Publishing has also had to adapt to maximize the potential reach of this medium. As a result magazine audiences have evolved from the standard model of one-to-many (one product, many readers) to many-to-many. The latter now has numerous platforms with varied content reaching a mass audience.

Readers are no longer passive. They want a conversation with the people who put their magazine together. Setting up a title without a Twitter or Facebook page is likely to affect the impact your magazine has on its intended audience – so you must build in provision for social media from the very start.

Once a presence on social media sites is established it must be publicized so that your audience can find you. Include your Facebook and Twitter user ID on all stationery such as email signatures and letter headings, inside every issue of your magazine and by putting icon links on the website.

Below are the key sites where you need to operate. However, bear in mind that progress is rapid so be ready to adapt should a new medium emerge.

**Facebook:** A great platform to communicate with your audience and keep the dialogue going. Not only can you publicize events and features in each issue, but also create a community among your readers and encourage them to interact with each other.

It also has the potential to generate reader content as well as features ideas. Look at the wall – what are your readers talking about? Do they have issues or problems they can't solve? By tapping into this you are being proactive and engaging your audience.

For example, an editor of a travel magazine might ask readers for the best holiday story or destination while a writers' publication might ask its readers for self-publishing experiences.

Today an audience is likely to value Vox Pops – they want to know about other readers' stories and their experiences. If they have the resources, editors can organize Facebook chats with their readers in real time. This has become hugely popular and helps to maintain reader loyalty.

There is also revenue potential with sponsored Facebook messages. Be careful not to overdo this, as it can be off-putting to your audience and affect your credibility.

**Twitter:** A great publicity tool that can really boost your popularity as well as promote content and competitions. To make this work your editorial team needs to tweet on a daily basis coordinating tweets with online, digital and print content. Build up your followers to boost your output. Re-tweets can also have a big impact and get your audience involved.

Revenue opportunities also exist on Twitter. Increasingly, magazines can offer sponsored backgrounds and tweets to their advertisers. While this can boost income, caution is advised. Choose your partners with care. For example a writing magazine offering such a deal to a vanity publisher could lose its reputation by association. This would be likely impact on circulation, which in the long term could result in a far greater loss in revenue.

Other social media sites include:

**Tumblr:** This platform is great for blogs, but keep the content short and sweet. In essence its aim is to tell a story in pictures so keep the content visual.

**Pinterest:** Is a virtual scrapbook where you can organize and share content as well as connecting with a Facebook and Twitter account. It has a real potential for any magazine that contains a how-to section such creative or B2B titles. Each entry shows the number of pins (users who have looked at the entry and pinned on their own board). Users can also share an item by re-pinning or tweeting as well as leaving a comment or clicking like.

**Google+:** Like Facebook only it enables more user control. Despite being in its infancy many editors are setting up on Google+. *Good Housekeeping* is one such title, which has four tabs – posts, about, photos and videos.

A word of warning – when building your title's social media presence, do monitor input and output constantly. Just as it has the power to enhance your magazine, it can also wreak havoc. An angry reader can damage your reputation if ignored. If there are negative comments on your walls or tweets respond immediately to limit any damage to your magazine's reputation.

Also, just as in print, there are legal issues to be aware of such as defamation. If in doubt always take immediate action by removing potentially damaging content from the site, then seek legal counsel.

## Exploring revenue potential

At the time of writing there is much division in the industry between charging for online content and allowing readers access free of charge. The options are:

- Offering free online content and using adverts to generate revenue.

- Having a proportion or taster content free, then charging for more detailed access.

- Making online content subscription only.

During the 2012 News:rewired conference, on *Making digital journalism sustainable*, organized by Journalism.co.uk, key speakers were keen to share their experiences on making publications successful.

One such speaker was Alicia Adams, digital editor of *The Times*, who acknowledged how the dynamics of media had changed with the evolution of smart phones and tablets. *The Times* now has 130,000 digital and 170,000 print subscribers in addition to the 470,000 news-stand sales. Alicia explained how the business model has evolved with many lessons learned with regards to pay walls. 'A change in the business model changes how we think about the relationship we have with our readers. Thinking about what happens to content when it reaches the audience and being able to retain existing readers. Understanding the value is crucial – a business imperative. Bring in the traffic and work to keep advertisers happy.'

One initiative for retaining *Times* readers was creating a live hub as a companion to the Olympics – letting their audience shape content with their stories, picture galleries, tweets and comments.

Following on from Alicia, Dennis Mortensen, chief executive and founder of Visual Revenue reiterated the necessity of drawing revenue from digital and online content. He felt it was essential to: 'Monetize your readers – keep them well served. Have a hero spot. Promote a story on the home page as this has the most revenue opportunity. The first story on the home page must be the most important one (known in newspaper terms as the leader) and it needs to get comments.' To Dennis, it is about predicting which stories will bring in the most traffic and comments. 'Make the channel sustainable' (Mortensen, 2012).

However every publication is different in terms of effective business models and the audience. John Barnes managing director of the technology and digital division at Incisive Media emphasized the importance of building on trust and quality content – advising delegates not to 'always compete on volume'. Using their B2B title, *Legal Week*, as an example he urged editors to: 'Build a loyal set of readers who keep returning to the site. It is less about reach and more about engagement. Make the experience curated – iPads, are the elective opportunity for engagement as content is the same as print in terms of article style, but integrated with the web to aid further engagement. With iPads readers are able to consume content, then expand and comment.'

At News:rewired conference in 2011, editor of the B2B title *Property Week*, Giles Barrie, stated that the free module with ancillary branding is a good thing. This perspective continues to be a working model for publications. Viewers should register on the second click and pay on the sixth, thus providing them with taster content, while the publisher can capture data for future use. (Barrie, 2011).

Currently many mainstream publishers are following this trend by offering free content online, along with some mobile apps. However, some publishing houses have introduced subscription charges. This seems to work particularly well with B2B publications, where specialist knowledge is at a premium.

The *Financial Times'* *(FT)* website, ft.com, saw a 79 per cent year-on-year increase in registered users in 2010, taking the total to more than three million. There has also been a reported 50 per cent increase in digital subscriptions on 2009, with 207,000 registering, and 900,000 downloads of *FT* apps on mobile phones and tablet devices for the period. But the *FT* is required reading in financial houses and is predominantly bought by companies not individuals. Hence it is not price sensitive.

Before deciding whether or not to charge for online content, look at your publication's content. Does it have specialist information that is likely to enhance your readers' wealth, business or career? If the answer is yes, then an online subscription is more likely to succeed.

That said, the demand for apps has grown substantially and will continue to do so. Apps have good revenue potential, but they must offer a service, tool or resource. First a publisher can charge for the initial app to enable the downloads of digital issues, then add a fee for each issue. In addition to this there is much potential for developing apps alongside content. For example if *The Stage* magazine – a B2B for actors and performers – were to run a contacts' app then they would be selling valuable information and readers would pay. Mainstream and niche titles can also make money from apps. A food magazine could sell an exclusive recipe and shopping app, while a writing magazine could develop a resource tool. Again it is about knowing your market and developing an app, which offers readers an added extra that they need.

# Summary

This chapter has shown that in today's tough climate clearly defined publishing strategies are a must. Successful publishing is about embracing technology and developing creative strategies for all three mediums – print, digital and online, while not alienating the reader.

Thus magazines should be available across platforms and editorial, treated as a complete package with content being fluid as opposed to regurgitated. It is important to understand that digital and print are not the same. Aside from distribution, the digital version has a greater capacity with its ability to embed online content such as links or videos. This gives it an advantage and more potential to earn more from advertising revenue.

An effective online strategy would be to build the site as a sampler for publishing products, in other words used as a sales pitch with taster content to entice readers to buy either a digital or print edition. However, social media should take its place on the periphery of the magazine – its focus being to enhance that sense of community within the publication while providing a forum for views.

While many new tools have evolved in publishing, some old values remain in place – the ability to engage your reader and provide quality content.

# INDUSTRY INPUT

**Sara Cremer, managing director of Redwood Publishing reveals her tips for successful publishing strategies and explains how mobile and interactive platforms will play an increasing role in the way content is consumed.**

**Figure 4.1** *Sara Cremer, CEO Redwood*

*In the next five years both mobile phone and tablet formats will thrive. The second trend will be towards more complex interactivity in content. At the moment, when we say 'interactive' what we often mean is 'has some video in it', which isn't very interactive at all. More content will become truly interactive, allowing 'readers' to play with it, reorder it and consume it in exactly the way they want. Remix culture – the ability for users to take content, chop it and make new things from it – will be really important.*

*A third, and almost opposite trend will be a revival in using traditional story telling techniques to communicate. Just as we're going through a phase now when games (through gamification) is seen as a valid way to communicate, so the traditional 'sit back and enjoy' narrative will make a re-appearance.*

*There hasn't been a successful model for how content has been paid for: newspapers, for example, have, for sometime, had mixed models of freesheets, low-cost/high-volume tabloids, and smaller circulation (but higher cost) broadsheets. Similarly, there will be no single model of payment for content in the digital space.*

*Pay per view content can exist outside the B2B market where either the technology allows it (for example: iPad magazines) or the content is so compelling that it's incredibly valuable.*

*It's worth noting that some content in the consumer space is paid for: for example, avatar designs on Xbox, or streamed events for World of Warcraft players. But . . . and it's a big but . . . the content has to be unique, because if your content is unique then people are more likely to pay for it. If someone else is doing similar content, yours had better be absolutely unique in quality if you're going to make it valuable enough to pay. Being 20 per cent better than a free alternative isn't enough: you need to be 100 per cent better.*

*Productions costs for digital editions are not necessarily cheaper than print. If you want good quality content you still need to have good quality contributors so you're not losing any staff costs. Depending on how interactive your content is (how much video, how many tools, flash modules, response mechanisms etc.) you will need to bring in new skills, which are not those of the traditional print magazine team. Costs simply depend on how many fireworks you put into the digital version, the only thing that you can be sure of is that you take out the print, paper and postage/distribution costs.*

*The secret to producing a strong digital title is absolutely NOT to treat it just as a version of the print magazine that you can see on screen. This is a totally different medium and the ideas and content should be created for the digital space (for examples, see our versions of* Electric! *And the* Electric! *E-zine. They are clearly the same brand, have the same tone, the same core values but they deliver all of that in a way that is appropriate to the channel). What is important though is to use the same journalistic skills of understanding your audience and knowing how to talk to them and engage their attention.*

## ACTION PLAN

Discuss your publishing strategies with your editorial team. Look at your audience research to gain a clear understanding of how they will read your publication and what they want. Once you have set out clear objectives assess the following:

- Content provision across your chosen platforms.

- Productions costs of your chosen mediums.

- How much revenue is each medium likely to generate?

Now define your publishing strategies to include in the business plan.

# 5

# A sustainable business model

**B**ehind every successful magazine there is a solid business plan – it is a route-map to success. Its function is to map progress from the initial concept to where you see the title sitting in five years' time. From planning to execution, this tool provides insight, direction and focus. It will also turn research into valuable data, help to determine staff needs and set out future plans.

The primary purpose is to help secure funding. No bank manager or investor will offer funds until they have scrutinized your business plan and are happy that it is realistic in its forecasts.

## Why develop business plan?

When an idea for a magazine first evolves, thoughts often focus around the visual and editorial as opposed to its profitability. If it is to succeed, a publisher must build solid strategies from the start. Setting out objectives and strategies on paper allows the business to be tested before any heavy expenses are incurred.

But is a business plan essential? Tim Danton, editorial director and deputy MD of Dennis Technology says: 'Of course a good business plan is important, but don't think for a moment that what you create in the comfort of a small room after a few weeks of spreadsheet-bashing will be what ends up driving revenue for your magazine. All the launches I've been involved in have had moments of crisis when we've realized that we've made an incorrect assumption, and we've had to adapt and change – something even established brands have to do periodically.'

Freelance UK's website reiterates the importance of a good business plan, describing it as an essential tool crucial for securing investment: 'Potential investors will look at the strength of your plan to reach a decision. Your business will not be considered without a well-thought out, business plan with realistic projects. It must sell the company as a whole, not the concept' (Freelance UK, 2013).

While you may have come up with a great publishing concept, is your company the right one to turn it into profit and secure a healthy return for investors? What will a business plan prove? Freelance UK identified the following six reasons to write a business plan:

1  Focus your efforts, set objectives and company direction.

2  Identify pitfalls before they happen.

3  Set realistic targets which allow flexibility without compromising core objectives.

4  Enable you to track your growth.

5  Structure the financial side of your business.

6  Raise finance.

Raising finance is one of the most important reasons. Starting a magazine usually incurs considerable expense, therefore the publisher must seek funding to get started. A good business plan will not only explain the product, but also provide a strategy for success and development. It will also identify whether there is a point to abort the project or an exit plan for either salvation or handsome profit.

However, business plans vary massively with each publication, explains Tim Danton. 'It boils down to how do I get money, when will I get money, how much money will I have to spend, and how on earth do I get the message out to potential readers that they want buy this thing I'm producing?'

The entire set-up, from concept to production, must be estimated realistically – beginning with the start-up figures to estimating monthly expenditure once the magazine is up and running. These estimates will show how much capital is needed to set up, as well as predicted running expenses and potential income. This will help the publisher to see how much investment is needed.

Start-up capital is usually made up from a percentage of the publisher's own money, a bank loan and investment. In *The Best Laid Business Plans*, Barrow (2001, p.6) states:

> I spend quite a lot of time working with bank managers, helping them to understand small business. They often ask me how I would convince someone of the need for a business plan. I take a purely selfish view on any venture that involves money – especially my own. I would want the maximum insurance I could have that my business idea was going to work

and that I would not lose a penny of my own money or need any more than I had anticipated. The business planning process gives me the chance to make my mistakes on paper before I am tempted to make them for real.

Barrow reinforces the rationale behind setting out a comprehensive business plan before trading. It must be well researched, set clear objectives with strategies to implement these to give your business the best chance of success.

When compiling your plan, start with financing the idea by answering the following questions:

- Is the magazine likely to sell and attract advertisers?

- Where will most of the revenue come from?

- Has it the potential to be profitable? If so, how and when?

- How will the magazine survive that crucial first two years?

Do this before you write the business plan. If you cannot answer any of the above, the concept needs a rethink.

# Defining objectives

While ideas are crucial, it is impossible to succeed without clear objectives and strategies. Business strategies should mark out success indicators while flagging up potential dangers. As a publisher, your goal is to build a successful title that utilizes print, online and digital in equal measure. But the first task is to define your key business objectives by asking two questions:

- Where do you see the magazine in five years' time?

- How do you intend to get to that point?

Once you have this set out, it is then necessary to consider the pitfalls and opportunities along the way in equal measure. This will facilitate strategies for taking the publication from concept to launch. Tools used by business owners and entrepreneurs to work out such strategies include:

- **PESTLE** (**P**olitical, **E**conomic, **S**ociological, **T**echnological, **L**egal, **E**nvironmental).

- **SWOT** analysis (**S**trengths, **W**eaknesses, **O**pportunities and **T**hreats).

There are scores of acronyms setting out formulae for business. Not all are accurate.

However, when working on a launch campaign proposal for *Vegetarian Living* a PESTLE was used. As part of the research undertaken, we examined the environment outside of the magazine and subsequently drew the publisher's attention to economic, environmental and social strengths, weaknesses, opportunities and threats.

The original PESTLE compiled for *Vegetarian Living* is shown in Table 5.1. It differentiates between threats, opportunities, weaknesses and strengths. This enables both plus and negative points to be clearly identified. Once highlighted, an action plan to counteract potential problems and maximize opportunities can be put in place.

**Table 5.1**  PESTLE for *Vegetarian Living*

| | |
|---|---|
| **POLITICAL** | ○ **A new government** – could add VAT to magazines but this might be offset with carbon footprint initiative. |
| | ❖ **Educational value** – if in line with government initiatives could be eligible for a grant. |
| **ECONOMIC** | ➤ **A rise in fuel duty** – could impact on distribution costs. |
| | ○ **W-shaped recession** – fall in sales as consumers cut back. |
| | ¤ **Niche market** – readers need an informative, reliable product. |
| **SOCIOLOGICAL** | ○ **Change to the way audiences consumes** – long-term could threaten sustainability. |
| | ¤ **Collaboration of resources** – reciprocal deals with societies groups. |
| | ❖ **Create a community focus** – feature small, local groups in each issue. |
| | ➤ **Potential biases** – towards animal cruelty organizations could alienate readers. |
| **TECHNOLOGICAL** | ○ **Lack of technological investment** – could lead to excluding audience participation. |
| | ❖ **Shift to interactive media** – reach a wider audience by creating eBooks, iPhone apps, mobile magazine readers, online interactive readership. |
| | ¤ **Utilizing social media forms** – Facebook, Twitter, blogs, forums. |

**Table 5.1** (Continued)

| | |
|---|---|
| **LEGAL** | ○ **Changes to the data protection legislation** – may impact reaching new readers or buying in databases for mailshots. |
| | ❖ **Building brand trust** – to ensure readers trust advertisements and editorial content. |
| **ENVIRONMENTAL** | ○ **Rival publications** – enhance their existing products. |
| | ❖ **Opportunity to expand** – into lifestyle section to offer a hybrid product. |
| | ➢ **Mainstream magazine distribution sales in decline** – this could impact on niche markets. |

○ = threats

❖ = opportunities

➢ = weaknesses

¤ = strengths

All the factors above need to be addressed in the business plan. Of course these will vary as every magazine is different, but the general gist such as competitors, expansion, and building a trusted brand is similar.

A major factor in the PESTLE for *Vegetarian Living* is that this was formulated before the demand for iPads and tablets. Hence there is little focus on this. Today a PESTLE for any magazine should heavily focus on developing technology. With the tablet market expanding so rapidly it is logical that within the next five to ten years the majority of readers will be consuming content on a device. Digital production is rapidly expanding and may well mean the end of mass print editions before the next decade.

# Revenue streams and funding

Your concept may be successful in terms of attracting a loyal readership, but it must generate sufficient revenue to pay for itself and make a profit. Previously magazines were sustained mostly by advertising, plus income from news-stand and subscription sales. But the old model is changing. Advertising revenue has decreased while production costs have gone up.

Advertising revenues are also shrinking. Previously the corporate sector relied on media advertising campaigns to reach their public. However, with rapid technological developments – such as websites and social media – most companies now have their own media outlets such as customer publications and online applications so do not rely so heavily on outside advertising.

The result is that magazines – as well as the rest of the media – must find additional sources of revenue to sustain them.

Sustainability is the key. Publishers can no longer just produce one product – a magazine. Instead, copy is produced for many formats, all with fresh content. The replication ratio between print and online is approximate 20 per cent duplication: 80 per cent new content. Signposting is crucial. For example readers or users depending on the medium – print, online, digital – are continually directed. A print publication must direct its readers to apps and a digital version as well as online and social media, while online content must signpost print editions, social media sites and apps.

The repercussions of such demands are that many magazines are now running at a loss as much of the content is provided free. Advertising income combined with news-stand and subscription sales is insufficient to sustain the business model. Unless more revenue can be generated many new publications will struggle. According to Tim Danton several revenue streams are the key to success. 'Advertising is of course the most common,' says Tim. 'But if you can add other streams such as events and brand extensions (one-off guides, for instance, such as *PC Pro*'s guide to Windows 8) then you'll give yourself more security.'

Do not, however, believe that secondary income can justify a publication. The core revenue must do that and peripheral or secondary income should be the icing on the cake.

So how can magazines make money? Through content seems to be the logical answer. Readers now consume a large amount of free content such as blogs, newsletters, Tweets, Facebook posts. Can a publisher turn these into income streams? Yes, there are many opportunities. Here are a few examples:

- **Advertising:** There are now opportunities to sell adverts on websites, newsletters and social media sites. Also many companies will sponsor social media pages or newsletters.

- **Advertorials:** Storytelling is big in advertising. For magazines this translates by turning an advert into a feature.

- **Paywalls:** Although some publishers shy way from setting up a paywall on their site, it is possible to get an audience to pay for some content. However, this must have an actual or perceived value. The *Financial Times* achieves this with distinction.

- **Newsletters:** These have two revenue possibilities – from sponsorship and advertising potential, but also through selling the database of subscriber's details.

- **Sponsorship:** Creating consumer demand will enable a publisher to sell sponsorship of competitions. This is fast becoming popular in the specialized and lifestyle sectors.

For example BBC's *Delicious Magazine*, which according to its media pack has a monthly circulation of 94,044, offers potential advertisers comprehensive print and online advertising. In addition, *Delicious* further explores revenue opportunities by selling competition sponsorship at £2,000, e-newsletter advert at £2,000, or solus e-newsletter at the rate of £4,000. Prices for video creation and hosting start at £5,000, while the cost of recipe or article sponsorship is from £2,500 (Delicious Magazine, 2013).

Before you get carried away by the success of BBC publications remember they have free marketing – backing of the biggest broadcasting network in the world, funded by public money.

---

## CASE STUDY

An interesting model of maximizing online advertising revenue is the-beauty-pages.com, which demonstrates additional opportunities.

Launched in 2008, statistics from a recent media kit show this online beauty magazine per month has 20,000 unique users, 100,000 page hits and 2,500 subscribers. An insert shown below, taken from the-beauty-pages.com's media pack demonstrates how the publisher is maximizing advertising revenue opportunities by offering the following deals:

- **Option 1 – advertorial:** Your brand will be included in the 'Breaking News' section of the website. Between 200 and 500 words written in editorial style, with up to three images. Advertorial will stay on the website for a whole month and will be featured on website homepage for the first week. A summary and link will be sent to database in weekly email. Bespoke advertorials can be created to support a branding campaign, with four follow-on advertorials in a monthly period.
  Current Prices: Single Advertorial £350
  Four follow-on Advertorials: £1200.

- **Option 2 – advertorial blog:** Your brand will be included in the 'Blogs' section of the website. Between 300 and 1,000 words written in zeditorial style with up to three images. Advertorial will stay on the website for a month and will be featured on website homepage for the first week. A summary and link will be sent to database in weekly email. Bespoke advertorials can be created to support a branding campaign, with up to 12 follow-on advertorials featuring on a monthly or fortnightly basis.
  Current Prices: Single Advertorial Blog £350

Six follow-on Advertorial Blogs: £1,500
12 follow-on Advertorial Blogs: £2,750.

- **Option 3 – dedicated email:** A stand-alone email sent to our entire database. Between 200–500 words, including up to four images. Current Prices: Dedicated Email £350.

- **Option 4 – competition:** Provide us with a competition prize worth between £500 and £1000. Brand logo included on the competition page for one month, plus 200 words brand info. Inclusion on weekly email, sent to database four times in month of competition.

As shown above there are numerous opportunities to make money from online advertising, but creativity is the key. However, some of the above examples may bring into question a site's integrity, so it is up to the editor to ensure ethical standards are maintained.

Another potential online revenue source is paywalls, although successful paywall models are still emerging. The *New York Times* introduced a paywall in 2011. According to a report by Jonathan Cook in the *European Magazine* many readers were upset at having to pay for access after the first 20 articles, reduced to just 10 a year later. Two years on the paywall has been acknowledged as a 'surprising success' by the *Huffington Post*. Cook states that recent financial reports show a circulation increase relative to the same quarter the previous year. (Cook, 2013).

If subscriptions to the *New York Times'* paywall continue to grow then it is logical that this model could be implemented widely across the magazine sector around the world. However, publishers should remember that any content behind a paywall must have a perceived value to create a demand.

In Britain, Rupert Murdoch followed suit with *The Times* and *Sunday Times*, but has found it hard going. This is because the magnificent BBC site is free at the point of consumption. Only the *Financial Times* among UK newspapers makes a significant profit by using paywalls. Even now the *Financial Times* finds it is competing with the global reach of Bloomberg.

Brand extensions provide another opportunity to boost income streams. With *Writers' Forum* these included producing a book (*FAQ's for Writers*), self-publishing and novel writing competitions.

Many magazines are now developing ideas that have a synergy with their title.

*Good Housekeeping* was perhaps one of the first titles to do this with their product range. In 2011 *Glamour* marked its tenth birthday by teaming up with ten high street stores, including Reiss, French Connection and Marks & Spencer, to design limited edition *Glamour* dresses.

Brand extensions are as much about revenue opportunities as they are about raising a title's profile. Increased popularity boosts news-stand sales, which makes the title more attractive to potential advertisers.

# Formatting business plans

A business plan is a professional document, therefore must be set out accordingly. A few ideas jotted down on the back of an envelope will not do, neither will a few notes typed on an A4 sheet. The plan must be in-depth and document the core structure of the business.

There are many free templates available from online sources or banks in their business start-up packs. Alternatively set up a document up from scratch using Word, which also has some templates. Useful links can be found in the Resources section of this book. Once set up, the plan must be available as a digital and print document.

To achieve a professional format, consistency is a must. Use the same fonts throughout. Standardize all headings, sub-headings, tables and bullet points. Include your logo to ensure consistent branding in all the content. This should be the masthead of the magazine to reinforce the product's identity. Also include extras such as borders to ensure the finished document looks professionally presented. Images such as a jpeg of the cover or double page spread may also be inserted in the product section to reinforce identity.

Below is a list of the essential sections.

- **Title page:** This should also contain a short, sharp vision statement.

- **Executive summary:** An overview of the plan designed to give the reader the core essentials at a glance. It should contain a mission statement, main objectives, marketing strategy, an overview of the proposed title including circulation and editorial direction, plus a summary of potential revenue streams. In addition information must include details of key personnel.

- **Contents page:** Should be simply laid out listing all the sections to enable the reader to navigate the document easily.

- **Introduction:** Set out an overview of the business plan, but do not repeat the Executive Summary. This should include how the concept evolved and identify where gaps in the market exist. It should also state the stage the business is currently at – perhaps incorporating a timeline from start (initial concept) – to launch. Highlight your star personnel in this section, but direct readers to the staff plan. Lastly it should contain a brief synopsis of how you intend to progress.

- **The product:** Make this section comprehensive. It needs to cover the magazine as one product across platform as opposed to several in different formats. The new title must be introduced as: print, digital and online. For example when marketing, many retail outlets now work as one unit across different mediums and have the strapline under their logo – in store | online | mobile.

Make the section visual by inserting a front cover and screen shot of the home page to reinforce the magazine's style, tone and identity. Explain the rationale for the magazine in detail – from the unique selling point to formats, frequency, distribution, audience and reader profiles to potential advertisers and future plans. Do include an overview of content in the form of editorial pillars that will sustain the magazine.

- **Market analysis:** Must demonstrate in-depth research of current trends and your title's position within the market. It should incorporate predicted magazine trends, market testing relating to surveys and focus groups as well as the data gained from these. Also include a detailed analysis of your closest rivals, looking at their product across platform, circulation and online analytics plus their revenue streams and advertisers.

- **Business strategy:** This explores how the business will be run therefore needs to have a **PESTLE** in addition to a **SWOT** report. Business strategy covers distribution, marketing, strategic partnerships, product pricing, sales and revenue streams.

- **Staff:** Outline your management team, including a synopses of key personnel such as the publisher, editor, deputy, advertising sales manager and distribution director. Each synopsis should summarize their relevant experience, industry achievements and salary details. Also insert a staffing plan, illustrated using a chart, and estimate how many freelance writers may be used during the course of the year.

- **Financial overview:** Itemize the level of investment needed and where the other start-up capital will be sourced as well as any potential grants for which the magazine may qualify. Don't forget to include your own cash input, which should be around 40 per cent of the total cost. Financial summaries detailing start-up costs, cash flow plus profit and loss should go in the appendices.

- **Appendices:** Pilot issue, media kit, screenshot of web page and financial summaries.

The minefield is always how much to spend on promotion – usually it is best to put what money you have into the product and utilize good ideas and PR as much as possible for promotion.

Remember the information you provide must be carefully researched and prepared.

# Financial summaries

Setting out your business finances is a priority. As a publisher you will need to know your set-up costs aka capital expenditure – the cash needed to set up the magazine, as well as day-to-day expenditure and potential revenue. This will give you an idea of how much capital will be needed so that cash flow can be managed in those early months before income starts to flow. Generally, when setting up a business a percentage of that capital will come from each of following sources:

- Private investors (such as Business Angels).

- Bank loan.

- Publisher's own money.

- Grants.

However, before applying for loans, grants or investments, a publisher must know how much is needed to get started and to cover running costs for up to six months. Therefore producing financial summaries are essential. But how detailed should these be? According to Tim Danton: 'Different people will have different strategies for this, but I find it useful to go into a lot of detail. It can help you appreciate a detail of the launch process you might not have thought about previously. Stop when you feel like you're guessing.'

It is such detail that will help you to balance cash flow. Knowing your expenditure and projecting potential income is crucial. A business owner must know there will be sufficient funds to sustain the company.

When starting out, a publisher should have the following as accounts spreadsheets:

1 **Capital expenditure:** A summary of all the business start-up costs.

2 **Expenditure budget:** This should be an estimation of business expenses for the first six months.

3 **Income targets:** Set realistic targets of projected revenue for the first six months.

4 **Cash flow forecasts**: This provides a detailed picture of expenditure and income.

Here's an approximate example in sterling (based on a publishing company located in the south, setting up a publication of average quality with 20,000 print run) of what the financial summaries should include.

**Table 5.2**   Capital expenditure (ex VAT)

| Item | £ |
|---|---|
| Serviced business premises (deposit & first month's rent) | £1,200 |
| **Equipment:** 5 iMacs & 2 Macbook Pros with MS Office + Adobe CS6, 2 iPads and 2 laser printers | £17,346.30 |
| Digital cameras (2 Canon SLRs) | £600 |
| Website (domain, hosting and build) | £4,000 |
| **TOTAL** | **£23,146.30** |

**Table 5.3**   Expenditure budget (one month)

| tem | £ |
|---|---|
| Print order (20,000) | £7,600 |
| Distribution costs (including promotion payments) | £8,000 |
| Editorial package (articles/photos) | £2,000 |
| General overheads (staff/stationary/mobile phones) | £10,200 |
| Insurance | £2,000 |
| Finance and professional fees | £1,000 |
| Contingency (20% of budget) | £3,300 |
| **TOTAL** | **£34,100** |

**Table 5.4**   Projected income (one month)

| tem | £ |
|---|---|
| *Copies sold 12,000@ £1.75 (50% of £3.50) | £21,000 |
| Subscriptions 200 @ £32 | £6,400 |
| Digital sales 1,000 @ £1.50 | £1,500 |
| Advertising revenue (net) | £7,500 |
| **TOTAL** | **£36,400** |

*estimate based on copy sales of 60% of the print run

The tables (see Tables 5.2, 5.3 and 5.4) give an approximate estimation of costs and potential income. Every magazine is different therefore costs must be estimated accordingly.

Don't forget to take into account that income owed isn't necessarily paid immediately. For example, payments from news-stand sales are made three months in arrears by the distributor while revenue from advertising sales may come in up to two months after the issue has gone to press. Therefore a publisher must allow flexibility in the cash flow to allow for this. A rigorous credit control system is essential from the start.

## Future leads the way

In the UK, Future Publishing seems to have developed a good business model to take the company forward in uncertain times. Despite sales falling in consumer magazines, sales for digital editions have doubled for some of this publisher's titles.

Perhaps its biggest success story is their monthly gadget magazine *T3*. The iPad edition of *T3* was first launched in October 2010: it is aimed at ABC1 males, aged 26–45 who are obsessed with the latest technology. Editorial features high quality content both in print and digital. The *T3* interactive edition includes 'a 360-degree, hands-on product photography, breaking news, interactive reviews and stunning image galleries'.

According to Future: '*T3* interactive iPad edition has been the UK's most successful lifestyle app, the highest-grossing app on Apple's Newsstand and the ninth-highest grossing iPad app on the entire App Store last year, beating off competition from *The Sunday Times* and *Empire*. *T3* also recently launched the first fully interactive digital edition into the Android Market' (Future, 2012).

On its website, Future cites ABC audited circulation figures for *T3* as: '70,556 out of which 49,006 are print copies, 7,327 standard digital editions and 14,223 interactive digital editions'. Announcing the figures in a press release, *T3* group publishing director Nial Ferguson said: '*T3* now sells 70,556 editions every month. This is 24 per cent up on last year and 16 per cent up on its highest ever ABC figure. The growth has come entirely from the new digital publishing landscape as over 30 per cent – or 21,550 editions sold – are now digital. This is a phenomenal result and all credit to the innovative and tireless work put in by editor Luke Peters and the *T3* team' (Future, 2012).

Future's Editor-in-Chief of Digital Editions, Mike Goldsmith, explains the rationale behind *T3*:

Launched back in September 1996, *T3* was purely print-only product. It stood for Tomorrow's Technology Today, was a spin-off from Future

Publishing's short-lived science title *Frontiers* and the cover featured the first DVD player to be imported into the UK – so a digital edition for iPad wasn't even a twinkle in its eye.

But 17 years later, you can see the brand has gone through countless changes in editorial tone and design, moving from pure technology to modern lifestyle and now comes with a website and iPad edition just as valuable as the print parent in reaching global audiences. Things change – and will continue to do so.

Coming up with the pricing structure for the app and digital edition was difficult.

Along with *Wired, Popular Science, Sports Illustrated* and others, *T3* was one of the first fully interactive editions – and in the first quarter of 2011, one of only four iPad titles to have subscriptions enabled as a test for the launch of Newsstand on iOS in Oct 2011.

How much to charge for a single issue and then a subscription? We didn't know as, apart from publishing digital replicas on Zinio (a newspaper and magazine app for Apple and Android products), there was zero precedent. So we based it on Zinio, the price of apps, the amount of content, our existing cover price in print . . . and then quickly changed it, tried various price promotions, launched a print + digital bundle, learnt to drop back issue prices based on sales patterns . . .

The lesson is: what you 'come up with' and what you 'end up with' are very different things, especially in digital. From a business perspective the biggest learning curve taking *T3* digital was ignoring the horror stories that surround any launch, print or digital. Also is the sheer importance that the digital edition has taken on. The boost to circulation that Newsstand gave, the validated circulation certificate from ABC and subsequent commercial attention from the agencies has lead to the iPad edition being a leading part of *T3*'s multi-channel strategy – so a learning curve well worth taking.

It is a lesson that Future has learned well. Despite achieving a reported six million downloads in the first six weeks of Apple's Newsstand digital app launch in 2011 (Marshall, 2012), Future Plc appeared to be on a downward spiral as the company's share price went down to 9.53p in 2012. Yet as I write, the share price is making a definite comeback indicating that press reports are correct in predicting Future as the leader of the digital revolution. As of March 2013, its share price is holding steady at around 20p.

With its latest innovations and award-winning digital products, Future appears to leading the way forward in an uncertain climate by working towards a sustainable business model to secure a way forward for the magazine industry. As the company has shown, in order to survive publishers have to start bringing in revenue from their digital content.

# Summary

As reflected in this chapter, a sustainable business model is dependent on the many components of a business plan. Such plans are crucial not only to secure funding, but for mapping the direction the company should take. It should not only include the essentials to document the business – such as the product, staff and finance – but also strategies for taking the company forward. An entrepreneur needs to know where they want to be – not just tomorrow but in five years' time. More important is the journey to that destination, explaining how they intend to achieve this.

These are difficult times for publishing, but there is a way forward and your business model might just be it. So think laterally, make your financial figures as realistic as possible – underestimating will leave you short on funds, while overestimating could suggest you don't have a grasp on the finances. Also take the advice of professionals. Appointing a financial director – even as a part-time non-executive – may seem costly at the time, but it is likely to be a sound investment.

But most of all think about how you want to develop the magazine, particularly the digital aspect. Technology is advancing at a rapid pace, so consider what your reader will want in three or five years' time. That might be personalized content, if so how will you deliver? And, how will you plan for the additional investment needed further down the line.

At the heart of everything you do – including the business plan – must be your reader. As Tim Danton, Editorial Director and Deputy MD of Dennis Technology, explains, they are the key to a successful magazine:

> To know who your reader is – and know that what you'll be offering them is something they'd be willing to buy. The mistake many people make is to produce a magazine that caters to their own interests, but fail to realize that there are only 5,000 other people like them in the UK, of whom only a few per cent are ever likely to buy the magazine itself.

Whether you are a budding writer, entrepreneur or sportsperson, goal setting is fundamental to achieving success.

Although the publisher may deviate at times from the business plan, it is an effective tool for setting up and taking a company forward. The more information it contains, the smoother your path to success will be.

As the Chinese say, no battle plan ever survives contact with the enemy – and no business plan survives contact with reality. But you must have one, be flexible and build in as many contingency factors as you can.

# INDUSTRY INPUT

**Figure 5.1** *Mike Goldsmith*

**Mike Goldsmith, Editor-in-Chief of Digital Editions at Future, shares his thoughts on what makes a sustainable business model.**

*Business models for magazines are likely to change substantially during the next five years. The majority of change will inevitably be around the multi-device opportunities that digital offers. Rather than it being perceived as a simple marketing opportunity, digital now represents a wide variety of revenue streams.*

*In just 18 months, the global opportunities around digital editions and the iPad have led to some of Future's titles having larger digital subscription bases than in print. The future lies in 360 degree commissioning – print products enhanced for tablet by exploiting content already commissioned for website, podcast, YouTube etc. or just capturing content at the commissioning stage (film your interviews and cover shoots etc.). Live events can also be a rich source of additional content.*

*What makes a magazine financially viable? Understanding your audience, indispensable content, communicating your brand and having a multi-channel strategy. Business models come and go but you need to totally understand who the consumers of your content are, what they want and how they want it. The real win is to keep asking that question plus do something with the answers.*

*In print, the two biggest expenses you are likely come across are staff costs (and the subsequent overheads) and paper (more expensive than it's ever been). You can see why digital – with its content feeds, new ad budgets, global audiences and low staffing levels (with the added option for working from home) – is so attractive.*

*Up until recently, there has not been guaranteed revenue coming from digital to rival that from print's cover price. But a wider variety of online solutions (yes, including paywalls), digital editions plus the increased CTR (click through rates) around tablets are changing that.*

*While some magazines may develop successful paywalls, this model won't work well for others. It really depends on the audience you're targeting. If you're chasing a large, mainstream audience to sell to large, mainstream advertisers, your publication will be free. If you're targeting a smaller but valuable audience of enthusiasts, you can sustain a higher price point.*

*The best news is that digital – and digital editions – increases the reach of both these models. The App Store now enables you to publish titles to 155 countries with the push of a button. You are now a global publisher but likely publishing a UK-specific title. Such a big opportunity needs an equally big shift in strategy.*

*What is the best way to make money from digital? There's a question – so let's put a date on it. In 2013, I work for what is still a magazine publisher. We are migrating to digital as while annual print sales still stand at 24 million magazines, but we know that long-term the print industry is in decline. Right now, digital accounts for 54 per cent of our total ad revenues based on a web portfolio that attracts more than 50 million unique visitors a month online.*

*Future makes $1 million a month from copy sales on digital editions, led by sales of T3, the UK's number one iPad magazine. Some of our magazines now have more digital subscribers than print ones. Of our total revenues, digital now accounts for 23 per cent. All this is in a constant state of flux as the iPad is barely three-years-old.*

*So the best way to make money from digital? Just be 'in' digital and keep adapting.*

*Print and digital formats can still coexist in the long-term, especially in the enthusiast/specialist markets, which now make even more sense with digital's global reach. Digital editions are still so early in their evolution, it's hard to predict where they will settle down but it's likely to involve high frequency, lower price-point and a live element. Print titles, however, may end up more expensive and bought somewhere other than the high street. However, enthusiasts are just that – and as long as a specialist product is right for these audiences, they will buy both.*

*It's always been important to have a solid business plan before setting up a magazine, but in 2013 rather than the word 'solid', I'd use the word 'agile'. The impact of digital, be it iPad, connected TV or smartphone, means that everything changes all the time – pricing model, ad model, distribution, exports, the lot.*

*Previously, publishers could look to precedent in their own business or to rivals as they were dealing with one channel – print. Not anymore. Right now, the only precedent is that everything changed yesterday and it might change again today. Your business model needs to be able to adapt to something new all the time.*

*A business plan for any new title needs to demonstrate that the magazine will be viable and sustainable. In your initial pitch to investors, the initial editorial premise, content mix, market research, SWOTs on rivals, advertising research, marketing campaign and financials. Launch costs and projected revenues on all that plus risk/exposure.*

*But just how detailed should the plan's financial summaries be? For a launch, you should be looking at basing your proposal on a standard publishing top sheet – staffing and freelance, projected ad revenues, copy sales, launch costs, marketing, travel and expenses etc. – for the first three years. Get some proper publishing input.*

*Summarize that initial investment based on set-up and launch (year one), paying back your costs and breaking even (year two) and then into profit (year three). Although if you could replace the word 'year' with 'month', you'd be a lot more likely to get your project green-lit!*

*Setting out a vision in your business proposal for future development is a must. What kind of future however, should be based on where your industry, audience and advertisers are going as much as what your vision might be.*

*When publishing a new title you need a plan. Talk to the audience as soon as you can and as much as you can, make sure you consider every channel be it digital or live.*

*Our contemporary craft title, Mollie Makes, was based on identifying a growing subset of our existing crafting audience. We reached out to them via dedicated community management and built a solid online following before we'd even launched – 26,000 Facebook fans, 10,000 Twitter followers and countless YouTube views. That translated into a properly engaged and loyal audience who wanted the project to succeed. This in turn led to Mollie Makes breaking Future's new subscription record, achieving 3,000 subscribers before issue two went on sale.*

*We've subsequently continued that strategy and grown the title into a set of high-price bookazines in related areas (baking, sewing etc.), a weekly iPad project-based title in Gathered . . . by Mollie Makes, plus we are currently looking further afield in what Mollie could mean in different countries and languages.*

*My advice to someone thinking about starting up a new magazine? Do lots of research. Content is relatively easy to come by (there will also be enthusiasts wanting to create something and wanting a by-line on it!), brand strategy changes with the wind and figuring out advertising strategies could take up 25 hours a day, all day. Instead, spend all your time researching, talking to and 'recruiting' your audience – it's these people who will stay with you when advertisers, trends and social media strategies leave.*

## ACTION PLAN

Find a suitable template for your business plan then write it. When complete, produce a comprehensive financial summary with a cash flow forecast. The financial summary must include the following:

- Capital expenditure (initial start-up costs).

- Expenditure for the first six months (or issues if a monthly title).

- Target income for first six months (based on realistic estimate from revenue streams).

**Tip:** When estimating expenditure, you will need to get quotes. In business you must get the best detail in terms of quality and price. Get three quotes for printing and office space.

---

# 6

# Branding and editorial concepts

**B**randing is about building an instantly recognizable product. In magazine terms, that means sexy, purposeful and trusted. But how is a brand actually created?

One of the world's leading experts on branding, Jean-Noël Kapferer, PhD, a Professor at HEC Paris, defines it as: 'a product or service becomes a brand when customers and non-customers have an emotional relationship with, or perception of the product or service based on differentiation, relevance, knowledge and esteem' (Blakes Marketing, 1998: 7).

Magazines need editorial consistency across all content to create an identity. To achieve this there has to be a definitive house-style that is consistent with the title's brand values. An example which perhaps best illustrates this point is the BBC's magazine, *Who Do You Think You Are?* It is part of a successful, global brand across four mediums – print, digital, online and TV. While all of its products are unique to each platform, they share that same identity – thus the Who Do You Think You Are? brand is instantly recognizable.

In this chapter we will look at developing a magazine as a brand from core values and to building a strong, iconic image that will stand out on the news-stands. Achieving a consistent house-style is central to a brand's visual identity, while avoiding a repetitive layout will also be covered.

## Brand characteristics

Blakes Marketing Practice working with the Professional Publishers Association states in its *Magazines As Brands* Report (1998), that there are four key characteristics of branding:

- Functionality
- Awareness

## Table 6.1

| Functionality | Awareness | Personality | Values |
|---|---|---|---|
| • Purpose | • Promotion | • Editorial | • Longevity |
| • Relevance | • Distribution | • Subject matter | • Consistency |
| • Usability | • Longevity | • Tone | • Editorial quality |
| • Accessibility | | • Writers | • Esteem/Respect |
| • Frequency | | • Packaging | • Customer Care |
| • Price | | • Binding | • Editorial |
| • Differentiation | | • Paper quality | • Subscriptions |
| | | • Photos | • Adverts |
| | | • Value for money | |

- Personality
- Values.

These will shape a title and determine whether or not it will be successful. Table 6.1 has been based on Blakes' Four Dimensions of the Magazine Brand.

As this table illustrates, each dimension is reflected in content and appearance – not just on its relationship with the reader. Furthermore, Blakes Marketing suggests that: 'the strength of a publication is dependent on the relative proportions of these characteristics, with strong brands demonstrating high levels of personality and values' (Blakes Marketing, 1998).

However, the report also argues that awareness, while a prerequisite of a strong brand, adds no value on its own. Awareness contributes only through methodology of the promotional aspects.

Despite being more than ten years old, Blake's model is effective in determining successful branding within a magazine. Each of the four dimensions is connected and thus must be incorporated into the magazine's identity. For example, the cover price, which falls under functionality, is central to a publication's identity. A high cover price of £3.50 or more defines the audience category, such as the sought after premium band ABC, who usually have a high disposable income. Whereas mid- to lower-priced titles denote the CDE grouping low-end market. This in turn affects:

- How the magazine is promoted.

- Its personality in terms of content and packaging.

- Values of editorial quality, advertisers and strategic partners.

Alignment of those four dimensions is crucial when building a sustainable brand. As well as having an identity, a brand must create a need in the consumer. This enables the publisher to set a clear path for the magazine's financial future.

# Building your brand

When developing a magazine, it is necessary to think of it as a brand, building content around a central ethos, with the title's identity at the core. Branding is reflected in:

- **A magazine's core values** – reflects its ethical boundaries, moral obligations to readers, and value of the content.

- **Cover price** – is your product high- or low-end, where does it fall in terms of audience classification, ABC1 or DE?

- **Design** – achieving a consistent house-style in print, digital and online.

- **USP** – needs to align your product's perceived ideals with its core values.

- **Promotion** – must reflect your title's identity in style and tone.

- **Advertising/sponsorship** – all advertisements and strategic partners need to match the product's core values.

Katy Dunn, editor of *Hinge* magazine, has worked on numerous publications including *Grand Designs Magazine*. For her, branding is about consistency, 'people need to know where your magazine stands' and the trust, which comes from consistency and knowing your audience. 'Be everywhere, do social media, online, and blogging. Be recognized for doing one thing well, rather than lots of things averagely.'

A publisher must define core pillars before developing the concept. Aligning these values and ensuring they set the standard for content and design is the first step towards building trust and a good reputation. This needs to be reflected in the title's name to form the basis of your brand's identity both for readers and advertisers. Remember brands are all about trust and reputation.

Examples of iconic, trusted British magazines include *Radio Times, Reader's Digest* and *Good Housekeeping*, whereas global-brand counterparts – recognized around the world – are *National Geographic, Time* and *Vogue*. All have values, which translates as trusted content.

---

### CASE STUDY – *RADIO TIMES*

Despite currently facing competition from numerous rivals on the news-stands, the *Radio Times,* launched in 1923, has built a reputation for providing trusted content on TV, radio and film. It is a brand readers rely on. According to the latest figures from BRAD, it is read by more than two million people, with an average print circulation of 865,562 per issue and a ratio of 52:48 female/male ABC1 readers. While the *Radio Times* has a strong circulation today this figure is far below its peak – before the advent of the *TV Times* and other similar publications – when the circulation was around eight million copies a week.

Its BRAD profile describes the publication as 'A premium guide for multi-channel listings with in-depth coverage of the best on TV, radio and film' (2013). Households across the UK regard the magazine as being the definitive guide to weekly TV and radio programmes. Trust is central to its identity.

To reinforce the brand's values, the title publishes The *Radio Times* Promise in every issue: '*Radio Times* provides trusted, independent journalism that has been gathered without fear or favour from television, radio and entertainment companies. We cherish our editorial integrity and independence as we strive to give you accurate and discerning guidance to the very best of broadcasting and film.' This further demonstrates the value of setting out clear brand values and ensuring these align with content. It is this strategy that has made the *Radio Times* both popular and sustainable, despite fierce competition in a tough economic market.

---

## Visual aspects of branding

Magazines must stand out from competitors by having a unique identity. This starts with the masthead (your magazine's title). It needs to be distinctive and instantly recognizable from 10 feet – the distance a shopper might be from the shelves in a shop or supermarket. Below (Figure 6.1) are three iconic covers, where the masthead is instantly recognizable even if the rest of the cover is concealed.

Each cover has a clear identity – in terms of the masthead and cover layout. However, it is essential to recognize the differences between issues of a magazine, so the cover looks fresh and vibrant every time. For example if you

**Figure 6.1** *a)* Writer's Digest *June cover, b)* Reader's Digest *cover, c)* Oldie *cover*

**Figure 6.2**  *a)* Writer's Digest *Feb cover, b)* Writer's Digest *June cover*

were to compare the February and June 2012 covers of *Writer's Digest* magazine (Figure 6.2), they would be the same, but different.

Both covers have the same masthead in a banner across the top, then a central image that takes up three quarters of the page and is right aligned. The cover lines also follow a consistent style on every issue. The differences are subtle, but sufficiently distinctive for each issue to be unique.

Visual branding is about ensuring that a magazine cover stands out. Consumer and specialist publications need covers that make a sales impact, where numerous titles within a subject are competing for readers. Today it is as much about selling a brand as it is about content. To achieve a clear identity a cover needs:

- **A strong masthead** – title of the magazine that is recognizable away from the cover.

- **To be busy** – which gives a perceived content value.

- **Have distinctive** haptics – how the magazine looks and feels in terms of paper, layout and house-style.

- **Buy-me cover lines** – such as 'how to . . .' which create a need within the reader.

- **A strong sell** – an overall feeling that the title is designed specifically for individuals.

For B2B publications or subscription-only titles there is less emphasis on covers. Because there are no sales within a retail environment it does not need to be part of the business model. However, it is crucial that branding – in terms of consistency in cover design – is apparent, even if it does not have to define the product.

This needs to be consistent across all products – print, digital, online and social media outputs. For example, do headings in the title's digital pages reflect the style of those in the print format? What about panels – are they boxed out or shaded? How are pull – or drop-in – quotes defined? Will feature layouts keep to the same grids – across two or three columns and will this differ with each section? Also little stylized symbols such as putting an icon at the end of each article/story to signify the end can make a big impact and should be unique to your title.

Visual branding applies to everything connected to the publication – this includes:

- **Masthead** – when used anywhere such as apps, subscription adverts, newsletters, press releases, correspondence, email signatures and social media content must be the same as it appears on your magazine cover reinforcing the title's identity.

- **Online identities** – this must be publicized as much as possible. Make sure that your Facebook, Twitter, other social media accounts and website addresses appear on staff email signatures, inside the magazine, on all correspondence and online.

- **House-style** – this must be consistent in the layout and contents applying to print and digital products, apps, website and e-newsletters. Don't forget to include small icons such as symbols unique to your title's content.

Remember consistency is paramount. Staff must be directed to observe visual brand concepts as well as the values. Style guides need to be set up to reflect this, everyone in the company must have a copy and adhere to it.

# Editorial consistency

Once a visual identity has been established, the format for content takes shape. One of the first jobs is to define key editorial pillars, or themes on which to peg your content. For example when *Writers' Forum* was relaunched on the news-stand the team felt it important to identify the key themes on which content would be commissioned. These were:

- 'How to' articles
- Writing courses
- Author profiles
- Self-publishing
- Fiction
- Poetry
- Marketing features.

This gave the team a basic framework covering the key aspects of the subject. As well as consideration to the reader, this framework was also developed to maximize advertising sales. For example it was no accident that the marketing themes reflected categories for advertising sales.

Over the years *Writer's Forum* has included many peripheral items such as writers' working environments, technology and even a nod to festivities with its annual 'Christmas presents for writers' spread. However, the editorial pillars remained the basis on which copy was commissioned.

Equally important are decisions on the flow of content. How many sections the magazine will contain, where will regular articles/items sit and what will be the prime locations for advertising? These choices include setting a format for regular editorial slots, columnists and cover stories or key features to appear in the magazine.

Creating a flat plan is the only way to set out an issue. In every editorial office you will find a flat plan pinned up on the wall or available on the team's computers. It is usually put together in either Microsoft Word or InDesign using a series of boxes to represent the magazine pages. It is a diagram or map of the issue – magazine covers and inside pages – detailing what content or which advert should be on what page. It also will show sections, pages specifically allocated to advertising as well as regular slots such as 'Hello from Editor', contents pages and regular editorial slots. The remaining gaps will be filled in as each issue evolves.

The flat plan is a crucial planning tool. It clearly identifies blank pages yet to be allocated a feature, filler or advert while enabling the editor to rejig the content should a problem arise. What causes a rejig? Numerous problems such as an advertiser dropping out at the last minute leaving a spare page, a feature needing a longer spread or an essential article, which turns up just as the issue is about to go to press.

Editorial strategy is not all about planning where content will go in the magazine. It's about creating a unique voice that will keep readers buying the publication. Being known for either having a popular columnist or creating a unique editorial concept will not only boost readership, but also enhance the quality of the magazine. Here consistency is essential – once a regular editorial piece is established then readers should be able to find this quickly in the same place every month.

One example of this is the lifestyle magazine *Easy Living*, published by Condé Nast, which at the time led the way with a page called 'My life in books'. This regular editorial piece featured a well-known person, who talked about their favourite books, which had made an impact on their life. Soon other lifestyle titles followed suit with similar style features. Now the angle 'My life in . . .' takes many forms.

Other aspects such as setting an average feature length and style of writing also contribute to the quality of the title, creating consistency. Will the editorial incorporate one or two in-depth pieces of 2,000 words or will features be capped at between 1,000 and 1,200 words? How do you make such decisions? This depends on the nature of your title. Lifestyle magazines might err on short features, while business publications are more likely to include in-depth, investigative features of around 2,000 words. It is also dependent upon the readers' needs – short entertaining and informative content verses investigative, long articles, which demand concentration. The discipline of following style is essential and nobody does it better than *Time* magazine.

## Aligning content

Ensuring content is aligned across your brand can be difficult. Too much repetition must be avoided, particularly in online and social media forums. In both cases the editorial must be fresh. Each platform must have a purpose and signpost of mediums. Online content must sell the digital and print edition of the magazine, as should its social media forums. The publication – digital and print – also needs to direct readers to the web. All content must reflect the magazine as a brand – so consistency is crucial.

During her time on *Grand Designs* Katy Dunn had first-hand experience of multi-product branding. She explains how the editorial team aligned the magazine with the Grand Designs' brand:

Superficially by using the Channel 4/*Grand Designs'* logo and Kevin McCloud's face on the cover. I say superficially, but actually it was crucial for the news-stand profile – one look and potential readers 'got it'. McCloud's face was a shortcut to building trust in the magazine as the TV programme had already set up the relationship.

The tone and content of the magazine had a distinct identity under the umbrella of the Grand Designs brand. We would feature at least one 'TV house' per issue and the editorial team liaised with programme producers to schedule the best times to include the houses, but that's as far as it went. The magazine was allowed to be autonomous.

The profile of the TV show was crucial in differentiating the magazine from the rest of the homes magazines on the news-stands – it helped with the initial pick-up rate. However, it was important for the magazine to be more than just an extension of the TV show. We wanted the magazine to be useful as well as beautiful and ultimately it was the quality and depth of the research and information provided that kept our readers returning.

We toyed with trying to match the *Homes and Gardens* brigade for gloss, but ultimately that wasn't what the brand was about, it was about authenticity, substance rather than gloss. And anyway, we didn't have the budget.

Effective branding entails ensuring that, while each issue contains new copy, the layout and formula are effectively the same. Defining a content strategy across the brand is more difficult. 'Usually it's pretty clear what content suits which platform,' explains Bill Dunn, editor-in-chief at Redwood Publishing.

'Although increasingly editors are asked to make savings by rolling content across several platforms. This has a huge impact on everyone and makes shoots longer as photographers jostle with directors of photography (for video) and journalists.'

To achieve brand identity across content, Bill recommends setting out what your magazine stands for at the start. 'In its heyday *FHM* used to interrogate feature ideas by asking "Is it funny, sexy or useful?" Everything else got binned. Try writing two or three words that encapsulate your brand and then apply that "filter" method to editorial ideas – it can work for any title.' As an editor, Bill says his most successful strategy was knowing his readers, and employing the ideas filter.

He also advises never saving a good idea for next issue. 'If you use up all your good ideas, you'll think of more. If you sit on them you get constipated. And you could get run over by a bus tomorrow.'

*Stylist* is a free title published by Shortlist Media targeted at female commuters. It has an average weekly circulation of 431,266 (BRAD) and is hugely successful. In April 2012 *Stylist* launched its first tablet edition on

Google Currents – an app which enables users to have free, digital magazine and newspaper editions on their phone or tablet. It currently has 274,990 subscribers (Google Currents). The *Stylist* website boasts 300,000 page impressions of which 30,000 are unique users or browsers.

In every issue its formula is the same, but always uses a new theme. Judging by its circulation figures, the formula has been extremely successful across print and digital, though online actual web users equal only 10 per cent of the print circulation. Stylist has shown that a free magazine can be a quality product with a high-end readership. Again branding has played a key part in this. The magazine has distinctive layouts with icons to highlight quotes and the end of articles – all unique to *Stylist*.

# Digital editions

With the development of the iPad and subsequent tablets, digital editions are now feasible and exploited as paid-for-content. As discussed in Chapter 4, digital editions are similar to the print version. However, digital versions allow far more possibilities such as embedding video or links into the pages thus enhancing the user's experience and enabling the reader to build a library of issues without the bulk of print versions.

As with print, when creating a digital edition it is important to remember this is just an extension of the magazine, the only key difference is format. Therefore it must replicate brand identity with a consistent style, tone and voice. The layout should mirror the print edition but include some extras. Additional copy, which is embedded, such as video, also needs to reflect the publication's identity style and tone.

The opportunity with digital is to create a more interactive edition. It is likely that most digital users will be multi-tasking, perhaps on the move. Therefore their attention span may be less than if they were at home with a cup of coffee. They are also likely to be technologically competent and want to engage with the article they are reading. Here exists an opportunity to tailor the content accordingly by ending with a question to encourage feedback and contributions to threads on its Facebook page or tweeting.

As a result the digital editorial strategy differs from the print edition. It must be more flexible to maximize the version's full potential. The editorial content guidelines should be set accordingly. Features and content must incorporate interactive elements as well as prompts in the copy to encourage reader responses. All staff know the digital guidelines and follow them. It is crucial the team has a clear picture of the product they are producing and that it aligns to the magazine's identity.

# Brand extensions

Although not defined as such, brand extensions have provided a way of exploiting magazines for years and take many forms. For example, *Writing Magazine* began a newsletter and short correspondence courses – this not only made the magazine popular, but also provided a cushion against times when circulation dipped. *Good Housekeeping* is another magazine which used this strategy of endorsing products and eventually selling these to their readers.

Today, brand extensions are frequently a necessity. *NME* expanded to incorporate a radio station, events and TV. The BBC, while a non-profit making organization as a broadcaster, does profit from its magazines. Its titles, such as *Top Gear* and *Who Do You Think You Are?* have been established alongside popular television programmes to exploit the brand. Given its free TV and radio exposure, beyond the resources of most publishers, it can hardly fail.

Under the Cosmo brand, Hearst publishes *Cosmopolitan, Cosmo Campus* and *Body*. Other extension include Cosmo The One, a dating site, and Cosmo Shop.

Why are publishers so keen to maximize their brands? Many know it makes shrewd business sense, particularly during a tough economic climate where magazine sales are down and advertising revenue is falling. For others it is about keeping ahead of their rivals. Other considerations include the period following the rapid development of technology where publishing houses have not quite worked out a successful business model to exploit their online content.

When developing brand extensions how far should you go? As with creating a brand it is really about trust and balance, providing additional services that will not only increase revenue, but also offer readers a product or service that gives added value. Any extension must be built around the magazine, which is why the best models to analyse are probably those such as *Writing Magazine* or its hugely successful American counterpart, *Writers' Digest*.

# Summary

As explored in this chapter, branding impacts on every aspect of a magazine, encompassing visual, content, reputation and associated partners. The first step when creating a brand is to define its core values, then build content and layout around these. Consistency is the key and must be taken across all content – print, digital, online, as well as any other products associated with the publication such as e-newsletters.

However, the work doesn't end just because a brand is established. It is crucial to maintain and review it on a regular basis. Usually this is better as evolution rather than revolution.

Also significant changes to the publication – or brand extensions – should not be made without considering the brand as a whole. For example a total relaunch would have to re-evaluate existing brand values and not just be a makeover of cover and content. *Company* magazine's relaunch reinforces this point. The title changed on every level, taking on a fresh identity with its scrapbook style reflecting the re-emergence of scrapbooking with sites such as Pinterest. It demonstrates an attempt to engage with trends and modern practices.

Other aspects, such as taking advertising sponsorships or forming strategic, reciprocal partnerships also reflect brand values. A publisher must ensure that their core values align. For example a writing magazine forming a partnership with a vanity publisher would impact severely on the title's values – readers may lose faith and move to a rival publication.

Thus when developing a magazine think in terms of the brand. Remember that establishing and keeping strong core values will ensure the product is not only sustainable but also trusted by its readers.

# INDUSTRY INPUT

**Figure 6.3** *Jessica Strawser, photo by Christine Polomsky*

**Jessica Strawser, editor of *Writer's Digest*, reveals the secrets of editorial consistency, the importance of creating a community for readers and offers advice on how to turn a magazine into a brand.**

*It's almost impossible for one editor alone to ensure consistency and brand identity across all media. If your online efforts are successful, you quickly find that it's much too big of a job for one person. The key is to put other editors in place who are on board with your brand's integrity and mission – and who understand your audience.*

*Not only do we have a dedicated online editor who is instrumental in that extension of the* Writer's Digest *brand, but every editor on our team has a hand in building and maintaining our vibrant social media presence and online-exclusive content. My role is to ensure the goals of those efforts are well defined and clearly communicated to everyone involved.*

*What do readers like most about* Writer's Digest*? It's often said that writing is a solitary endeavour, but I think the magazine fosters a sort of camaraderie, not just among our immediate readership, but the writing community at large.*

*All of our issues feature interviews with bestselling authors, who often reveal they are humble individuals grateful for their success and generous in sharing what they've learned along the way. They are not afraid to admit that they still struggle with some of the very things aspiring writers face – whether that's the agony of creative blocks, or of rejection, or self-doubt. It's refreshing, inspiring and reassuring.*

*We also celebrate the success of debut authors, feature submissions from our readers in light-hearted contests and columns, while inviting further discussion online. The magazine aims to always provide inspiration alongside information and work to foster a feeling of community. I think our readers seem to respond to that above all else.*

*Our approach to organizing our content flow is a key aspect of what sets* Writer's Digest *apart from our competitors. Every issue has comprised a themed feature package. A lot of thought, analysis and planning goes into each year's editorial calendar well ahead of time, and then we aim to put together the most comprehensive coverage of each topic that we have space to print. From there, I try to order the features in the way I'd want to come to them as a reader.*

*Sometimes, we start with the simplest approaches to the topic and then move on to progressively complex or advanced articles. Other times, we'll aim for a chronological approach – for example, starting with articles on writing a manuscript, followed by articles on revising it, followed by articles on submitting it. The feature well, as with many other magazines, follows an up-front section of more bite-sized, trend- or time-driven columns, and the book concludes with some of our more informational departments.*

*Our online content is organized very differently. A key goal being to present information so that readers can find exactly what they're looking for in terms of specific topics or single articles quickly. The magazine is designed as more of a reading – or at the very least –browsing experience, from start to finish.*

*Technology has doubly impacted* Writer's Digest *readers in particular because of the way it has affected publishing – the very industry that they aspire to be a part of. The very definition of what it means to be a published author is changing, and more control is shifting into the hands of the authors, in large part because of innovations in eBooks and self-publishing technologies and the rise of online-exclusive venues for quality work.*

*The impact is probably greater than anyone can even fully grasp. It has effected how they consume* Writer's Digest *as we now have digital issues and digital subscriptions, available as PDF downloads and for e-readers such as the Kindle. But the vast majority of our readers still prefer print. As writers, most of our readers do still aspire to be published in print.*

*How magazine content will be consumed in ten years' time could vary widely by magazine depending on the audience it serves and what that audience prefers. More and more, the readers dictate the medium. Publishing houses that do not keep pace with advances in technology will eventually be left behind. It's as simple as that. My sense is that this is currently much more important for books than it is for magazines, but time will tell whether or not that's correct.*

*Technology has also enabled us to develop our existing brand extensions. We are fortunate to have long been a part of a diverse and well-defined brand:* Writer's Digest Books, Writer's Market *(both the annual print books and the online subscription database WritersMarket.com), and* Writer's Digest University *(formerly Writer's Online Workshops) have all been around for decades.*

*More recent brand extensions are not extensions of the magazine alone but of the entire* Writer's Digest *community. Of note, we now have popular conferences in New York City as well as on the West Coast, an enormously successful line-up of live webinars, which then become on-demand webinars, as well as a subscription-driven* Writer's Digest *Tutorials hub of online video instruction.*

*What's the best way when launching a new title to build a brand? Know your target reader. Always keep the needs and wants of that reader at the forefront of every decision you make – whether it's a new paid service or product that's been months in the making, or a single off-the-cuff tweet or Facebook post on a Saturday afternoon.*

## ACTION PLAN

Develop a clear editorial strategy for your title across platform – print, digital and online.

When undertaking this task you must identify those key editorial pillars that will provide the core content with sufficient stimulus and variety to sustain content. Do not neglect to ensure that your editorial strategy appeals not only to readers, but also to your advertisers. They must be complementary – after all the advertising pages of *Vogue* or *Country Life* hold nearly as much appeal to the readers as the editorial content.

Also explore brand extensions. Start by analysing the most successful magazines then take a closer look at those titles that are similar to your publication. Now identify at least two possible extensions that will boost your title's popularity and increase revenue potential.

# 7

# Distribution strategies

**P**roducing an excellent magazine that fills a gap in the market won't guarantee success without the right distribution plan. It is fundamental to making the business model work. It impacts on everything. Good distribution equals sales and circulation, which in turn will enable the publisher to secure strong advertising revenue.

According to a report by distributors COMAG: 'Every year there are more than 1,000 proposed new magazine launches, but only one in three makes it to publication and the news-stand. Out of approximately 100 new titles which launch each year only half become established magazines' (COMAG, 2013).

Competition is fierce, particularly on the news-stand, but there are numerous distribution models to choose from. Make sure you opt for the one that fits your audience – be it news-stand, targeted, subscription-only, door-to-door or street, or targeted venue distribution for free titles.

This chapter will guide you through the necessary stages – from deciding the best distribution method to appointing a distributor.

## Distribution methods

Before deciding on your key strategies, think about that first print run. How many copies of the magazine should you begin with? This ultimately depends on your target audience and distribution methods.

Distributing your title doesn't mean it has to go through the news-stands, but to succeed it is probably best to use a distributor. Their advice will be invaluable. Small publishers now employ a circulation specialist on a consultancy basis to maximize sales. Larger outfits appoint somebody full-time.

Distribution options are as follows:

- **Wholesale only:** through retail outlets such as WHSmith, newsagents and supermarkets. This method must be done via a distributor. The total cost of this equates to 50 per cent of the cover price, plus payments to each retail outlet that stock the magazine. This is unique to each title as it is dependent on factors such as the type of publication, the tier of stores the publisher is targeting such as large or travel outlets and how many competitors are stocked.

- **Wholesale and subscription sales:** Usually 80/20 split – 80 per cent to wholesale while 20 per cent go to subscribers.

- **Target outlets only:** This works for specialist magazines that are only distributed to specific outlets – those that have a synergy with the title. For example *Natural Health* magazine is available from health food shops as well as on the news-stands.

- **Digital:** Distribution is done through channels. The current main ones are Apple Newsstand, Blackberry Newsstand and Kindle Fire. These sell issues or subscriptions on behalf of the publisher. However, a publisher can create an app (known as the fourth channel, Branded Apps), which enables readers to buy copies or subscriptions direct from the publisher.

- **Subscription only:** All copies are sold to those readers who pay for a set number of issues upfront. This could be three, six or 12 issues. Promotion is usually done via direct mail or online by targeting specific groups.

- **Controlled circulation:** This mostly applies to customer publishing. Those are magazines that are produced solely for customers of a business and distribution is usually measured. For example any *Healthy & Beauty* Boots customer magazine has a barcode and cover price of £1, but is free to Advantage card customers. However, the publication cannot just be picked up and taken – customers must take it to the till to pay either the cover price or show their loyalty card.

- **Local distribution:** Copies are usually free and mass distributed to specific locations using a distribution company or privately with a man and van. They can be a local magazine or national. Successful national free magazines include *Shortlist* and *Stylist*, published by Shortlist Media. These are delivered to various venues in cities in the UK – from railway and tube stations to university campuses.

Which strategy you pick depends on the type of magazine, the genre and your target audience. Every magazine should have its own strategy. For example on *Writers' Forum* we went for a combination of news-stand and subscription, targeting potential subscribers by sending out mailshots to every writers' circle in the UK offering their members an exclusive subscription rate. The team also participated in writers' conferences both in the UK, Europe and the States. At these events, numerous subscriptions were sold. If you can sell 1,000 subscriptions at £36 each that gives you £36,000 in advance sales, a superb boost to your cash flow figures.

Today there are even more opportunities. As a result the distribution model for *Writers' Forum* would be likely to consist of news-stand, subscription, digital and targeted distribution to stationers such as Ryman and Staples plus university campus shops.

A magazine not only has to find potential readers but also be easily accessible. When relaunching *Weddings Today* in 2005, taking it from an annual to quarterly publication, our distributors took it to the news-stands. However, today with so much competition, that may not have been the best strategy.

There is far more opportunity for targeted distribution and also digital making the magazine more convenient to consume. As more smaller retail outlets consider expanding to include a small selection of magazines relating to their subject it is likely that *Weddings Today* may well have been accepted by bridal shops. This would have put it ahead of the competition. The bride-to-be would not be searching through dozens of magazines in the supermarket or other magazine retailer, instead it would be next to the cashier desk enticing the browsers or buyers to pick up a copy.

Digital distribution also increases circulation potential. Being able to read your favourite magazine on a tablet and buy items reviewed or advertised in the edition will please both readers and advertisers alike.

## What a distributor does

Before engaging a distributor, it is crucial to understand the trade. A distributor's purpose is to get a magazine out to retail outlets, then promote the title to entice new readers. The process works as a five-tier chain, starting with the publisher and ending with the consumer as shown in Figure 7.1.

It is the distributor's job to persuade buyers in retail outlets such as newsagents and supermarkets, as well as targeted outlets (if appropriate) to stock the title. Magazines are distributed into retail outlets by a wholesaler. Currently there are around 40 wholesalers in the UK at present, with the majority owned by Menzies and Smiths News.

Publisher → Distributor → Wholesaler → Retailer → Consumers (readers)

**Figure 7.1**

When distributing a magazine wholesalers work through branches, each branch serves a postcode area, distributing to up to 1,500 outlets within that vicinity. There are around 54,000 retail outlets in the UK (double those a generation ago) with almost a third of those owned by retail chains, which according to COMAG, account for 70 per cent of all magazine sales.

However, before wholesalers become involved it is up to the distributor to assess the magazine and research its potential viability, before pitching it to retail buyers. Getting buyers to take on a new title is no mean feat as they see hundreds of titles every year. According to figures from COMAG, of the new titles pitched to distributors each year only 10 per cent are chosen by retail buyers.

Once a distribution company has taken on a magazine it will offer advice on covers, layout and content. It is advisable to listen to any advice a distributor gives you as they see numerous titles every week and know the magazine market. But their views are not infallible. Listen and make up your own mind.

The distributer will also negotiate with the publisher to determine the percentage of the cover price to be remitted. Key factors that will influence negotiations are:

- Potential copy sales.

- Publication frequency.

- Cover price.

- Cost of carriage.

Remember a distributor not only has valuable contacts among buyers, but also will know how best to promote your title – particularly if it will be sold on the news-stands. The distributor also monitors sales and are able to supply publishers with a valuable breakdown of data detailing each issue's sales, showing outlets where the title is performing best and those where sales are poor.

This uses a variety of methods from telephone audit panels to tracking of EPoS (Electronic Point of Sale) data. The latter will show a detailed account of the sales figures, which outlets sell the most copies and highlight where sales are poor. It will also highlight how your title is performing compared to similar magazines in the sector.

## News-stand supply

Launching a title on the news-stand requires in-depth research and market analysis. Knowing exactly where the magazine will sit in the sector is crucial.

A publisher must also have a detailed knowledge of how many direct and peripheral competitors there are as well as an overview of rival publications' content. These factors will increase the chances of retail buyers agreeing to stock your magazine. Buyers are unlikely to take on a publication if the market is saturated.

There are pros and cons to the news-stand strategy. First, the advantages include reaching a wider audience. While digital subscriptions are growing, many people still prefer to buy their magazine either from a newsagents or supermarket when doing the weekly shop. Secondly the magazine may appear more professional simply by appearing in that environment. Titles not available in stores may attract scepticism from potential advertisers.

Lastly – although expensive – there are many promotional opportunities in-store to attract new readers. Once acquired a new reader has the potential to become a subscriber. Such opportunities include preferred shelf position, guaranteed number of facings, a 'shelftalker' usually positioned under the magazine display signposting the issue and a PoS (point of sale) stand near the tills or by the magazine stands. Prices for such promotions vary from retailer to retailer and publishers may be able to negotiate deals.

As the number of outlets has doubled in a generation the general level of magazine circulation should have increased. Not so. When there were 28,000 newsagents alone circulation was a more easily defined business. But once garages and supermarkets joined the outlets firm orders for titles fell away.

Supermarkets refused to stock niche titles unless a publisher paid for expensive promotion schemes. Soon newsagent chains decided to follow suit and began to sell premium slots to publishers. This was fine for major publishers, but the kiss of death for many smaller titles.

WHSmith, which underwent many management upheavals as it lost ground, began to de-list magazines which failed to sell a minimum number of copies in each shop. At one time the number was 30.

The absurdity of this policy soon became evident.

Supermarkets could occasionally be persuaded to take a new title, but they still tended to treat newspapers, magazines and books like tins of beans.

However, *Writer's Forum* launched a unique promotion with Sainsbury's, offering a fly/cruise holiday in New York as a short story prize limited to Sainsbury's' customers. This was scheduled for six months but was so successful the supermarket stocked the title for two years. Copies of *Writer's Forum* in Sainsbury's carried a special band promoting the offer.

When competing on the news-stand, competition can be fierce. Publishers are competing in a heavily populated market. Also this method of distribution can be expensive, especially when factoring in promotional activities such as PoS and preferred shelf positioning. Not to mention the extra payments made to retail buyers for stocking the title.

The cost of news-stand distribution works out at around 50 per cent of the cover price. But this is without taking into account payments to retail outlets and additional promotional activities. Based on a percentage of the cover, price a breakdown of distribution costs are as illustrated in Figure 7.2.

As illustrated in Figure 7.2, the publisher will receive around 50 per cent of the cover price for net sales after fees are taken out. However, payment is not immediate, the publisher won't receive the income from the sales for 60 days.

A distributor's payment cycle works in two tranches. The first payment is made 35 days after the end of the month of publication, with the balance following 30 days later. For example with *Writers' Forum*, if the July issue went on sale in June, then the first payment (50 per cent of estimated net sales) would be made in August with the balance being paid in October.

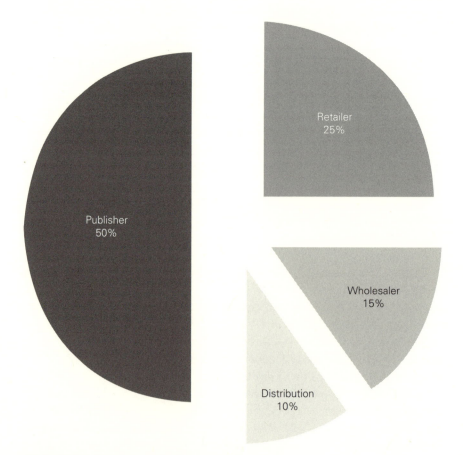

**Figure 7.2** *Breakdown of distribution costs*

Distribution costs and subsequent income from consumer sales must be factored in to your business plan expenditure. Take payment dates into account too, as this will affect cash flow.

Remember, that – like many products – magazines are sold on a sale or return basis (SOR). At the end of the on-sale period – usually three weeks for monthly title – unsold copies are returned to the wholesaler where they are destroyed, unless returns are requested and carriage paid for by the publisher. The balance is then credited to back to the wholesaler by the distributor, which adjusts the remittance on the final balance payable 60 days after the issue went on sale.

An ISSN (International Standard Serial Number) must have been obtained before a magazine can be sold on the news-stand. This is the standardized international code that allows the identification of any serial publication. Only when a publisher has an ISSN can a barcode be purchased. Barcodes are usually inserted during production on the front cover for easy scanning at the checkout. It is imperative that the cover is of the highest quality, with a great cover image and cover-lines so that it stands out among the competition.

Targeted distribution is another option, which can be incorporated into a news-stand strategy. Some publishers are now using sole or part targeted distribution as part of their overall plan. This is where specific retail outlets that have a synergy with the title stock it. This method is ideally suited to the specialist magazine. For example some health food stores such as GNC and Holland & Barratt are now stocking a few heath titles near the tills.

## Syndication rights

Distributing magazines to overseas retail outlets is expensive. Unless the magazine is known worldwide and is part of an established publishing house, it is unlikely to be worth exporting it to numerous countries. According to COMAG: 'Many overseas markets operate to much lower efficiencies than in the UK and it would be quite normal for a magazine to only sell 30 per cent of copies supplied' (COMAG, 2013).

Generally it is more profitable for the publisher to sell overseas subscriptions directly to readers. That said, specialist publications are worth exporting if affiliated with local events.

For example, a few of the *Writers' Forum* editorial team would attend the Santa Barbara Writers' Conference in California and therefore would collect a few readers. Also a few of our advertisers ran various writing holidays and conferences in Europe, again copies would be supplied to the nearest cities or towns.

Circulation enterprise is too often neglected by publishers, who tend to let the distributors 'get on with it'.

Magazine circulation for specialist titles should be planned with military precision. First you need a large-scale map of the UK. Use red pins for major outlets, blue for minor, green for your top 20 and black for the 20 worst selling areas. Now work out the reasons for yourself. Check the circulation in the catchment area and the number of outlets.

For example *Writer's Forum* always sold well in Guildford in Surrey and Harrogate in East Yorkshire. Why? Simply because those areas also enjoyed vigorous writing circles. One area we should have done well in was Cornwall, but we never did.

Having gathered the reasons for the variations, what should you do? The natural inclination is to attack the weak areas. Wrong. Follow instead the advice of Clausewitz and other great military philosophers who advise on *abandoning weak points and reinforcing strengths*.

Whenever that policy has been followed it has succeed, but the graveyard of magazines is testimony to those who continue to invest good money in a bad strategy.

# Distributing local/free magazines

With the emergence of popular titles such as *Shortlist* and *Stylist*, free magazines are no longer seen as poor quality. However, just because they are free, doesn't mean there won't be any distribution costs. Nor should the publisher be restricted to a few men and vans, although in some cases this is by far the most viable option.

Free titles offer many alternative circulation options to the news-stand. But to be successful they mostly still need to be distributed and publicized. For local magazines that target a particular area, one option is to take up space in the free publication display boards in supermarkets, garages and convenience stores. This offers nationwide access, but at present can only be arranged through a distribution company. Display stands are usually situated by the entrance and stock a variety of local, free publications.

If it's a national magazine, another strategy might be to organize key distribution points across the UK to reach your core audience. *Cosmopolitan*, then owned by NatMags, launched a brand extension titled, *Cosmo on Campus*, in October 2010.

With a print run of 250,000, NatMags distributed copies to 65 university campuses in the UK, targeting 750,000 female students. Cosmopolitan's publishing director Justine Southall told *Marketing Week*: 'that the initiative is about recruiting readers to Cosmo and to the print medium. It's about bringing content that is relevant at that stage of life to build loyalty to Cosmo and recruit new readers' (Baker, 2010).

As part of the distribution strategy, NatMags appointed 'hand picked' Cosmo Ambassadors to hand out copies of *Cosmo on Campus* to the target audience. Now owned by Hearst Magazines, the magazine is still distributed the same way and according to Hearst's website has the same print run.

*Stylist Magazine*, owned by ShortList Media, is a free weekly title targeting female commuters. Every Wednesday it is distributed to more than 400,000 readers in nine UK cities – London, Brighton, Edinburgh, Glasgow, Manchester, Liverpool, Newcastle, Leeds and Birmingham. It is a phenomenal success story of how a free magazine, distributed to key locations can be valued by readers and advertisers. *MediaWeek* reported that: 'According to industry figures, Stylist sold 199 pages of ads across the four issues in September. Some of the biggest advertisers in September were Marks & Spencer, with 14 pages; L'Oreal with 10 pages and John Lewis with 10 pages of ads. According to rate card figures, Stylist generated £1.5m in ad revenues in the month. But there is likely to be a substantial discount to this figure. Media buying sources said the overall ad figure in September was around £1m' (Batten, 2012).

These two examples demonstrate that free titles can be hugely successful targeting a specific audience with the right distribution strategy. Local (free) magazines can also work well, but again, distribution must be carefully mapped out.

Remember distribution costs must be recouped from income, be it from advertising revenue or copy sales. Whether using a service such as the Royal Mail where the magazine is sent to every household with a particular postcode, or delivered door-to-door by an army of workers – a publisher must create a need for the magazine. If few people read it, then advertisers won't get a response and the title will fail.

## Digital distribution

Digital magazines can be cheap or expensive to distribute depending on the method chosen by the publisher. Every magazine is unique, so a digital distribution strategy must be created specifically for the type of audience the magazine will be targeting. Other factors to consider may include how the user prefers to access content, how much they are prepared to pay for it and whether or not they intend to subscribe.

For example, the strategy for independent publishers who have produced a free magazine but are restricted by limited resources and need to keep costs down will be very different from that of a big publishing house launching a lifestyle or specialist title. The small independent publisher's best option is to publish the magazine as an interactive PDF on the title's website or on a site such as Issuu.

Issuu is one of the leading digital publishing platforms, where publishers – small or large – can publish a digital version of their publication for free. The downside of the free account is that it has fewer tools and features, such as you can't increase the size of viewer to fit the screen, and there is an advertising side bar. A more professional option is an Issuu Pro account aimed at professionals with additional publishing power and no advertising. At the time of writing costs for an Issuu Pro account were advertised as $19 a month or $228 (roughly £145) annually.

According to the website, Issuu's mission is to: 'empower individuals, companies, and institutions to publish their documents across all digital platforms.' It claims to be the 'fastest growing digital publishing platform in the world' with 210,000 new magazines published every month (Issuu, 2013). It targets a worldwide audience and claims to attract 52 million readers per month with 3.4 billion monthly impressions. As a result, Issuu is used by tutors at universities and colleges around the globe as a platform on which to publish student work.

Free digital magazines can also be distributed through the title's website or sent out via email to those who have signed up for a subscription. Distribution can be promoted via social media sites, targeted emails using existing or bought-in databases and through reciprocal links with advertisers, suppliers or affiliates or third parties with whom the publisher has a link.

For those looking to invest in digital circulation, opting for the digital news-stands may be a better strategy. News-stands are apps that are downloaded on to specific devices such as iPads, Kindles or other Android devices. When downloaded the app works as a magazine store, which appears as a newsagent's shelf on the device. Readers can buy single issues or subscribe to magazines from the store. They are also able to create a library of past and current digitals. Magazine editions, once purchased and downloaded from a news-stand app, do not require an internet connection to be viewed. The exception is those titles with interactive parts built into the issue, then a connection will be required.

The main news-stand options are:

- **Apple Newsstand** – specifically for those readers who have an iPad or iPhone.

- **Blackberry** – the latest app now allows Blackberry users to purchase magazines, which can be downloaded on to their device.

- **Kindle Fire** – now has its own news-stand, which works in the same way as the others.

- **Branded apps** – publishers can create their own app allowing their magazines either as subscriptions, single or back issues to be purchased by the reader.

- **Pocketmags** – a digital news-stand that enables publishers reach to reach their readers with Apple computers, iPhones and iPads or PC and Android devices such as smart phones and tablets.

Digital copies should not be restricted to single-issue sales. Publishers should offer more options such as short and long-term subscriptions – from three to 12 issues. Also readers should have an opportunity to purchase gift subscriptions for their friends or relatives. As with print copy sales, every issue must be promoted as should the opportunity for readers to subscribe.

# Building print subscriptions

These can be handled two ways. Either in-house by the publisher or out-sourced to a subscription specialist, who will market, promote and handle the sales. Digital or print subscribers are crucial to a magazine by boosting cash flow as issues are paid up for to a year in advance and building reader loyalty.

A large subscriber list provides a publisher with a direct-target database through which to advertise brand extensions or new products. Advertising clients also like to access magazine subscribers. Advertisers who take inserts know these are guaranteed to generate a response. Those same inserts on news-stand editions may go in the bin provided by the retailer.

Building a solid subscription list is one of the most challenging aspects of magazine distribution. Unless it's a B2B or specialist magazine, it is extremely hard to entice readers to subscribe. The reasons are numerous, but in all likelihood it boils down to choice.

During a seminar on distribution, I asked a group of my second year magazine journalism students how many of them subscribe to a magazine. Only two people out of 22 put their hands up, of those two both subscribed to special interest magazines. The rest it seems mostly bought lifestyle titles. Those who didn't subscribe were at first reluctant to admit the real reasons behind their decision, but after some prompting most responded with one of three following reasons:

- Prefer to choose a different lifestyle title each time.

- Don't want to pay money up front.

- Didn't want to commit in case they got bored with the publication.

That day, I held four such seminars. The ratio of response was mostly the same. Even when it was pointed out how much money they could save, the cash-strapped students still admitted they would be reluctant to subscribe. I have included this anecdote to illustrate just how hard it is to get subscribers.

Despite being a writing magazine, *Writer's Forum* also struggled to get beyond 5,000 subscribers. Yet some of our highest subscription sales came from literary events at which the editorial team would have a stand and subsequently meet the readers. Readers like to feel involved with the magazine, at such events many would-be writers would come up to the stand for a chat. That chat usually led to the purchase of a subscription. The next year that subscriber would come back to renew – and of course – a chat.

Building a subscription list takes cunning. Readers will only subscribe if they feel they are getting value for money, therefore it is important to incentivize and spell out the deal. Below are five ways to build a subscription list:

1  **Incentives:** offer readers a deal, say around 20 per cent off the cover price.

2  **Advertise:** Let readers and their friends know about the deal. Put an advert in every issue, on the website and on the magazine's social media pages. Also think about using direct-target mailshots and reciprocal deals with magazines, which aren't competitors.

3  **Sell:** Make sure your subscription advert gives readers reasons to buy.

4  **Freebies:** Offer new subscribers a free gift but make sure that gift has a synergy with the title.

5  **Reciprocal promotions:** Work well particularly with specialist titles. For example on *Writers' Forum* we offered those who belonged to a writing circle an exclusive rate. On *Vegetarian Living*, members of the Vegetarian Society were also offered an exclusive subscription rate. These type of deals must be beneficial for both parties involved and there must be synergy.

Once a publisher has built up a good subscriber list, he or she must work hard at retention. All lapses must be contacted to find out why and perhaps be persuaded to reengage. It is crucial that existing subscribers are made to feel as important as new ones. Don't just offer your best deal to new readers. Focus on retaining your existing readership and above all, create a sense of community.

## CASE STUDY – *EASY LIVING* vs *CANDIS*

Both of these are lifestyle titles and have begun to embrace the digital age, but that is where the similarity ends. This case study will evaluate both titles and demonstrate how each title has developed its own strategy for success.

Launched in April 2005, Condé Nast's *Easy Living Magazine* was aimed at ABC1, women aged 30–59. It had an initial print run of 600,000, but circulation targets were between 150,000 and 200,000 copies (Darby, 2004), although it actually achieved more than 170,000 (Turvill, 2012). It was the first lifestyle magazine to divide content into colour-coded sections.

Following a downturn in circulation of 7.1 per cent year on year, recording 158,038 circulation for 2011 (Turvill, 2012), the title and its website were relaunched in March 2012. Designed to attract a younger audience with a new look and more emphasis on fashion, the print edition went on sale with a special cover price of £2. In a *Press Gazette* report, *Easy Living's* editor Deborah Joseph said: 'We have redesigned and introduced more fashion, more pages and a more newsy feel.'

Yet looking at the circulation figures a year later in 2013, the relaunch doesn't appear to have worked as figures are down even further. According to its media kit, it has a combined digital and print circulation of 150,854 and 317,000 readers and 64,993 subscribers. When broken down the figures show the average print circulation was 150,020 while the digital edition sales amounted to just 834 as stated in PPA's Combined Circulation Chart (Dec 2012). Surprisingly it has had more success online, attracting 1,554,944 average page impressions per month with 313,550 average unique users per month. (Easy Living Media Kit, 2013) With poor digital sales and an ever-decreasing print circulation, it would appear the distribution strategies need a re-think. Or has this title had its day as a magazine and should the publisher focus on building the online aspect?

Like *Easy Living*, *Candis* is a lifestyle title aimed at the 40-something woman published by Newhall Publication. But that is where any similarity ends – this title is built around a community and charitable donations.

Its story begins in 1962, when after losing two close relatives to cancer, Joseph K. Douglas set up the Cancer and Polio Research Fund (CPRF). By 1971, a fortnightly newsletter priced at 15 pence was published to report the work of the CPRF and sold door-to-door. By 1985 the newsletter had become a magazine distributed to members. In 1986 the newly formed Newhall Publications organized a competition for readers to come up with a new catchier name. *Candis* was a clear winner. By the late 1990s a new-look *Candis* had grown into a 124-page, full-colour, subscription magazine.

Today the magazine has more than 200,000 subscribers. Like *Easy Living* its editorial coverage includes celebrity interviews, fashion, trends and a how-to section. In fact the two magazines share many editorial pillars as well as a fall in copy sales. At its peak in 2007, *Candis* was selling more than 300,000 copies. Now, perhaps due to the combination of the recession and a saturation of the women's lifestyle market *Candis* has gradually failed to evolve to meet current trends.

# Summary

As this chapter illustrates there are numerous strategies for successfully distributing a magazine. But it is not a case of one size fits all. Each magazine is different and therefore requires its own distribution plan. Pricing too is an important part of the plan. Whether you decide to opt for a cover price, or produce a free magazine will depend on your target audience – and how you plan to circulate the title.

For example free titles are perhaps best distributed via selected outlets as detailed in this chapter, as currently there are no free titles on the shelves of retail outlets selling print issues. However, that may change in the future if predictions that all newspapers will be free by 2020 come true. Yet there are numerous distribution options for free digital titles. For example there are numerous, good quality free magazines available on digital news-stands from Pockmags to Google Currents.

Whatever your distribution strategy, make sure you plan carefully, take advice and research the market before the launch.

# INDUSTRY INPUT

**Figure 7.3** *Patrick Knight*

**Patrick Knight, Strategic Development Director of Pocketmags, shares his expertise on distributing digital editions.**

*One of, if not the main benefits of digital is the distribution. There are minimal or no lead times, you can deliver an edition globally instantly and readers can pay the same amount wherever they are (and not have to wait weeks to receive an international edition) and there is no wastage.*

*The simplest method for taking a print edition digital is to deliver a replica edition online and in apps. For resource versus return (for small/ niche audience titles) this is often the most feasible solution as even with a great product, if the potential audience is small then custom/ bespoke apps and editions can soon price costly. Also this way you can work up to enhanced PDF and then custom editions based on response. On the flip side if you want to make a splash rather than complimentary income the 'custom' products/ editions, designed for digital, are the way forward. The financial risk involved, however, is generally significantly higher, as is the design commitment.*

*How much should a publisher charge for a digital edition? Prices have to be based on the Apple pricing tiers, their standardized tier based pricing which allows Apple to offer rounded prices in each international App Store, for example if you use tier 1 this will mean $0.99, £0.69, 0.79, so you can't pick and choose your exact price. Also due to each tier being linked to the $ price sometimes UK pricing suffers, e.g. there is a £2.49, £2.99, £3.99, £4.49, £4.99. Many people want to offer a slight reduction on print, often meaning £3.49 but this doesn't exist.*

*At Pocketmags we generally recommend keeping the single issue lower but close to print and then offering your savings in the recurring subscriptions. For example £3.99 a single issue, but £2.99 if on a monthly recurring purchase or £23.99 on an annual recurring purchase.*

*When working out the financial costs involved, how much of the budget a publisher allocates to digital distribution is impossible to say. Some digital editions provide 40 per cent of a title's income and/or circulation, while others provide less than one per cent. I would say be sensible and don't over commit by spending thousands on an app/first issue and then be left in a hole if it's not instantly recouped.*

*Magazine app publishers can help with genre specific experience and sites like App Annie can give you a feel for what competitors are doing (relative to others).*

*A clear breakdown of the costs is difficult to allocate. Often a publisher will have two purchase options – upfront/licence fee and then fixed fee per issue (or just an annual cost) or a lower setup fee then a revenue share. For people starting out the revenue share/shared risk can often be preferable, particularly with processes where you're getting more than just 'app technology then you're doing everything – submit, design, manage', i.e. when you're getting a practically fully managed service.*

*When launching a free title issue downloads will be incomparably higher as often publishers can get thousands of app downloads but only tens of paid issue downloads, showing the audience is there. The tough thing is making them stick, and come back for more, and monetizing the free product. It depends how you gauge successful, downloads or revenue, if the former, yes, if the latter, this will depend on your advertising sales team.*

*Publishers have to be proactive when promoting a digital launch. You have a window of opportunity when the app goes live when you're featured in the new section. As many marketing/PR pushes and mentions as possible need to coincide with this as your numbers will be the highest they will be from organic discovery whilst they are in a featured position. If the combined coverage can get you on to one of the charts then once you are there you have a great chance of staying there. Otherwise there is a risk of descending into the App Store obscurity that now exists, due to how many apps are available and all marketing resources/coverage are left being those which you are driving. To try to build the coverage when first released send an email blast to everyone you can, get active in suitable forums, put it in your print when on the way and released, get on social media, send links and/or comp access to relevant blogs, run draws for free subscriptions etc. Be creative!*

*Many of the promotional tools at a publisher's disposal in this regard are free, or the cost of the time of the person who designs/sends/posts etc. There are numerous small app marketing agencies who have big claims of reach at pretty reasonable costs, but even on your own there are numerous resources which you can use at no/very little additional cost.*

*Often publishers assume the digital will take care of itself as earnings will tick along without a great deal of promotion. But it's vital that marketing and design time are spent on the digital and it's not an afterthought as campaigns and promotions do work if done correctly and can really boost profile and income.*

*How will the digital market evolve in the next five years? The industry is taking shape currently but I can't help but think that in five years the digital 'magazine' concept could be very different. Younger generations seem to be more about instant bites of content, the 'issue' concept is changing and brands looking to maintain ad revenue will look for longer engagement than the monthly cycle, even if the core product still stems from this.*

*My advice to a publisher wanting to launch a new magazine? Assess what your realistic goals are, project realistically and don't overstretch. An expensive app project can very quickly become a labour of love rather than the pot of gold it was envisaged as, so be realistic about the potential and plan carefully how you'll get it in front of an audience; making the app is the 'easy' part.*

## ACTION PLAN

Develop a distribution plan. Set circulation targets first, then decide on your print run before setting out a distribution strategy for print and digital editions. Evaluate your competitor's methods and approach distributors before deciding how you will circulate the magazine.

Research the following options and cost them before deciding which will strategies will work best for your title:

- News-stands (print and digital).
- Subscription opportunities.
- Local and targeted distribution.

# 8

# Your team

*I must follow the people. Am I not their leader?*

BENJAMIN DISRAELI

**C**hoosing the right team increases a magazine's chances of surviving that all-important first two years. You must have people who are passionate and love the title. Editorial staff also need to be interested in the title's sector otherwise they won't put their heart and soul into making it work.

Taking on an editor who doesn't like exercise to work on a new health lifestyle magazine is not a wise choice. He or she is unlikely to have the interest or the dedication to make it successful. The same goes for the rest of the team. Behind the scenes on any successful magazine is a dedicated team. A team who loves the title and believes it has the potential to outperform competitors. Do not employ those who are average in attitude. Look for energy and passion. Remember, skills can always been enhanced, but a can-do attitude is either there or it is not.

When starting on *Writer's Forum,* I loved the industry, the genre and was obsessive in my dedication. I probably would have worked for free had I been financially self-sufficient. Those character traits are what you, as a publisher, should be looking for – hunger, energy and someone who loves their job.

Publishers are leaders and managers. Your task as a publisher will be to set out your magazine's ethos and general development by leading the whole team – editorial, circulation and advertising sales. However, remember, even if you are brilliant, you are only as strong as the team supporting you.

How many staff you are likely to need and where to find great people are vital questions. Salary scales, costs involved and professional development to maximize your investment in the people you employ demand strategic thinking. By the end of this chapter you will know who you need to hire and why.

# The publisher – leader and manager

As a publisher about to launch a new title, you will have vision. It is likely that you are creative, have a good head for business and know how you want the title to evolve. Any skills you lack must be learned or bought in. Financial management is a good example as it is a specialized area that few are unable to grasp sufficiently to build long-term security to ensure maximum growth.

Vision and a head for business won't necessarily make you a leader or even a manager. The former is natural talent, but the latter is something many learn by experience.

While an editor manages the editorial team, it is the publisher who leads. Part of good leadership is about knowing how closely to manage them. There are many kinds of leadership styles, but the main four are:

1 **Dictators** – it's his way or the highway. This leader doesn't usually like to be challenged on any decision nor does he (or she) give staff any autonomy. Very difficult to work for, unless you are a people pleaser or can stay at arm's length.

2 **Procrastinators** – this one is never going to make a decision quickly, which may result in lost opportunities and stagnation for the magazine. Working with this type of leader can be frustrating.

3 **Everyone's friend** – typically doesn't like upsetting anyone, even if they are doing a bad job. Also unable to set boss/staff boundaries in the workplace. As a result the staff don't know where they stand and often have little respect for this style of leadership. This boss may also be two-faced as he or she is unable to confront staff problems.

4 **High flyers** – this boss is confident. He or she knows what they want out of the team and is apt to get good results. Will listen to experts and embrace creativity and ideas. He or she is willing to give good people the autonomy to take the publication forward.

So which of the four are you? Perhaps you are a mixture of all four. Identifying your leadership style early will help you overcome potential weaknesses. This is crucial, a good leader is a realistic one and relishes challenges. An effective leader will thrive on problems – they are simply challenges that always have solutions. And this is where creativity comes into play. And beware of two dangerous personalities: those who always laugh at your jokes and the 'yes sir, no sir, three bags full sir' types.

Table 8.1 highlights the differences between good and bad leadership.

While a leader inspires, a good manager instils order and productivity. The latter is a necessity in any publishing house. Managers – whether in editorial or

**Table 8.1**

| Leadership | Key skills | Core traits |
|---|---|---|
| Strong | • Organized<br>• Strategic<br>• Delegator<br>• Communicator<br>• Good listener | Inspirational, charismatic, motivated, focused, decisive, strategic, reflective, balanced, honest, reliable, has integrity and is intelligent. |
| Poor | • Disorganized<br>• Not strategic<br>• Uncommunicative<br>• Poor listener<br>• Can't problem-solve | Unfocused, indecisive, unmotivated, unable to communicate, inflexible, is unable to develop people and lacks interpersonal skills. |

advertising sales – need to organize the workload and the team effectively. It is their responsibility to ensure that deadlines are met, content is checked and that the magazine is delivered to the printer or uploaded on time. The managers on your magazine must get the best out of their teams so good communication is essential. Poor management costs money in time and output.

The editors/managers on your title must know what you expect from them. Whether they micromanage depends on the size of the publication. If it's a small team, then they will have far more interaction. If working for a larger organization where an editorial department can have 20 or more staff, daily contact will be less intense, but should be regular with timed agendas.

An editor must, on some levels, micromanage. He or she will be legally responsible for the content of the magazine, therefore must know what is on every page. The advertising sales manager also has a similar responsibility and must check all the adverts for errors or legal problems. Thus an ability to deal with people and communicate effectively are skills all managers must possess.

## How many staff do you need?

This depends on the size of your publication. It is about cost and sustainability. If you are producing a small magazine of around 72 pages, with a monthly circulation of up to 20,000 then you can probably make do with a basic team until your title is able to support expansion.

Three periodicals that achieved success through a successful formula using a small launch team were: *Slimming Magazine, CAR* and *Choice*.

*Slimming* had the benefit of a husband and wife team: Tom and Audrey Eyton. Tom was a dour Lancastrian chief sub-editor who knew his way around

Fleet Street and insisted on the most exacting sub-editing standards. Legend has it that Hugh Hefner walked out of *Esquire* and founded *Playboy* because they refused to increase his salary, but it is a fact that Tom quit the *Daily Telegraph* when they offered a miserly, inadequate salary increase.

Together with his wife Audrey, a talented women's magazine writer, they launched *Slimming* to a chorus of disapproval: did they not know that every newspaper ran slimming articles? Did they not know that no woman would pick up a magazine from the bookstall which hinted that she was overweight?

With Tom's ruthless streak ensuring that the business side worked and Audrey's flair for capturing her audience the magazine boomed and opened the way for imitators.

Even more derision was heaped upon Fraser and Frankel when they launched *CAR* magazine. The market was awash with motoring titles. 'There was no room for another one' cried the experts in the advertising agencies.

It didn't take long for *CAR* magazine to become the best in the field. The quality of writing and enterprise in reporting new models before they were in the showrooms assured a devoted readership. It was their quality of writing which took motoring journalism to new levels, not to mention their courage in standing up to manufacturers who they upset with some devastating and honest reviews.

Then there was *Choice*, a magazine devoted to retirement planning produced by a hard up charity with £36,000 of debt.

John Jenkins and John Kemp acquired it for its debts and within two years had turned it into a money-spinner. Kemp and Jenkins, both senior *Daily Telegraph* journalists freely admitted that although they shared an abundance of editorial talent they were weak on other skills needed in publishing.

'But we learned fast,' said Kemp.

They poached an ace advertisement director from the *Daily Mail*, embraced new technology with messianic fervour and shot *Choice* into the top 100 magazines in the UK with a subscription list of 60,000 and used it as the cornerstone of a publishing company with 11 titles.

They too heard the dismal Jimmies saying the idea would never work. Exploitation? Image? The title spawned profitable books on money and retirement, health as well as a wealth of easy-to-read books on understanding occupational pensions and state benefits. In addition the magazine launched retirement holidays and lectures for major companies who were encouraging staff to take early retirement.

All three titles – *Slimming, CAR* and *Choice* – were sold and made fortunes for their six founders.

All had one thing in common – partners who believed in and trusted each other. Such partnerships are rare but it is far better than going it alone. Before you admit anybody to a directorship you must be doubly sure of his or her loyalty. It's an unpleasant fact that divorce is usually much easier to handle than getting rid of a rogue director.

One enterprise which began as a cooperative with six partners, all directors, signed a rule that each director – and that included the editorial duo – had to generate four times their annual salary in the first year or lose their jobs. It worked.

A more recent example is *Writers' Forum,* which was launched on the news-stands with a team of six. That team comprised of the publisher/editor, deputy editor, two editorial assistants plus an advertising sales manager. There was also a part-time secretary. Although the magazine was produced in-house, the team was adequate for the size of the publishing company. Why? Because we were extremely efficient and worked as a team. Employing additional staff would have put a strain on the budget.

Communication was our key strength. Everyone was clear on their role and was willing to go beyond their duties if necessary. This example demonstrates the power of a small team. In this situation, the communication chain was short and perhaps more effective than on a larger publication, which may employ a team of 20.

A large team works in a medium- to large-size publishing house, which produces many titles. Because of this, costs are lower as resources are shared across the business. But when starting out, employing too many people before the business has had a chance to grow can put unnecessary pressure on your finances. This in turn could threaten your long-term sustainability. Your staff budget must be carefully scrutinized. Everyone you employ needs to bring value to the magazine making them almost self-sufficient in terms of generating their salary.

The first step is to produce a staffing plan. Decide how many people you will need for each of the following areas:

- **Editorial posts:** editing, commissioning copy, subbing, production and planning issues. These are salaried posts, but you can fill editorial assistants' positions with interns, although if longer than a month you should pay them a basic wage.

- **Online/social media positions:** Editing, subbing, writing, uploading and updating content. If full-time, this must be a salaried post.

- **Production posts**: Produces print and digital layouts, perhaps video editing and podcasting. As full-time, this should be a salaried post.

- **Advertising:** Selling, submitting copy, checking adverts and general admin. Usually paid a low basic wage plus 15 per cent commission.

- **Office admin:** Supporting editorial and sales staff. Can be paid on an hourly basis if flexibility is required.

- **Accounting:** Bookkeeping, invoicing, VAT and tax etc. Usually contracted out to independent firm.

Your initial staffing plan will cover all of the above areas. The key is deciding how many employees you need in each role, and if some roles can be effectively combined. Too few staff and the quality of your magazine will suffer, but too many will impact on your budget.

Here is a staffing plan for a small publishing company. It is based on Writers' International Ltd, which published three titles.

Based on the staffing plan, a publisher would need a minimum of six staff to start a magazine. This includes the administration side such as bookkeeping, accounting and secretarial support; key positions which if overlooked will put unnecessary strain on your editorial and sales staff.

When you have your staff plan, allocate a salary to each position. Remember that editorial salaries vary in the industry. These are dependent on where you are based and the size of your publishing company. For example – if a publishing company, similar in size to Bauer Media, based in London, was recruiting an editor for one of its titles the salary is likely to around £50,000 plus a benefits package. Yet the salary for the same position for a small publishing house based in the South West is likely to be between £28,000 and £32,000.

**Figure 8.1** *Staffing plan*

Defining your wage budget requires research. Look at job advertisements for editorial posts across a range of titles and compare salaries offered. Once you have this data decide on your own pay scales based on the above factors. However, you must also take into account tax, holiday and employer's National Insurance contributions, which can equate to 30 per cent on top of the gross salary.

Now, workplace pensions are another factor to take into account. The Pensions Act 2008 in the UK has introduced mandatory workplace pensions. This requires every employer to enrol all eligible jobholders into a qualifying workplace pension arrangement. The scheme is being introduced gradually, starting with largest employers in October 2012. Unless part of a large organization, your publishing business will fall into the smallest employers bracket, which requires employees to be enrolled by 2014. As an employer your contribution to pensions will be around 1 per cent. This figure must be included in your salary budget.

# Defining roles

Traditionally roles were straightforward on most magazines, with gatherers (writers), producers (sub-editors) and managers (editors). But in today's digital age the boundaries are merged. For example, gatherers can now be content editors who not only source and develop stories, but also edit their own work and upload copy to social media and the web. Now writers are also producers too. While a magazine used to have one editor, today it is likely to have several. These include a content editor for online and social media, section editors as well as an editor who is responsible overall for print, digital and online editions.

Your title must be sustainable in the long term and that means having a multi-skilled team. Technology is moving fast, how content is consumed is changing rapidly. Staff on any publication should be able to handle a variety of jobs from features and online content to shooting short video clips and providing updates on social media.

An except from the *Press Gazette* (2008) defines the role of a job description: 'This job description summarizes the main aspects of the job, but does not cover all the duties that the jobholder may be required to perform . . . It is not intended to restrict the scope of the job, but clearly to define its starting point.'

Therefore first step in hiring a team is to define each role, clarify everyone's contribution in an editorial office. Here is a guide to the six key roles on a magazine:

- **The editor:** Sets the strategy, tone and voice of the publication and is the front man or woman. He or she hires/fires staff, manages the department, oversees the editorial budget for content and pictures, worries about circulation, runs the editorial conference and chooses the cover. This post requires raw talent to give the magazine verve and a strong voice.

- **Deputy editor:** Knows everything that goes on in the day-to-day running of the magazine and takes over if the editor is away. He or she will allocate tasks, coordinate coverage across platforms, run the office diary, check copy, liaise with sub-editors, report to the editor. This post needs a brilliant organizer who is able to manage the team and production effectively.

- **Chief sub-editor/production editor:** These used to be separate roles, but in today's tough climate they have been combined. Generally this role requires managing the editorial assistants, section editors and writers, policing deadlines, design quality and content. May write the headlines, coverlines or *sells* as they are sometimes called. He or she will report to the editor and get final approval before an issue goes to press. A talented sub-editor with design skills will fit this post.

- **Online content editors:** Must have strong social media skills and a proven track record in web writing skills. He or she will be responsible for online stories, updating content online and on social media as well as policing the site's forums for unacceptable or slanderous content uploaded by visitors. This role would suit a graduate with some experience who has a sharp eye for errors and the ability to make a story go viral.

- **Feature writers:** need to be able to generate ideas and approach old favourites such as seasonal pieces with fresh vigour. A good feature writer should have lots of cuttings, great contacts and a style of writing that suits your magazine.

- **Editorial assistant:** The most junior position – ideally a graduate in their first job. Typically an editorial assistant with a can-do attitude, will approach any task with enthusiasm and be able to write good copy, talk to PR companies and undertake some administrative task. Despite being a junior role, this is a demanding post, which requires a passionate starter who is able to undertake tasks with the minimum of supervision.

Some roles can be combined such as the editor and deputy, but a few such as the publisher and editor – must not. These are two different roles as previously explained. Bookkeepers are not the same as general administrators. The former has specialist skills while the latter is more general. Also the advertising department must not be combined with editorial otherwise the inevitable bias this would cause could result in a compromise of brand values.

# How to source good people

The ability to recruit bright, ambitious people is essential. Whether targeting a recent graduate or an editor with a flare for content and a good track record in building circulation – the right team will produce a great magazine. People with a can-do attitude, solid skillset and creative flare will enhance your business.

When a magazine concept is in the developmental stages, picking the right team can be difficult. Staff must be carefully chosen, ensuring each recruit will fit in to your environment. But how do you find that perfect editor or the high-flying advertising executive? And how do you persuade them to join your business?

First, start with the job specification. Having a clear idea of what each role entails will help you to define the core skills you need for that post. Get this right before recruiting. Traditionally advertising the job, then interviewing is a recruiting method that many editors have relied upon. However, this does not always give a true profile of the individual, because you don't get to see how candidates perform on the job or how they would interact with colleagues.

One of the most expensive ways to recruit is to headhunt. First research talented, successful people on similar titles that you would like to employ. Look at their current position such as likely benefits and current salary to gauge their needs. Then make an approach with a better offer. The downside of this might be that the candidate will want a considerable incentive to move and this may not be feasible.

However, in these situations it often helps to have someone who knows the person you want to poach. This way you can glean the necessary personal information, which will increase your chances of successfully engaging them. At Writers' International the publisher was able to recruit a fantastic advertising sales executive this way. Initial research through a mutual contact revealed the person was unhappy working in their current job and looking for a new challenge.

Another option is to recruit someone you have previously worked with or from a pool of graduates who have completed work experience or a paid internship on the magazine. By doing this you can assess their skills, creativity, reaction to problems and attitude sufficiently to decide whether they would suit your publication. This strategy is extremely successful and has been used by many editors. It works for both parties as the graduate gets coveted experience and contacts, while the publisher is able to see how the person will fit in with the rest of the team.

On *Writer's Forum* and *Weddings Today* we would often recruit this way and it proved to be successful. Indeed, the young graduate, who was promoted to assistant editor when I left, started out a few years before as a work experience placement. Having proved her worth, she was then taken on as a part-time editorial assistant until she graduated when she joined the magazine full-time and soon progressed when the opportunity arose.

Secure the right person for each job. Aim to build a balanced team of people with specialist skills and those who are multi-skilled. But don't be tempted to take on too many multitaskers, remember specialists specialize.

# Staff development

Staff loyalty is a bonus in any firm. Once a team is established, a publisher should look at developing existing staff before hiring new people. Adding to your staff's skillset will not only increase output, but also ensure that your team remain loyal and aren't tempted to move on too quickly as soon as they have sufficient experience.

Editorial trainer and lecturer, David Mascord feels the best way to encourage staff development is to develop a culture in your team that encourages people to take time to learn – both informally and formally.

'It's all too easy for staff to get so tied in to the production schedule that they feel they can't make time for learning and training,' he says, admitting he can recall cancelling courses or not taking opportunities for that reason.

He advises employers to make staff feel that 'training' doesn't always have to be about attending a formal course. 'Allow team members to take, say, a half day every month to do some personal learning. This might mean they take part in a physical or online seminar, experiment with some production software or maybe do some reading. Ask them to come back with some key points to pass on to their colleagues.'

Running informal 'skills-sharing sessions', led by a different team member each time is also effective.

They need last no longer than 45 minutes and can be schooled to happen every fortnight on a specific day. This format is proving particularly successful among magazine teams working in multi-platform environments. Individual team members might demonstrate tips and tricks in InDesign, using social media tools, writing and designing for tablet users – and other subjects that have become more prevalent in recent years.

If you're the manager you also need to 'model' the behaviour you want to promote: be seen to be investing time in your own development too. If you don't do it too, others will think it's not important.

When it comes to allocating a training budget, how much per person is sufficient? 'A few years ago in the UK, major publishers with multiple magazine brands were devoting between £250 and £500 per employee annually to training. That equated to one to two days training per employee per year and would cover training in craft skills and developing management abilities', explains David, adding that now budgets are tight it is difficult to assess.

However, he suggests identifying gaps in skillsets by asking five key questions, rather than identifying a sum of money per head. The questions are:

1  What do we need people to be skilled in, in order to achieve our objectives?

2  How will we prioritise these needs?

3  What training can we do ourselves and what do we need to outsource?

4  What is the likely cost?

5  What can we reasonably budget for?

Once you have the answers to the questions above, identify those skills, which can be taught in-house by a team member or yourself, and those that can't. For the latter, decide on a budget, then look for professional courses such as those run by The Periodicals Training Council.

The key is to develop your training budget to meet your needs as a publisher and that of your staff.

# Freelance contributors

Why use freelance contributors when you have an editorial staff? Having a talented pool of freelancers who have good ideas, are able to stick to the brief and deliver their copy on time, is a great resource. Not only will it enhance your publication, but also ensure your content is fresh.

Sourcing good freelancers takes time. It usually starts of with recommendations from colleagues or contacts. Sometimes professional writers will spot your magazine and approach you directly. Occasionally a budding writer will send in a great idea on spec and deliver good content.

A main benefit of using freelancers is that if you need copy in a hurry and the editorial team is too busy, help is just a phone call away. All commissioning editors build a pool of reliable, contacts, noting their specialist areas, ability and fees. Being able to contact a trusted writer to get an article at short notice is crucial.

It is worth nurturing your contributors. By helping budding writers evolve into regular contributors you may be rewarded with a continual stream of new ideas from someone who has grown with the magazine.

But how closely should you brief them? Generally a professional freelance would have seen and analysed several issues of a magazine before sending a pitch to the editor. However, it is good practice to have a set of contributor's guideline to send out. This should include the average word length, format and additional content for online contributions. *Reader's Digest* briefings were once a model of clarity and detail.

If you commission directly without receiving a pitch then you must be clear about the content you want and ensure the writer understands the brief. Not using copy from a freelance you have commissioned means you will be required to pay them. This is what's known in the trade as a kill fee. It is a percentage of their rate, usually around 30 to 50 per cent.

Rates for freelancers vary according to the size of the magazine. The NUJ (National Union of Journalists) suggests writers submitting a 1,000 word article to a medium-size glossy magazine can expect around £700. For a smaller consumer title the rate is about £400. The lowest recommended rate for a small title is £250. But many get away with paying less.

However, like most things, payment is negotiable. How much you pay your writers depends on your budget and their experience, contacts and standard of writing. Unlike employees, freelance writers are responsible for their tax, National Insurance and pension arrangements.

Sometimes staff feature writers are recruited from the freelance pool so build up your contacts and nurture those budding writers with potential. One day they may become a colleague.

# Summary

Throughout this chapter we have examined staffing needs, how to find good people and keep them motivated. To build a strong team, which is going to take your title forward you must first know what you want in employees – and this means identifying your staffing needs.

It is also good practice to develop a loose job description to assess the skills candidates will need. Do this before starting the recruitment process. Remember, personality and the right attitude and energy in candidates are as important as skillsets. For a magazine to evolve, the team must get on well and be able to communicate effectively. A team, which has personality clashes and power struggles, may prove unproductive and be a drain on resources. Creative tension needs a strong choke chain.

'Recruit for attitude first and skill second,' advises David Mascord.

The industry is changing fast and you need team members who are open to change and willing to take on new things.

It's all very well having a great feature writer turning our brilliant 3,000 word features. But they are no good to you if they are a stick in the mud when you need them to adapt. It's far better to take on someone who has a 'can-do' attitude and then train them in any skills they lack.

When you have a team who are energized and work well together, do your best to keep them. Staff retention levels are as important as the recruitment process. While people will always want to move on eventually, make sure they don't leave because they don't like working for you or feel they are not suitably recompensed for their efforts. A happy team is a productive one.

# INDUSTRY INPUT

**Margi Conklin, editor-in-chief of the *New York Post*'s *Page Six Magazine*, explains her recruitment strategy and reveals that a can-do attitude is a must for any editorial team.**

*Recruiting for* Page Six Magazine *is usually always done through word of mouth. People I trust will recommend others who I meet and, if they fit the bill, I'll offer them a contract to work on one issue of the magazine. It's only published three times a year, so employment on the magazine is short and temporary.*

**Figure 8.2** *Margi Conklin*

*When interviewing, the skills I look for in a candidate depends on the job. For an experienced editor, I want someone who, first of all, understands the DNA of the product. They will have had years of experience writing and/or editing for other publications, be organized and calm under pressure. The right candidate will also be able to work with lots of different personalities and juggle many projects at once.*

*As we don't have big budgets, thinking creatively around problems is essential. For an entry-level position, I want someone with energy, enthusiasm, natural intelligence, a sense of initiative and the willingness to take on any job, however menial, with a smile.*

*Using interns can be rewarding. Some are more trouble than they're worth; others are invaluable. It's all about the quality of the intern. The smart ones who are willing to learn while bringing people- and office-skills to the job are tremendously useful. But those who feel entitled to run the place, believe they are better than their superiors and don't know a thing about journalism are pointless.*

*Sometimes difficult people can produce fantastic work. For example, I have put up with brilliant writers who are a nightmare to deal with because they can deliver unparalleled results. But these people are extremely rare. Most people's talents are somewhere between mediocre and good, so a terrific never-say-no personality is essential.*

*Ensuring new people fit in to a team is essential. The features department is a fun place to work, so I want someone who demonstrates a sense of humor and energy. Someone who smiles and gets the joke, but isn't overly giggly, which might indicate a lack of substance. I also need people who take direction well, so I'm looking for someone who listens more than they talk in an interview.*

*During my career I have made some great recruitment decisions. My current editorial assistant at the newspaper is an excellent example. There were 2,000 applicants for the job, but he stood out because he had an enormous amount of work experience on top of having completed his four-year university course in three years. He proved he had a flair for writing and a passion for media, but also was deferential to superiors and understood he'd have to do menial jobs like finding toner for the printer to win the position. He's the best assistant I've ever had.*

*I made a few recruitment mistakes when I was launching* Page Six Magazine *as a weekly. I had to hire people fast to meet the two-month launch deadline, and this meant I wasn't able to vet everyone as thoroughly as possible. In some instances, I had to settle for people who could just do the job, rather than perform at the very highest level demanded from the job. As a result, I had a lot of turnover.*

*Building an editorial team should ideally be done in a slow and considered way. Find individuals who complement each other. You want people who can bring different, unique things to the table rather than the same things. It takes time to understand the strengths and weaknesses of your existing team, so you can work out what you need and don't need from new hires. I like to spend at least two months looking for a new writer.*

*Communication on any publication is crucial. I have regular meetings with key players and make sure the right people are copied in on emails regarding story direction. Ideas meetings take place every Monday, when rotating members of the full team get a chance to contribute their thoughts. I also reply to every email I get from my team. I want them to know I am available and willing to give feedback at all times.*

*To keep the team motivated I also offer regular praise, which I share every Friday on a team email listing web traffic numbers along with other highlights of the week. It's also important to assign the right stories to the right writers, so they perform at their highest level and enjoy their work, rather than flounder with pieces that confound them. I also try to challenge people with new work when appropriate, and promote as much as possible from within.*

*Staff training can be important, especially when it comes to new technology, such as social media or writing headlines for the web. These are things traditional journalists need to be updated on and it needs to be done through training. But the best training in journalism is just doing the job over and over again.*

*New publishers looking to recruit staff should outline what roles are needed first, and what responsibilities you need to assign to these roles. Ask everyone you trust who you would recommend. Interview as many people as possible – sometimes the wrong person for one job is the right one for another.*

*Take your time when making your decisions; think it through and discuss the pros and cons of each candidate with a key member of your team if possible. Give candidates editing and writing tests, also ask for ideas to see how they think.*

*I believe in acting on your gut, but when hiring new people it's better to do so based on as much information as possible. Making a bad hire can be costly not just for you as a manager, but for the entire team, so it's important to get it right.*

## ACTION PLAN

You must work out a complete staffing plan including the salary you will pay for each role. Take the following three steps to decide how many employees you will engage and how much you will pay them.

1  **Discuss:** How many staff you need to produce your magazine. Don't forget areas such as administration, bookkeeping and advertising sales.

2  **Research:** Salaries of small and large publications to gauge how much of the budget you should allocate for each role.

3  **Build:** Your staffing plan.

When including salaries in your financial summaries in a business plan, don't forget to add an additional 30 per cent to permanent employee salaries, these do not apply to freelance rates.

# 9

# Advertising and other revenue streams

As publishing has become a multi-platform operation so the sources of revenue have multiplied. This is born not only out of necessity, as advertisers have a greater choice of media to exploit and reach their target audiences, but also because survival and profit may well depend on peripheral income.

Traditionally, anything other than income from advertising, sales, and subscriptions was regarded as a little extra cream for the bottom line. Commercially minded managers soon picked up on the idea of merchandizing, roadshows, exhibitions and the exploitation of databases.

When digital age opportunities forced their way into management thinking, it soon became clear that these sources of income, once regarded as peripheral, were producing the lion's share of income.

## A brief history

Traditionally magazines have derived income from:

- Advertising.
- Cover price.
- Subscription sales.

But more astute publishers have also recognized the value of exporting an image and maximizing a brand. An outstanding example in its heyday was *Reader's Digest*, which published in 70 countries and totalled sales of 17 million copies a month in the USA alone and two million in Britain.

As *The New York Times* (Romenesko, 2010) reported after *Reader's Digest* filed for Chapter 11 hearings regarding bankruptcy:

At one time, everyone at *Reader's Digest* got Fridays off in May, and a week of paid travel to visit anywhere in the country. There were free garden plots at the magazine's headquarters for those who couldn't grow tomatoes at home. These perks are noted in '*Reader's Digest*, the Local Magazine that Conquered the World,' an exhibit that opened at the New Castle Historical Society in Chappaqua, NY.

The publishers knew all about maximizing image and brand long before these became buzzwords in Madison Avenue. A survivor from that era is Condé Nast's *Vogue* with editions from its American launch being published in the United Kingdom, France, Italy, Germany, Japan and many other nations.

But *Vogue* does not rest on its century-old tradition. Condé Nast was the first major publisher to deliver subscriptions for the iPad, starting with *The New Yorker*. The company has since rolled out iPad subscriptions for nine of its titles.

Now there are far more opportunities to maximize magazine content across a variety of outlets. While it is relatively easy to lock into new media outlets, an overriding essential is to collect revenue from these and to utilize them without damaging the core business.

Possibly the longest pedigree for a magazine which has adapted to changing times and is thriving today is *Cosmopolitan*. It was launched in 1886 by Schlicht & Field of New York. Paul Schlicht told his readers that his publication was a 'first-class family magazine', adding (Schlicht, 1886 – via Princeton.edu, 2013):

> There will be a department devoted exclusively to the interests of women, with articles on fashions, on household decoration, on cooking, and the care and management of children.

*Cosmopolitan*'s circulation reached 25,000 that year, but by March 1888, Schlicht & Field were no longer in business. John Brisben Walker acquired the magazine in 1889. That same year, he dispatched Elizabeth Bisland on a race around the world against Nellie Bly as a publicity stunt.

E. D. Walker, formerly with *Harper's Monthly*, took over as the new editor, introducing colour illustrations, serials and book reviews. It became a leading market for fiction, featuring Rudyard Kipling, Jack London, Willa Cather and Edith Wharton. The magazine's circulation climbed to 75,000 by 1892.

In 1897, H. G. Wells' *The War of the Worlds* was serialized, as was his *The First Men in the Moon* (1900). In 1905, William Randolph Hearst purchased the *Harper's Monthly* for US$400,000 – around £7.5 million at today's prices.

It continued to have an eye for great fiction and contributors included Sinclair Lewis, A. J. Cronin, George Bernard Shaw and Upton Sinclair. Hearst knew instinctively that if you put the money into talented writers it would pay huge dividends in the magazine market.

The magazine also set new standards in design with illustrators Francis Attwood, Dean Cornwell, James Montgomery Flagg and Harrison Fisher.

# Building a sustainable title

With a circulation of 1,700,000 in the 1930s, *Cosmopolitan* had an advertising income of $5,000,000. Emphasizing fiction in the 1940s, it was subtitled *The Four-Book Magazine* since the first section had one novelette, six or eight short stories, two serials, six to eight articles and eight or nine special features, while the other three sections featured two novels and a digest of current non-fiction books. During World War II, sales peaked at 2,000,000 (Audit Bureau of Circulation).

The magazine began to run less fiction during the 1950s. Circulation dropped to slightly over a million by 1955, a time when magazines were overshadowed during the rise of paperbacks and television. The Golden Age of magazines seemed to come to an end as mass-market consumer publications gave way to special interest magazines targeting specialized audiences.

Cosmopolitan's circulation continued to decline for another decade until *Sex and the Single Girl* author, Helen Gurley Brown, became chief editor in 1965. Not only was she an author, but she had clawed her way to the top in Madison Avenue as an advertising copywriter. Not only could Helen write – she knew how to market a product.

Editorial and advertising were joined by an umbilical cord in which they became not only mutually supportive by virtually incestuous.

The magazine was renamed again *Cosmopolitan* in 1967, and it was refocused as a magazine for women. The birth of you-can-have-it-all philosophy was spearheaded by Helen Gurley Brown's *Cosmopolitan*.

It focused on young women and published articles that discussed sexual issues. Fan mail begging for Brown's advice on many subjects concerning women's behaviour, sexual encounters, health and beauty flooded her after the book was released. Brown sent the message that a woman should have men complement her life, not take it over. Enjoying sex without shame was also a message she proclaimed.

Like all great innovators Brown had her critics. The magazine ran a near-nude centrefold of actor Burt Reynolds in April 1972, causing great controversy. But clever Helen knew the publicity was worth a fortune in getting new readers and keeping ahead of its imitators.

The UK edition of *Cosmopolitan*, which began in 1972, was well known for sexual explicitness, with strong sexual language, male nudity and coverage of subjects such as rape.

*Cosmopolitan* has 63 international editions worldwide published in 32 languages with distribution in more than 100 countries making it the largest-selling young women's magazine in the world.

Some international editions are published under licences or as joint ventures. International editions are published in Argentina, Armenia, Australia, Azerbaijan, Brazil, Bulgaria, Central America, Chile, China, Colombia, Croatia, Cyprus, Czech Republic, Ecuador, Estonia, Finland, France, Germany, Greece, Hong Kong, Hungary, India, Indonesia, Israel, Italy, Kazakhstan, Korea, Latvia, Lithuania, Malaysia, Mexico, Mongolia, Netherlands, Norway, Peru, Philippines, Poland, Portugal, Puerto Rico, Romania, Russia, Serbia, Singapore, Slovenia, South Africa, Spain, Sweden, Taiwan, Thailand, Turkey, United Kingdom, US en Español, Ukraine, Venezuela and Vietnam.

Helen Gurley Brown claimed that until she published her bestseller, *Sex and the Single Girl:* 'If you were single with no engagement ring in sight, then you might as well go to the Grand Canyon and throw yourself in. If you were single and having sex, it was time to stick your head in the oven. . .' (via Kelsey, 2012).

Unsurprisingly her book, which encouraged a post-war generation of young women aching for change, to get a job, enjoy sex and not rush into marriage, went on to sell millions of copies.

Helen always followed her own advice. She held out on matrimony until 37, when she wed legendary film producer David Brown. She once wrote: 'I think marriage is insurance for the worst years of your life. During your best years you don't need a husband' (via Kelsey, 2012).

Her story is an inspirational guide to anybody who faces the usual barrage of 'it can't be done criticism'.

## Successes and failures

*Cosmo*, as it is affectionately known, has had its failures. While it has maximized the image and reach of the main magazine, some of its ventures – *Cosmopolitan Man* and children's titles have not run well and have been abandoned.

There seems to be an underlying philosophy at *Cosmopolitan*, which is even more appropriate than the one adopted by Helen Gurney Brown: abandon your weak positions and strengthen your strong ones.

Yet another great title from the United States came in 1923 from a couple of students at Yale University. Briton Hadden and Henry Luce launched *Time*, making it the first weekly news magazine in the United States.

They had met while chairman and managing editor of the student publication *Yale Daily News*. Hadden was happy-go-lucky character, who liked to tease Luce and saw *Time* as important but also fun.

In many ways their formulaic approach to serious matters set the tone for tight sub-editing across many continents when newspapers imitated the style to report serious matters in a way that ordinary people could understand. Lord Beaverbrook's *Daily Express*, at its height, slavishly copied the *Time* method of captions with the name of the subject in bold capitals underneath the picture and an italic lightface quotation from the individual underneath.

However, the *Express* drew the line at running inverted sentences and banned them from the paper.

Any student of magazine publishing should read *Time Inc.: The Intimate History of a Publishing Enterprise 1923–1941*. *Time* was one of the first major groups to realize that radio was a natural ally and not just a wicked competitor. *Time* and radio become interdependent and flourished greatly during the thirties and forties. Books too were another spin off and as the authority of *Time* grew – no American politician could dare ignore it – so did its profits. By the time of Henry Luce's death in 1967, the Time Inc. stock, which Luce owned, was worth about US$109 million. Not too bad for somebody who began with an idea while editing a student newspaper.

In 2007, *Time* moved from a Monday subscription/news-stand delivery to a schedule where the magazine goes on sale Fridays, and is delivered to subscribers on Saturday. Now subscribers to its paper magazines including *Time, Sports Illustrated* and *Fortune* have access to the iPad versions of these magazines for no extra charge. This is a strategy which doesn't appear to aid reader retention figures, as recently the circulation has declined in the face of competition from other media despite its attempts to combine print and online services for readers.

*Time* is also known for its signature red border, introduced in 1927. The border has only been changed thrice since 1927: the issue released shortly after the September 11 attacks on the United States featured a black border to symbolize mourning.

However, this edition was a special 'extra' edition published quickly for the breaking news of the event; the next regularly scheduled issue contained the red border. Additionally, the Earth Day issue on 28 April 2008, dedicated to environmental issues, contained a green border.

The most recent change in border was in the issue on 19 September 2011, commemorating the 10th anniversary of September 11 attacks by using a metallic, silver border.

Time's most famous feature throughout its history has been the annual 'Person of the Year' (formerly 'Man of the Year') cover story, in which *Time* recognizes the individual or group of individuals who have had the biggest impact on news headlines over the past 12 months. Apart from the great and the good, Hitler and Stalin have been among those featured.

In 2008 the Person of the Year was Barack Obama, with Sarah Palin as a runner-up. Obama is the twelfth US President honoured, following a line of every president since Franklin Roosevelt, with the exception of Gerald Ford.

What these great titles prove is that any successful magazine must invest in top grade editorial material and marketing management. One cannot live without the other.

## Maximizing sales opportunities

Another title that exploits its quality is *National Geographic*. For quality of its pictures and editorial, it has no equal. In 2011 the magazine was circulated worldwide in 34 language editions and had a global circulation of 8.2 million.

The first issue of *National Geographic Magazine* was published in October 1888, just nine months after the Society itself was founded. The hallmark of *National Geographic*, reinventing it from a text-oriented entity closer to a scientific journal, to a magazine famous for exclusive pictorial footage, was its January 1905 publication of several full-page pictures taken in Tibet in 1900–1901 by two explorers from the Russian Empire, Gombojab Tsybikov and Ovshe Norzunov. The June 1985 cover portrait of 13-year-old Afghan girl Sharbat Gula became one of the magazine's most recognizable images.

In later years its editorial focus has become more geopolitical with issues such as environment, deforestation, chemical pollution, global warming and endangered species being discussed.

In addition to being well known for articles about scenery, history and the most distant corners of the world, the magazine has been recognized for its book-like quality and its standard of photography. This standard makes it the home to some of the highest-quality photojournalism in the world. The magazine began to feature colour photography in the early twentieth century, when this technology was still rare.

During the 1930s, Luis Marden (1913–2003), a writer and photographer for *National Geographic*, convinced the magazine to allow its photographers to use small 35 mm cameras loaded with Kodachrome film over bulkier cameras with tripods and glass plates. In 1959, the magazine started publishing small photographs on its covers, later becoming larger photographs. *National Geographic* photography has quickly shifted to digital photography for both its magazine on paper and its website. In subsequent years, the magazine cover, while keeping its yellow border, shed its oak leaf trim and bare table of contents, for a large photograph taken from one of the month's articles inside. Issues of *National Geographic* are often retained and filed by subscribers.

As a spin off revenue activity in 2001, National Geographic released an eight-CD-ROM set containing all its maps from 1888 to December 2000. Printed versions are also available from NGMapcollection.com, but were not published as this is a 'not for profit' entity.

The magazine is currently published in 34 language editions around the world, including English on a worldwide basis, Arabic, Bulgarian, traditional and simplified character Chinese, Croatian, Czech, Danish, Dutch, Estonian, Finnish, French, German, Greek, Hebrew and an Orthodox Hebrew edition, Hungarian, Indonesian, Italian, Japanese, Korean, Lithuanian, Norwegian, Polish, two Portuguese language editions, Romanian, Russian, Serbian, Slovene, two Spanish language editions, Swedish, Thai and Turkish.

In contrast to the United States, where membership in the National Geographic Society was until recently the only way to receive the magazine, the worldwide editions are sold on news-stands in addition to regular subscriptions. In several countries, such as Hungary, Slovenia, Croatia and Turkey, *National Geographic* paved the way for a subscription model in addition to traditional news-stand sales.

The magazine is one of the few, which appears to have no serious competitor and it would be a brave entrepreneur to match its editorial and financial acumen. No other magazine has exploited TV as well as National Geographic.

National Geographic Television (NGT) is its documentary arm producing much of what you see on the National Geographic Channels as well as specials and series for other networks. From the well known National Geographic Specials that began in 1963 to its flagship National Geographic Explorer series today, NGT pursues the Society's mission of inspiring people to care about the planet.

A leader in high definition (HD) programming, NGT is widely recognized for the quality of its productions and has won more than 100 Emmy Awards. All production units – Explorer, Specials and Events, Natural History, Series Production and Science – are expanding, and the network is constantly seeking new talent; producers, writers and editors.

When it comes to a multi-media approach with an emphasis on photojournalism quality, National Geographic is usually reckoned to be at the top of any list.

# Website conundrum

As news-stand sales plummet, publishers – from national newspapers to specialist magazines – trumpet the number of hits received on their websites. But what interests advertisers greatly are statistics, which point to the conversion of this interest into sales.

It's a little like an analogy of shopping in London. Say 15,000 people walk past Selfridges in Oxford Street and glance in the windows. Some 3,000 enter the store and of these 2,000 make a purchase.

This conundrum, which affects every mass-market medium from tabloid newspapers to mailshots is under ever-increasing scrutiny. For the publisher there is a critical decision to be made on selling space on a website. Should it be incorporated in the standard rate card as an add on to advertising on the printed page – or should it have a separate rate card and appeal to potential advertisers who do not want or think they do not need to advertise on the printed page?

The decision will vary from title to title. Whatever the publisher decides, there is another fundamental decision to be made. Should the viewer pay to read the website or should it be free to view? The jury is still out on that decision. A specialist publication like the *Financial Times* can and does charge, and does profit from this policy. *The Times* is running a strong campaign to persuade its readers to pay for access.

Clearly the ones who do not charge build a bigger base much quicker than those who do. Top of British news websites is the BBC, free at the point of consumption and funded by taxpayers' money. While this situation exists many experts believe that newspapers will struggle and probably fail to persuade their readers to pay for website access.

Anyone launching a magazine would do well to analyse the potential readership and survey views. Most magazine publishers see their websites as providing an hors d'oeuvre for the printed version but this could reverse in the next ten years and a printed version will become the taster for the web version.

# Rights are important

An easier decision for the publisher is to recycle material in annuals, CDs or MP3s. Here the commissioning editor or whoever performs this role, has to make it clear that the publication wants to buy All Rights. This is in stark contrast to the traditional accepted practice of publishers obtaining first British Serial rights. It may well mean paying higher fees to freelance writers and it is a commercial decision for the publisher. Most experienced freelance writers are now acutely aware of their value.

One way around the dilemma is to specify what alternative media a publisher might use in recycling the material. For example, the writer may relinquish all rights with the exception of musical, stage and film. This may seem when odd when dealing with non-fiction but the blockbuster film Top Gun featuring Tom Cruise, began life as a feature in an American magazine.

Another solution may be to offer writers a share of income derived from onward sales. This is most common where exclusive photographs are featured. For example, a leading fashion photographer may have gained access and permission to photograph an actress in a variety of outfits created by a top fashion designer.

These could well be sold on to titles in non-competitive areas. A fee is agreed and a percentage of the proceeds go to the original photographer. On the other hand, the magazine may release a selection of pictures to a national newspaper, not only to defray its original cost, but also to tempt potential readers to buy their title and view the whole collection. Whatever the commissioning editor decides, it must be crystal clear in the contract exactly what is being bought.

## Spin off annuals

Imagine you are to launch a magazine for retirement planning. Let's call it *The Golden Age*. Each month you plan to cover specific items closely linked with subjects of primary interest to potential readers. These could cover:

- Investment
- Health
- Travel
- Gardening
- Hobbies
- Personality interviews.

At the end of the year you have at least 12 articles on each subject, which you can turn into a booklet: *The Golden Age of Financial Planning* or *The Golden Age of Travel* etc. The copy will need only light editing and updating, the illustrations have already been obtained and the series can be advertised on the title's website and in the pages of the magazine. Advertisers who have appeared in the magazine will be receptive to the booklets as they have a greater.retention value. Hence the return on capital is significantly greater in purchase terms.

Furthermore, you can employ digital print on demand and the downside risk is negligible. You could also employ a cover mount CD so beloved of news-stands and supermarket outlets. Healthy margins are assured providing you plan carefully.

# Syndication

American publishers have always been at the forefront of syndicating material thanks to the commercial acumen of the Hearst group. In how many countries have you seen Snoopy? This favourite cartoon character with his whimsical self-deprecating humour is read daily by millions in the United States and by millions more throughout the world. It's a whole industry with Snoopy mugs, towels, annuals and even a book on writing with his famous use of the phrase 'It was a dark and stormy night'.

The late George Schulz, his creator, was a wonderful man, modest to a fault and always willing to share his experiences with beginners. When it comes to revenue from syndication and spin-offs Snoopy became the Rockefeller of publishing. And all from one simple drawing.

But supposing you have a magazine devoted to martial arts. You can probably find several countries that do not possess such a title. You could interest potential publishers in such a title by offering them a complete package – copy and artwork – and regain half your editorial cost. The buyer would save greatly on having immediate material for much less than half the price once the saving on staff is taken into consideration.

Less obvious areas for revenue include merchandizing and sampling. Any manufacturer is willing to pay for test marketing a new product before launching it nationwide. This was greatly exploited by Tom Eyton when he launched *Slimming Magazine* in the UK.

Why would anybody buy a magazine devoted to slimming? After all, newspapers and women's magazines had done the subject to death. But Tom and Audrey Eyton thought differently and after a shaky start it went on to establish a whole new market.

Among its spin-offs were a slimming club, health spa, road show and testing programme for new products which food manufactures were happy to use. After all, you couldn't sell a calorie-free biscuit if a test group from *Slimming Magazine* thought it tasted like cardboard. Charges for the survey were based on a per capita basis depending on the depth of research required.

It's interesting to note that Tom left the *Daily Telegraph* as chief sub-editor because he was offered far less money than he was worth and went on to become a millionaire. A parallel with Hugh Heffner who walked out of *Esquire Magazine* to start *Playboy* after being refused a $25 increase in salary. The lesson? Entrepreneurs take risks.

# INDUSTRY INPUT

**Gill Hudson, editor of *Reader's Digest* discusses the impact technology and brand extensions have had on her readers and offers valuable advice to those thinking of developing a new title.**

*Constant adaptation is seen as essential at Reader's Digest. We had an iPad app as soon as the tablet was available in the UK. Long-established brands like ours can start to look very dated if we don't keep adapting. Rather brilliantly, our small size is the perfect fit for the iPad screen, so no resizing required for the reader! Like most other magazines, we also have a website, where we feature highlights of*

**Figure 9.1** *Gill Hudson*

*the magazine, plus some flick-through pages. And we have our own Twitter and Facebook following, too.*

*But it's really important not to put the medium over the message. Don't let the technical team take over. The fact is that if you don't have something your readers really want in the first place, it doesn't matter how cutting edge your delivery is. Digest readers, for example, are online a lot, but aren't huge Twitter or Facebook users, so if we push those platforms too hard, it actively turns readers off. You have to be sure that new developments are appropriate to your audience.*

*When it comes to revenue, technology has maintained levels more than it has increased them. Advertisers simply expect you to have additional platforms now, and it counts against you if you don't. That said, we have had some additional digital revenues, but they're still relatively small. Print continues to be the big revenue driver across the industry – at the moment, anyway . . .*

*Obviously advertising is a major source. As an editor I work very closely with the advertising sales team. We sit alongside each other, and I actively encourage that. It's important that everyone on the team, no matter which department they're in, understands the editorial vision for the magazine and all the different initiatives that are being worked on.*

*Achieving a balance between editorial and advertorial for me is straightforward. I set out my editorial agenda for each issue, and they sell ads on the basis of it. I don't really feel I have to 'achieve' a balance. You have to be commercially aware – obviously – otherwise you don't have a business. I've seen a lot of fledgling magazines fail because they simply don't offer enough reasons for advertisers to come on board. But* Digest *covers loads of bases – motoring, food, travel, health and more – so that's not a problem for us.*

*I often play an active role in helping get adverts in, because if we exceed our targets then the size of the magazine increases – and that means more editorial pages. What I won't do is mislead or confuse readers. They should always know whether they are reading editorial or advertising copy, otherwise they start to lose faith in the brand itself. If your readers don't believe in you, then you are undermining the key reason why advertisers would want to use you in the first place.*

*Have I ever had to compromise on this? It depends what you mean by compromise! For example, our advertising department recently asked if we could do a Christmas-food special in order to pitch the magazine to relevant food and drink advertisers, and help grow our revenue in that sector. We run food editorial anyway, so I was happy to come up with an idea for a special, and advertising were then able to take dummy pages out on the road with them, and brought in some new business on the back of it. If anyone thinks that's compromising, then they'd better get out of their ivory tower pretty damn quick otherwise they won't have a magazine to run their glorious editorial in at all.*

*That said I've seen some horrors in the fashion and beauty arenas. I remember one editor (and no, it wasn't me!) being ordered by her MD to rewrite her beauty pages because a key advertiser wanted more copy on their new fragrance.*

*Other revenue streams such as brand extensions have always been part of* Reader's Digest. *In fact, the magazine itself only accounts for around 20 per cent of the business. The rest comprises a mix of travel, music, books, financial services, lifestyle merchandize, healthcare and more, and that's been the case for years now. It's a really good basis for a business, because you're not dependent on just one revenue stream, and as long as you keep developing new streams, then if some of the older ones fall by the wayside, it's not so important. But magazines, in general, are now having to branch out into other areas in order to keep their income up. It's essential. Whereas you would once have clearly defined media territories – film, books, music, TV, etc. – the boundaries are becoming increasingly blurred. TV companies have got websites, click-through purchasing and user forums; retailers have magazines and video and chat rooms . . . everyone's parking their tanks on everybody else's lawns. That's why newcomers to the industry need to be able to turn their hand to just about anything.*

*The impact of these extensions on the readership is entirely positive – it keeps the brand fresh in people's minds, and introduces people to it who might not have encountered the magazine previously. This is absolutely crucial for a magazine like* Digest *that's mainly subscription-based – we have very little news-stand distribution, so there are few opportunities for potential readers to sample us via that route.*

*Reader's Digest's most successful brand extension is the 100-word story competition, now in its third year. We have thousands upon thousands of entries, providing us with a massive volume of tailor-made content that works across all platforms. Readers absolutely love it, and so do we. Perfect!*

*The most important thing is to keep coming up with fresh, well-executed ideas that are appropriate to your audience, and keep advertisers and readers excited about the brand. Easily said!*

*Magazines will continue to evolve. You just have to look at why the industry body has changed its name from Periodicals Publishers Association to Professional Publishers Association. While there will always be printed magazines in some form or other, the future will be much more about the brand – which will exist on any number of platforms, some of which haven't been invented yet. It won't be long before we'll all be our own media centres, chipped up and able to transmit and receive info and read it off any surface at all – from a nearby wall, a blank sheet of paper. . . or even our forearms.*

*My advice to anyone wanting to develop a new publication is get your business plan checked first by someone who's been there, done that. So many magazines go under within the first few issues because they simply haven't got the distribution sorted, a credible ad base, or a clearly defined audience. The attrition rate for new magazines is appalling, and it's not going to get easier any time soon. At least now you can build an online following first to make sure there really is a genuine audience for what you're offering before you risk the expense of going into print. If you want to go into print at all, that is.*

## ACTION PLAN

Remember that the rule of any business is to generate a profit, this is what will make your magazine sustainable. But it is how much profit a title can make that will determine the level of its success. Therefore when working out strategies be diverse and don't think in terms of limitations.

**Task:** Develop your revenue strategies. Come up with at least three key strategies for each of the following sectors. Ensure that these are sufficiently diverse to not only build revenue, but also to establish the title as a brand.

1 Advertising sales.

2 Circulation.

3 Online opportunities.

4 Brand extensions.

# 10

# Production: Print, digital and online

Getting to the production is an exciting part of the process. There is nothing like the buzz of putting together that first issue. Seeing some ideas pan out while others change shape. The finished magazine probably won't be as you first imagined. It should have evolved as ideas were developed or discarded.

While the first issue may not be perfect – all publications take time to reach maturity – it must have a strong identity across all platforms from the start. With the shift from print to digital the focus is now on the content, not the medium. No publisher in today's climate can ignore digital. Print, digital and mobile editions plus a website will maximize market coverage. Each of those must be branded – having a consistent identity throughout.

Take risks with those early issues and make the content unique and don't mirror competitors. It is that unique identity that will ensure the title is a success. Today content is a two-way conversation with the readership. From the start a magazine must be interactive in all areas.

## A pilot issue

Before launching a new title most publishers put together a pilot issue to test on potential readers, advertisers and wholesale buyers. Before they launched women's lifestyle titles, *Easy Living* and *Grazia*, pilot issues were handed out to commuters at main stations in London. Waterloo Station in London is where I have picked up many pilot issues including these two, both of which also contained a money-off coupon to persuade the reader to buy the launch issue.

Pilot issues are exciting. Developed after months of research then tested on a focus group, it marks important progress. Finally the magazine is moving from concept to publication. Although it will probably have fewer pages than the launch edition, a pilot issue will be the same in other aspects. Therefore it must include a digital edition and website along with the social media pages.

Like any other issue, the pilot edition starts with the flat plan, which is a map of the issue's content laid out as a diagram of small pages on two or three sheets of A4. The four covers are placed at the top, followed by the inside pages – all numbered and labelled with content and creator. Pages are then crossed off once finished. Although most flat plans are done on a computer there is much to be said for printing out a few large copies and pinning them on the walls of the editorial, advertising and production departments, just as the creation of an old-fashioned dummy with pages stuck in can save many errors which screen-tired eyes can miss.

Those of you who saw *The Devil Wears Prada* will recall that the editor's constant reference was 'the book' as she called the dummy.

A pilot issue needs to reflect the finished magazine as closely as possible. While a publisher doesn't need to print the full-size edition, it should be sufficient to give an indication of the size and feel of the publication. Decide how many pages you want to produce for the pilot. Ideally it should contain about 32 + 4 pages for a saddle-stitched issue, or 64 + 4 if producing a perfect-bound as sufficient pages will be needed for the spine.

Next think about the cover. First impressions count so it is important to get it right. Think about placement. News-stand title covers are busy and need a commanding presence in order to sell. But if it's a B2B or specialist title, then covers tend to be less busy with fewer cover lines. Subscription-only or free magazines covers are also more likely to be less consumer orientated as they don't have to stand out from the competition on a busy news-stand.

If launched on the news-stand, the magazine's cover must really make an impact to stand out among the hundreds of titles on display at a supermarket or retail outlet. To do this a cover (pilot, launch or other edition) must:

- **Be busy:** previewing several articles, thus giving it a greater perceived value.

- **Have a strong cover image**: with great pictures, perhaps an exclusive story.

- **Great sells:** cover lines that make the reader want to buy the issue.

Testing is essential. One tip is to produce a mock-up of the cover for testing. The first test is to put it on a wall then back pace about 10 ft. Critically analyse how it looks from a distance. Does it make an impact?

Another good trial is to take the mocked up cover to the news-stand shelves of a retail outlet and place it among its potential competitors. Evaluate how sits among other magazines? Does it look professional? Will it stand out? If the answer is no, then it is not good enough and you need to revise it.

Most magazines produce at least three mock-up covers for every issue. These are then debated at the editorial conference as well as subjected to the distance test. A pilot issue cover should have gone through several drafts to perfect it. Remember a cover must make an impact on the reader. Get the cover right and the rest of the magazine should flow.

The content and layout must be perfect with a logical flow of copy with a few sample adverts to demonstrate the title's value to potential advertisers. First decide where your sample adverts will go, then look at the flow of copy. Ideally it should flow as follows:

- Sample adverts.

- Contents page.

- News page.

- A few good features including a cover story and an interview. Reviews, if appropriate, are also good.

- House adverts.

A pilot edition is all about promotion. It can also generate readers' contributions (aka readers' letters) via post, email and social media postings for subsequent issues. House adverts are important as these can promote the launch issue, website and apps that will be launched at the same time. Do use lots of signposting in the pilot issue both in the content and the house adverts.

A 'Hello' from the editor is traditional – a mission statement for your public. It is the beginning of a relationship with your reader, so use the greeting page to start the conversation. The editor needs to build a rapport with the audience. But also use it to build excitement about the content, engaging those early readers.

A lively contents page is imperative. This is not just an index it must also promote features and highlight cover stories. Remember that a pilot issue's content must reflect brand identity. All articles should fit with those editorial pillars set out at the development stage. Think carefully about the order of articles and define cover stories – both on the contents page and on the layout – so that they stand out. The magazine needs strong brand identity throughout.

Despite being free, the pilot issue is a showcase therefore should be perfect as it is selling the content of future issues to the readers. Any mistakes could cost dearly in terms of reputation – particularly if seen by potential advertisers.

When distributing the pilot do publicize it. Include posts and tweets about it on your social media pages. Get everybody – readers and advertisers alike – excited about the forthcoming launch.

# Editorial essentials

While the pilot is being distributed, the launch issue will be progressing. At the early stages editorial pillars would have been decided upon and the first few issues mapped out, so the launch issue will have a starting point. The next stage is to decide how much of the content will be written in-house and what percentage will come from freelance contributors. It is likely that there is already a file of potential articles, which has been building up. Now the first issue can begin to take shape.

First decide on structure. Editorial should make up around 60 per cent of the content, leaving 40 per cent for advertising. If you haven't already done so decide on the average length of articles. Next think about how the content will flow. Will there be specific sections, if so how many? While some sections are useful and provide a solid structure, too many can result in a rigid publication. Caution is advised. Ideally the magazine should flow as follows:

- **Covers:** Aside from the front cover (FC), the inside front cover (IFC), inside back cover (IBC) and outside back cover (OBC) are premium positions for advertising. Remember these adverts must be visual, must compliment the magazine and make an impact. For the digital edition these must be interactive.

- **Early pages:** Start off with a 'Hello from the editor'; this should be followed by an advert on page two then contents. Readers' contributions in the form of emails, tweets and social status updates should be next. Do include a 'postbag' for letters if the magazine has older readers.

- **Adverts:** Allocate some pages for adverts only. The balance between advertising and editorial is a publisher's decision. Remember that advertisers do not like being lumped together at the beginning and the end of a magazine. They call these areas graveyards.

- **Features:** Start with a statement article to lead. The cover story can either lead or can go in the centre section as a spread if the title is saddle stitched.

- **Sections:** These will depend on the sector and genre of the title, but ideally have no more than three.

- **Middle:** This could have a themed focus, particularly if it is a specialist or seasonal-related title.

- **End:** Use this part for less important features/articles, but ensure that the last page has a memorable theme such as a 'last word' or profile.

Identifying the cover story early is crucial. Ideally covers are planned long in advance. A front cover of any title – particularly news-stand magazines – is the focal point so it must have depth and be strong enough to make an impact. Don't forget that it will also need suitable picture opportunities.

Other content will depend on the magazine. Is it Specialized? Themed? Seasonal? Seasonal-related lifestyle titles are perhaps the hardest to work on as coming up with fresh content for every Christmas, Valentine's Day, Easter and summer holidays can be challenging to say the least. However, specialized titles offer more variety in this aspect.

Although much of the content will be written in-house it is important to include commissioned pieces. Using three or four freelance articles in every issue will add variety as well as a fresh perspective to the house style. Although budget is a consideration don't skimp on these. Pay talented writers well, who can deliver copy on time, as this will raise the quality of content.

Consider taking on a well-known columnist – someone who will bring verve to the magazine and hopefully a following of loyal readers. He or she won't come cheap, but should be seen as an investment, which will pay dividends in terms of both content and additional publicity for the title.

# Sub-editing

A talented editor and team of sub-editors who work well together are invaluable. A strong team will ensure great content and fluid style throughout.

Like many areas in journalism sub-editing has a growing job description. Initially the role of a sub-editor was to fact-check, make sure the copy was legally accurate, correct any errors and generally edit it to give the piece more impact as well a headline and stand-first. Once done, it could then be cut to fit the layout template. Today the role has expanded. As there are few production editors left, a chief sub may now be responsible for much of the visual aspects on the page too. This involves laying out the pages as well as subbing them. The chief sub, while managing the sub-editors, may also be responsible for sorting out the flow of articles as well as policing deadlines and getting the copy to press on time.

For Fiona Forman, chief sub-editor at *Full House!*, a weekly lifestyle magazine the role is becoming more diverse as a result of downsizing due to the recession. 'Sub-editors are now often expected to write articles, edit and write website articles as well as updating social media sites.'

In addition to subbing, quality control and layout, the sub-editor must also focus on signposting. This is about ensuring a prominent feature gets maximum exposure by directing the reader online and to title's social media pages.

Checking a page for errors is also a big part of the sub's day-to-day tasks. However, while much of the checking can be done on screen, it is essential to do a final check on the printed page. Before going to press, pages must be printed off and thoroughly checked for the following:

- **Inaccuracies:** including typographical errors in the copy.

- **Missing items:** lines on the page, captions and any other anomalies.

- **Layout errors:** such as wrong fonts, type sizes, first-line indents or paragraph spacing.

All of the above are easy to miss on screen, but will standout on the printed page – as many have found to their cost when reading the issue just back from the printers and about to go on sale.

While every magazine has a different way of working most sub-editors' sections have a basic structure. In Fiona's experience the sub's team is likely to consist of a chief sub-editor, who oversees all copy for current and future issues, a senior sub, as well as a sub and junior sub-editor. Working methods follow a similar lines on most publications. As Fiona explains:

Copy is pre-subbed in Word, then designed (laid out usually in InDesign) and comes through from art as an InDesign layout. It is then worked on, and passed through for second read. But if a sub picks up a layout, it will then be read by another member of the subs desk, editing marks are made and it is passed back. The subbing marks are taken in by the person who originally subbed it, before being put through for final read by the chief sub-editor.

Pages are often sent to PR's/lawyers for approval. After it has been approved and final read, it is given to the editor and then passed back to the chief sub with the final editing marks. It is then passed to pictures and art to final. Once sent to repro, we print out the final proofs, read the cromalins and make second versions of any files that need changing before we sign off.

Sub desks are very busy, with a lot of copy constantly coming in and out, so it's essential to keep close track of everything, and we have trays for copy coming in, copy on second read, and copy back from the editor.

What's the best way to ensure smooth copy flow? 'Communication, flat plans and job bags,' says Fiona. 'Sub-editors must communicate with all departments to ensure they know where a particular layout is – it may be with art, pictures, features or the editor at any time.'

Fiona also cites flat plans as vital production tools.

They are constantly updated with changes, new versions are given to all staff every week – sometimes twice a week. Once a layout is in, it is marked off on the flat plan then marked again once it has been finalized. Mini versions are printed for the dummy board, so that everyone can see what's been finalized and art can check for colours.

Not forgetting the dummy issue – printed pages of the current edition, which are usually kept in a file in the office for constant reference. 'All magazine offices have a dummy,' explains Fiona. 'The dummy is given to the editor, so that they can see what's been sent to repro and what's remaining.'

However, for Fiona, job bags are the most effective way to organize production.

These are plastic zipped folders which has everything in it for each layout – the original copy, the edited copy, the read-back (if it's a real-life story, it is read back to the person featured in the story, and they often have changes), the various versions of the InDesign layout, as well as the contact sheet from pictures with all the pictures printed out and descriptions for each so that the sub-editors can write captions.

Each job bag has a sheet on the front with the issue number, page number and the name of who has first read and second read it, and it is then signed off by the chief sub-editor and the editor, pictures and art. Without job bags, it would be complete chaos.

What makes a good sub-editor? 'A good eye for detail, excellent organizational abilities and an unflappable demeanour,' explains Fiona.

Needing an eye for detail is echoed by Stuart Nissen, group production editor at Reed Business Information. He cites one of the core functions of a successful sub as: 'Being able to cut a story and write a headline to fit the allocated space without losing or changing its meaning. It sounds simple, but doing it quickly and consistently – and without upsetting the author – is a skill.'

Stuart also stresses the importance of re-reading copy. 'Every publication on any platform benefits from a *second pair of eyes*. After copy has been cut to fit and checked for literal errors, the sub-editor should be able to take a step back and ask what is being said.

Are there any contradictions in the story? Does the headline match what is actually being said? Does the message go against received wisdom, zeitgeist or other articles in the publication? What is the relationship between the story and all other elements on the page?

Stuart recalls how he was shown a newspaper page which had a story about a 'paedophiles' paradise' above an advert for Euro Disney.

An editor may choose to be unorthodox, but the sub-editor should make sure he does not do so by accident. A sub-editor should constantly be on the lookout for inaccuracies and potential libel, but during that *final read* they can become a hero.

I find that most of the libels that almost get published are introduced late in the production process. The story has been checked and approved by the lawyer, editor and writer then someone will 'improve' a headline or caption, or position the story next to something inappropriate. The editorial team relies on the sub-editor to spot this and shout above the clamour and stress of an impending publication deadline.

Another necessity, Stuart explains, is consistency:

Ensuring consistency of tone and style. The imposition of house style across copy from multiple contributors and commissioning editors has become more difficult in an age of high-volume web stories, blogs and reader comments. However, at the very least, style should be maintained within a publication to support the impression of quality and authority in the minds of the readers.

House style starts with accurate proofreading to remove misspellings and grammatical errors. Beyond this, decisions need to be made: do you use American or British spelling? Do you capitalize job titles? Which acronyms and abbreviations need to be spelt out at first use? To what degree do you use contractions in copy? The list of decisions that needs to be taken can seem endless and is not helped by the fact that dictionaries and online guides are inconsistent.

Remember sub-editors are highly skilled, can-do individuals who are capable of running the magazine if need be and thus require careful management after their initial training. Therefore caution is urged. Any editor who exerts too much control over a sub will lose that spontaneity that comes from great subbing. While the editor controls the general content, style and tone, a sub-editor is hired not only for their ability to organize, but their flair for writing great sells (or cover lines), headlines, stand-first and captions.

A sub's life may be a tough one, but no other job prepares a person better for becoming an editor.

## Producing a print edition

Most of the content planning, establishing the house style and setting up of style guides should have been done at the development stage. Therefore the first essential task (with each issue) is to produce a flat plan – a diagram of the issue showing the four covers (FC, IFC, IBC and OBC) and the inside pages.

A flat plan is a crucial tool for production as it is a map of the issue. It will highlight sections, show adverts and allow the editor or chief sub to rejig an issue should an advertiser drop out, or a feature not materialize. Pages are crossed off as they begin to fill, the issue's progress can then be seen at a glance.

When producing *Writer's Forum* I used to highlight blank pages on the flat plan in yellow to ensure these weren't missed. Strange as it sounds in those final days before going to press the odd blank page waiting to be filled can easily be forgotten, causing havoc when on the final count it is identified an hour before going to press. Hence experienced editors will develop their own strategies to prevent disasters occurring near to the deadline.

Other such strategies include having filler pages ready. When nearing to the press deadline rejigs often happen. It might be that an advertiser wants to be on a right-hand page instead of RoP (run of paper). Or perhaps an advertiser has dropped out or a feature is cut from three to two pages. This is when ready made fillers can be a godsend.

Fillers can be in-house adverts or short articles that are timeless. But caution is advised with the latter, most articles have a shelf life. When using such as a filler page ensure the content a) fits with the issue and b) is not out of date. Ensure that these fit seamlessly in with the flow of content otherwise the quality can deteriorate.

The majority of the content will have been planned in advance. But getting last minute submissions from freelance writers can really boost the issue, especially if the material is time-sensitive. Most magazines contain people pages – profiles or interviews plus reviews of related products, services, books, music and films. It is those people pages that can make the cover.

For example on *Writers' Forum* a regular contributor was able to secure a last minute interview with a well-known author who had just released a new book at a literary festival. Despite being only three days before the final deadline and a whole section that needed a rejig, we used it. Leaving it till the next issue would have lost the currency of the story. In fact it was such a great piece with a cover-worthy set of photos that we changed our cover story that month at the last minute too.

Flexibility is a must in publishing as is the ability to nurture a pool of talented in-house and freelance writers. Do this and the publication will grow in stature.

Yet once a magazine is established it is easy to become complacent. But a good editor must never be complacent, particularly when it comes to content. He or she should be willing to rejig if the right story comes in – even if it is at the last minute. It is that element of surprise that is the key to creating a strong magazine – one that keeps readers hungry for the next issue.

# In-house adverts

These are a must. Useful in-house advertisements include the title's website, apps and digital editions. While non-essential adverts that can be used as fillers might include other magazines in the publisher's stable and gift subscriptions. Signposts towards such adverts are essential, particularly for subscriptions and a preview of the next issue. Not only are these core ads essential for every edition, they are also crucial for promoting readership growth therefore it is important to nudge your readers subtly towards these and ensure they have the maximum impact.

Remember advertising is a sales tool. In-house adverts must be designed accordingly to maximize their impact. Useful adverts include subscriptions and forthcoming issues, which should both be full pages. Five points to creating a strong subscription advert are:

1   **Sales:** The advert must sell the title in the long-term.

2   **Marketing**: Offer the reader some incentives for subscribing such as a free gift or exclusive weekly/daily email.

3   **Savings**: Highlight the discount over a year, i.e. free postage, save 20 per cent of the cover price etc.

4   **Branding**: As with all products associated with a title, the page must be uniform to ensure consistent branding. Do include the latest cover and layout in the house style.

5   **Inspire**: Build reader loyalty, this can be done by creating a sense of community among subscribers.

Promoting the next issue is also crucial. Here it is important to create a sense of urgency (they don't want to miss it) and excitement about the content. Do include the cover, as well as a preview of the content. The on-sale date is also a must. Ideally this and the subscription advert should be placed near the back of the publication as it is important to get readers thinking about the next issue – and how they will purchase it.

# Taking it digital

A digital edition of the magazine should not differ in terms of the quality of editorial. Here the focus is on the reader experience. The nature of digital means that it can – and must – be interactive. Digital editions are about readers being able to consume media wherever they are. That might mean using a tablet during their daily commute or a smart phone to catch up on the latest industry news while taking a short break.

So what are the benefits, how should your content differ and what are the best methods to produce it?

According to Ian Betteridge, a digital content strategist at Redwood, publishers should start with the reader experience: 'Digital content isn't just consumed: it's interacted with. This means you need to think of it as part of a total user experience, and optimize it accordingly.'

In Ian's experience the best way to ensure a high standard of content is by: 'Giving yourself time to understand your audience and their needs, then creating something which meets those needs. Don't rely on gut instinct – use real data and information to give yourself insight into what people want.'

Creativity has surged with the onset of digital, increasing revenue streams with several strands. Not only can digital editions be viewed on most Apple and Android devices or online, the publisher can now create a variety of brand extensions in the form of apps to increase revenue and user engagement. Also more revenue can be made from advertising. Digital adverts can be interactive, having video embeds or live web links, therefore enabling the publisher to increase the rates.

Databases provide another revenue strand as digital has taken away the anonymity of purchasers. Those wanting to buy either a single issue or a subscription now have to submit their details. The result is that publishers are now gathering a rich amount of data, which can also be sold (with permission) to third parties or used in-house for advertising or competition purposes. Be careful to observe the Data Protection Act.

The production process for digital is far more demanding than print, for which pages are created then printed. 'Production for digital content,' Ian explains, 'should be split into the following four phases:

1   **Understanding**: Who are the audience? What platforms do they use? (There's no point creating an iPhone app, for example, if the people you want to reach all have Android phones.)

2   **Planning:** Create the plan for the content. What is it going to be? Is it a regular publication, or a one-off? How are you going to promote your project to your intended audience?

3   **Creating:** This is the fun bit where you get to make your project. Depending on the project, you might create the skeleton of the site or app by wire-framing it (creating, effectively, a sketch of the structure of the publication), and go through one or more phases of design and building.

4   **Measurement:** Is the content working? Is anyone reading or using it? Can you adjust it to achieve more visitors, or to increase the time that

someone spends with your content? Keep working on the content – it's all about continuous improvement, and measurement is core to that.'

With print software choices are narrow as editions are usually created using Adobe InDesign. But according to Ian, digital requires a different approach.

The best software to use to create digital content is the software which allows you to achieve your creative vision, and that will vary from project to project. There is no single piece of software, which meets the needs of every possible project. The best approach is to think about the platforms and levels of interaction you need to achieve, and use tools which work well on those platforms and also let you achieve your vision.

However, a digital edition must contribute to a richer user experience. Currently it is an extension of your magazine. But this will soon change. With technology constantly evolving digital is set to soon become the core product, with print editions slowly phasing out.

# Digital production

When designing content for tablets there are numerous options – depending on whether it is for an Android or Apple device. As an example of best practice when it comes to producing digital, we have decided to look on creating content for the pioneer of the tablet – iPad as, at the time of writing, it remains the market leader.

The first point to remember is that layouts or covers, which look fantastic on a glossy printed page can look poor on a high resolution iPad screen. One solution, according to Hill and Lashmar (2013), is: 'To design your magazine or newspaper for a tablet first and then convert the design for the less restrictive print output, unfortunately this is the opposite approach taken by many former print publishers. This approach also allows you to think creatively about the interactive possibilities provided by tablet computers which cannot be replicated on paper.'

One tool that enables users to build pages using Adobe's InDesign Package (CS4 or later) then output as a digital app for tablets or smart phones, is Mag+. While the tools (or plugins as they are known) are free to develop an iPad magazine or newspaper, which can be previewed on your device, there is a cost to publish it. This can be quite expensive – currently around $399 per month for unlimited issues, but restricted to one app, published on one device.

When looking to produce a digital edition, online experts Hill and Lashmar (2013) say the following points must be taken into consideration:

- **An infinite canvas:** The shape of the template is a vertical rectangle – as iPads provide an 'infinite canvas' where users scroll text up using touch and swipe gestures.

- **Allowing rotation:** Users hold their iPad either in landscape or portrait mode. As an app developer you can insist that content is viewed in particular formats – this is particularly common for gaming apps where the view is most commonly 'locked' to landscape mode.

- **Image quality issues**: For print work images should be at least 300 dots per inch (dpi). Lower resolution images can be used as the iPad 2's screen is 132 pixels per inch (ppi) and iPad 3 is slightly sharper at 264 ppi.

- **Fat finger syndrome:** iPad users have problems selecting individual lines of texts with their fingers on a touch screen. Mag+ has a tool that allows for a selection of a 'hotspot area' – a larger area of the page that can easily be clicked.

- **Add sound or video:** Video, particularly when in HD, looks stunning on tablets – so try to include some. You can show movies as part of an app design layout or allow users use to click the video to go full screen. Video can be streamed from another site (e.g. YouTube). Streaming keeps your app file size down, but users need to have internet access to stream video over the internet. The alternative is to embed a video file as part of the page. This will raise the file size of your publication, but will mean users can access video off-line.

The key to successful digital production is to build interaction, look at the screen template and consider how the user will be viewing content. Overall the design should be flexible to enable the user to rotate the screen.

## Online and social media

Websites should be seen as an extension of the magazine directing readers to the website and vice versa. It is an opportunity to expand content and therefore should be treated as such. When designing the site first consider why readers need a website and a magazine? Answering this will give you a starting point to develop your online content.

While there will be those who visit the site but don't buy the title, many of your users are likely to pick up an issue. At the same time not every reader will go online. Yet the majority will or at least should be directed towards online content. With so many available platforms publishers have to be careful not to regurgitate material online or through their social media sites.

The ideal ratio should be 80/20 – that's 80 per cent new content online with 20 per cent duplicated. Any duplication should act as a signpost to direct readers towards the website. Signposting is essential to all extensions of the brand – be it social media, print or digital. Consistency with brand identity is also important so that the magazine's style, tone and layout are reflected.

With online content consider how articles in the print and digital issues can be expanded upon. Today it's about storytelling, giving the reader a rich experience. For example a feature writer who interviews a well-known figure will not only gett material for the print edition, but also for the online version. Subsequently they may record a video clip using an iPad or iPhone. By including a short video clip or podcast along with some addition copy to introduce it, the two versions are very different. The interview goes into the print and digital issue, but also directs readers to the website for additional content and possibly a richer experience.

Online is not just a one-way conversation so tools for encouraging readers to participate must be embedded in the content. Such devices can include putting questions near the end of the article and reader polls – both will encourage the user to engage rather than just read. The more engagement, the stronger the site – both in terms of advertising potential and opportunities to include paid for content such as a paywall or members' only area with exclusive content and offers.

As with print production, sub-editing is a crucial aspect on online content. But what are the main differences?

'When subbing online copy you must always be aware that your headline and stand-first will become separated from their original context when pulled into search results or aggregated on news websites,' explains Stuart Nissen. Search engine optimization is a trick old sub-editors have to learn.

Graphics will be stripped out for email delivery, leaving the picture-dependent pun embarrassed in its isolation. Concepts of search engine optimization have moved on from the early days of packing your headline and copy with key words. While you still need to be explicit about your subject, imagine your headline appearing in a list of ten almost identical headlines and add some quirk or turn of phrase to make it stand out from the crowd.

Stuart also advises staying focused on the core users.

Online subs must also be aware that many readers will come to a story from a search engine and may have no interest in anything else in your publication, or indeed your market segment, other than what they have clicked on.

Management needs to make a strategic decision on how far writers and sub-editors should adapt their style to cater for these strangers. I would always advise staying focused on the needs of the target readership, but view every article as a potential doorway to the rest of your content.

Here Stuart shares his digital subbing experience.

Sub-editors should always look for opportunities to hyperlink from one story to another or perhaps have a list of related articles at the end of the piece so that the reader is always able to go forward from your article rather than back to the search engine results.

Unless you are using scrolling text boxes, digital sub-editors will still have the same space constraints seen in print publications. However, online stories can be as long or short as they need to be. Sub-editors need to beware as writers will often allow quotes that would be edited for a magazine to appear in full online, whether they are relevant or not. Working on business magazines, the most common example I see is the 'delighted managing director' in the final paragraph – whatever their company has done, the managing director will tell you in a marketing-vetted quote of their delight and then repeat the preceding story, but in speech marks. Cut it, no one cares.

Writers may also be scared to write short online and pad out their news with overlong background information. Subs should pare it back to the facts, perhaps hyperlinking to related stories and sources of information.

The greatest boon for a sub-editor when working on digital and online copy is the ability to hyperlink to other sources and keep the copy tight.

Social media is also a core part of a magazine's online penetration and should be thought of as part of the overall package and work interactively. For example, article tag lines can be tweeted and re-tweeted to give the publication maximum exposure. Readers can perhaps engage with the magazine by tweeting about articles or their related experiences. Facebook can be utilized to upload reader offers to create a community and publicize events.

Whichever medium you choose – YouTube, Tumblr, Storify, Flickr, Pinterest etc. – they must work in conjunction with each other – and the magazine. For example you can publish tweets, or Facebook Likes of the day, week or month as well as readers' emails in the magazine. This is a modern take on the traditional readers' letters page.

Make sure your website encourages users to follow the magazine's social media pages too. Don't forget you can also use social media for in-house advertising such as promoting the on-sale date for the next issue or a subscription gift offer.

Providing social media content costs money in terms of the hours spent updating it by your editorial assistants or sub-editors. Therefore it should not only be the hub of your publication, but needs to be seen as a potential revenue stream as advertisers may be keen to include this in their package.

# Summary

As demonstrated, producing an issue – be it the pilot or launch edition – requires diligent planning and checking, as well as creativity. The title needs a consistent and vibrant house style that reflects the ethos of the magazine as well as a strong brand identity throughout.

Those important early issues are the start of the editor's conversation with the reader. To build that relationship the content must encourage that reader to participate in that conversation. Content should be a two-way flow – outwards to the reader, then their response. A sense of community is also becoming important and not just with your readers. Get advertisers involved too – particularly with social media this will further contribute towards that sense of community.

As explored in this chapter, sub-editing is a crucial part of ensuring quality content – whether print, digital or online. According to Stuart Nissen:

> Quality content should be a perfect fusion of relevance and accessibility. However, as we cannot control every variable in the publishing communication model, the sub-editor must fall back on their experience to strike the correct balance: identify the message that you are trying to convey, assess the reader and their context, and tailor each act of communication to bring them together using all the tools at your disposal.

Digital editions are a crucial part of the production. For editors who want to take a magazine digital, Ian Betteridge advises using the process as an opportunity.

> Don't just try and reproduce your magazine in digital format: think about ways that you can use interactive tools to achieve something that's really native to the medium. Once your publication is live make the most of the measurement tools you have. You can monitor what's working and not working on a daily basis: unlike print, you can find out instantly what the most popular parts of your magazine are.

Finally think about deadlines. In the early stages of production make sure that all the deadlines are achievable. Build in an extra 48-hours or three days depending on the frequency of the title. Contingency planning for time is as important as a financial contingency. When setting deadlines work backwards.

Start with the on-sale date, followed by the distribution lead times and the press deadline when the issue goes to the printers. It is wise to liaise with your printer to ensure that printing slots are booked for the next six months. Once the magazine is established they can be booked up to a year in advance.

Never miss the press deadline as this will disrupt the production schedule and could result in missing the allocated printing slot. This will then impact on your on-sale date. Miss an on-sale date and the magazine will lose a week on the news-stands – and revenue you will never recover.

The keys to successful magazine production are organization, structure and a good sub-editing team.

# INDUSTRY INPUT

**Martyn Moore, former editor and journalist for Emap/Bauer shares his production expertise and reveals those important lessons only learned from experience.**

*Today with such a high volume of output it is getting harder to produce a new title. Editors need to understand the fundamental differences between print and digital. Although there are a thousand vital differences between the two mediums, we can best prepare future creators by getting*

**Figure 10.1** *Martyn Moore*

*them to look at the similarities: appeal, engagement and accuracy.*

*People will tell you that print is all about beautiful pages and longer reads – a slower, more thoughtful activity with really good pictures. But I see beautiful images on my tablet every day. I've also seen magazine pages designed to look like websites with tabs at the top that don't do anything. At that point I wonder what is going on.*

*Digital does seem to be about immediacy, news, data, lists, info, buying, cheapness (or free) and quick and easy. It does these things very well and because everything can be updated cheaply, standards have changed. It can be badly-written or 'not thought through'. It also has a 'temporary' feel due to the fast-moving nature of media today. In fact, most digital content will be more permanent that its printed equivalent and website archives will be throwing up bizarre articles from 1998 fifty years from now.*

*Print is information going one way, despite the joy of the letters page. Digital is more about branded communication – a branded community having a conversation. Print is about reading stories. Digital is about watching and listening to stories.*

*McLuhan was right when he said the medium is the message and I don't think you can take a traditional 'magazine' approach online. Traditional magazine producers have, by and large, been hopeless at doing digital.*

*The most important lessons I have learned about content are that only two things really matter: relevance and clarity. If readers find it interesting and it's well-written, well laid-out and easy to read and navigate, you're on to a winner. It's amazing how many specialist titles struggle with this. Many seem to be edited by enthusiasts with dreadful magazine skills.*

*An editor encounters many problems when launching a new title. It used to be that the bigger publishers were only interested in selling more than*

*100,000 copies a month. That got you into the supermarkets, guaranteed a quick return on investment and kept the shareholders/owner happy.*

*A magazine idea will come out of somebody's belief that lots of people will want to buy a magazine about 'X'. This needs to be demonstrated.*

*Some specialist titles proved to be difficult to pitch. For example a monthly magazine about old cars may have a market, but that doesn't make it exciting. Another problem is the lack of meaningful research. Focus groups are useful but it's hard to convey the whole package with feature spreads stuck on boards.*

*And then there's the advertising market.* Charity Shop Fashionistas *might be a great title but it will struggle to secure ad revenue. This will put the cover price well beyond the charity shopper target market. Determination, self-belief, hard work, positive feedback and strong numbers are the only formula to overcome those niggling doubts and problems that crop up when launching a new title.*

*Producing a pilot issue that has the broadest appeal possible is crucial. This is to encourage sampling and convey the breadth of coverage. The design needs to work very hard to convey the navigation and style messages. The editor's welcome, all the stand-firsts and intros need to be 'on message', supporting the editorial and market position.*

*It should also be as close as possible to the finished item. Although feedback from the readership will feed into product development, this is a bit late for market research. Magazines such as* Heat *found their place in the world eventually, but re-invention six issues in is a costly and stressful strategy.*

*The reader should be in no doubt about the magazine's position on issues they care about. Readers look for magazines that are 'on their side'; reflecting their ideas and opinions and helping them meet their challenges.*

*If your new magazine is mass market then you just have to get it into as many hands as possible. Free 'samplers' can work, as can whole issues given away free or cheap with a sister publication. If you're adopting the 'free-but-paid-for-advertising' model, choose your distribution areas and pick-up points carefully.*

*If you are hoping to get into Asda, Tesco and Sainsbury's good luck – it's a battlefield with lots of great magazines among the casualties. For those going down the specialist interest route, look at where people enjoy that interest. Consider specialist retailers such as cycle shops, garden centres, motorcycle dealers, visitor centres etc.*

*Market the brand online and sell subscriptions. Start a Facebook page and Tweet about it. Buy a mailing list. Offer a free issue or two and capture credit card payments early. If readers like it, you won't have to worry about them cancelling.*

*What makes a great launch issue in terms of the cover and content? Something that looks bold and new and fresh and exciting, yet familiar and trusted and 'my kind of magazine'.*

*A relaunched photography magazine had the cover lines: 'Never get an exposure wrong again' and 'David Bailey makes love daily'. If that doesn't grab photo enthusiasts, I don't know what will.*

*Although I've never launched a magazine my best experience was as editor-in-chief when my division launched Digital Photo magazine and that was fun. It was probably less fun for the actual editor.*

*I also managed the team that launched the Max Power website. Fast cars and sexy girls on the exciting new medium that would make us all millionaires ... what's not to like? And I got out just in time, too.*

*I've enjoyed plenty of relaunches. Bike and Classic Cars were the best. Invigorated the content and saw big sales increases.*

*Probably the worst experience was running a new launch project for a big publisher and it failed to get the backing of the board, which chose a genuinely better idea. But my project was researched really well and might still become a reality one day. So the disappointment was huge and I can't even talk about it because it's still secret.*

*Actually, Bike was my best and worst. Although the relaunch was a roaring success, the team I inherited weren't up for it. I'd robbed one of them of the editor's job and that always has to be handled carefully. But making things happen through force of will or just doing them myself was the making of me as an editor.*

*My advice to an editor who is about to launch a new title? Don't plan too many cosy evenings with loved ones for the next few months. Revisit everything a dozen times asking 'Can this be done different or better?' The answer is always 'Yes'.*

*Proofread everything. Ask yourself what every feature does and how it feeds into the vision. Check the flat plan. Revisit again. Is it clear? Is it relevant? Proofread again.*

*Get the best deputy you can find – a great journalist who shares your vision and will make things happen your way when you're not there. Your deputy will think like you, write like you, care like you and, when her or his ideas are better than yours, will be the one to take over from you.*

*Remember a great new magazine needs:*

- *A visionary, fearless editor who knows exactly what is wanted by ...*

- *An audience hungry for the content she or he consistently serves up for them.*

- *A large and growing pool of advertisers queuing up to sell sought-after products to this hungry audience.*

## ACTION PLAN

Plan and produce your pilot as a print and digital issue. To do this you will first need to decide on the number of pages it will contain, how many copies will be printed and how they will be distributed.

Once these decisions have been made you will need to:

- Produce a flat plan.

- Have layout and editorial style guides.

- Sufficient content to fill the issue.

- Lead features and a cover story.

- Adverts.

- In-house ads.

Remember your pilot will be your showcase, so don't skimp on quality either in terms of editorial or printing.

# 11

# A successful launch

**G**etting to the launch part will have meant hard work with early starts and long nights peppered with many highs and lows. A launch always brings a sense of hope, but also anxiety. No matter how much a magazine has been tested there is always that doubt – is it good enough? Will people buy/read it? That is the real test of any new product on the market.

Assuming you have developed a strong title – presumably someone would have told you by now if it wasn't up to the mark – its success will depend on a good launch strategy. Getting it right is crucial. Skimping on promotion is not cost effective as the end result is likely to be reflected in poor circulation, while overspending will result in poor returns.

This chapter will focus on developing a careful strategy, which will bring results for the first issue and those that follow. Promotion needs to be ongoing. New readers must always be found. There is no room for complacency.

## A low profile

Most magazine launches are kept secret. Alerting competitors to a new rival should not happen until the last possible minute. Many publishing houses keep the development team small and communication tight. Others whose participation is in the wider circle will be told on a need-to-know basis.

Steve Hill, now a senior lecturer at Southampton Solent University, has worked in the industry for nearly 20 years. He recalls some of his favourite launch experiences – and the secrecy that surrounded them:

EMAP launched both *Zoo Weekly* (now just *Zoo*) and *Heat*. It always developed magazines under top secrecy and information was communicated on a need-to-know basis. *Zoo* was known internally as Project Tyson (after Mike, he had just bit the ear off Evander Holyfield. It was felt that was a story that would appeal to the desired *Zoo* reader.) It was particularly hush-hush as, of course, we knew that IPC had a weekly lads magazine in the pipeline – i.e. *Nuts*.

I worked on Project Geoff, a beginners guide to the internet. We called it Geoff as we had in mind a middle aged, white, male – the type of people who were really getting into the internet. Plans of which were leaked to *Press Gazette*, much to our annoyance. We never found out who faxed it to *Press Gazette* or why.

*Heat* of course when it started looked nothing like the magazine you see today. It started out as a UK entertainment weekly. It would be bought by males and females and contained quite serious investigative pieces about the industry. It was a complete disaster. I subscribed to it because we all got subscriptions for £12 a year! Mark Frith came on board (previously he was at *Smash Hits!*, another EMAP mag) and made it what it is today – *OK!* aimed at younger females.

When EMAP launched publications we thought of multimedia right at the get go. We launched them as multimedia brands. So *Heat* started out in paper format, but swiftly moved to other media platforms – web, mobile, radio and on TV. They wanted to be wherever the user is – platform neutral. Similarly, both *Heat* and *Zoo* have been licensed abroad very successfully – so you will find versions of both in South Africa, Australia and in other countries.

Not only do Steve's experiences reinforce the need-to-know rule to ensure new launches are kept under wraps, it also demonstrates how much a magazine evolves as the initial concept is researched and tested.

## Objectives and timings

With any product launch comes in-depth planning. Set out clear objectives. Be specific in terms of copy sales and publicity. What do you want to achieve in terms of circulation? What about new subscribers? Only by setting clear objectives will you be able to develop tactics to achieve the objectives.

Objectives should also focus on building the magazine's profile. Think long term, a campaign should be planned for the first three issues. Planning lots of tactics solely for the launch issue is a mistake. A magazine needs to reinforce its presence, in those early months when readers aren't used to looking for it.

Launches are also about timing. When choosing a good time – as with all things magazines – think about your target audience. Who are they? How will the title be beneficial to them? Finding those readers is the first challenge. Persuading them to buy and/or read the title is the second. More often than not – provided the magazine is a quality product – its success will come down to the timing of the launch.

Traditionally spring and early autumn are the best times to launch magazines. But given the current make-do-and-mend trend, a new craft title is likely to do well if launched just before Christmas or in February. Launch timings require careful planning, particularly if it is a specialist title. Research the events/social calendar, carefully. Are there any upcoming events that will provide an ideal opportunity with dates? For example an optimum time to launch a high-end wedding magazine was during the build up to the royal wedding of Prince William and Kate Middleton in 2012.

While an ideal time for a writing magazine to make its debut is either spring or autumn when national writing conferences or events are in full swing and major prize-winners – such as the Man Booker – are announced. This strategy is likely to attract aspiring authors who are all fired up. Missing such dates means a lost opportunity.

We launched *Writers' Forum* as a bimonthly on the news-stand in April 2000. The rationale was that it was a time when many writers would be thinking about ways to enhance their skills. Therefore timing the launch amid the hub of writing events and conferences, which take place in spring and early summer would maximize early sales. The cover lines on our launch issue reflected this including: 'Holidays for writers: special report'. Other major selling points were the short story and poetry competitions. Writers could win prizes and get their work published.

Clear objectives and timing are the keys to successfully planning a launch. Don't forget to check that there won't be similar titles launching at the same time. If this happens try to bring your launch forward to gain the advantage. Above all be prepared for all eventualities. If things can go wrong they usually do – so build in flexibility.

## Promotion opportunities

With any news-stand title some of the launch budget should go to in-store promotions to attract potential readers who are browsing. This is particularly important with lifestyle magazines, as promotion primarily needs to focus on in-store sales.

Getting buyers to pick your title instead of rival publications will be a challenge. Not only does your new magazine have to standout, it has to have a unique selling point. This could prove difficult in a crowded market, but on the upside at least retailers will know where to position it. If an idea has been well researched, a gap in the market should have been apparent and the opportunity taken. The launch campaign must highlight this gap.

If launching a specialist title, then the focus needs to be on that strength. For example a publisher launching a new food magazine needs to stand out in an already saturated market. Many cooking magazines have launched with a cover mount gift. Now they have also started to divide into niche areas of food such as bread baking and cakes.

Launched in 2010 *Vegetarian Living* filled a gap, as it was the only other news-stand vegetarian publication on sale. When planning the launch the publisher organized an in-store campaign, which included PoS (point of sale) boxes as well as mailshots to vegetarian and vegan groups.

Any gap on the magazine news-stand equals an opportunity. Currently a gap exists within the writing genre as – not counting *Mslexia*, which specifically targets female writers and focuses more on work writing – there are only two mainstream national titles on sale – *Writers' Forum* and *Writing Magazine*. It is clear from the covers that both of these are aimed at older readers.

The latter is now the market leader with a circulation of 22,000 according to BRAD, although *Writers' Forum* is not far behind with a circulation of 18,000. *Writing Magazine*, has a stronger news-stand presence and offers more in terms of content. Yet there remains a gap in the market for younger writers aged 18–35.

But is it a gap for a traditional print and digital model or just an online version?

Any quality title launched to fill this gap would have a good chance of succeeding. Content focusing on opportunities and technology together with a vibrant, carefully targeted cover reflecting its intended audience would stand out amid the competition on the news-stand. Add a strong launch strategy with some well-chosen promotional activities and the potential for success is high.

To work out the best promotional tactics focus on promoting the magazine's strengths in the right environment. For example an in-store promotion for a magazine aimed at young writers may catch a few would-be authors, but the core activity should target university campuses and utilize social media.

When planning promotion tactics the questions to ask are: Where do likely readers congregate? What are the common links? The key to any successful launch is to first focus on finding those who might be interested, then build the campaign strategies, which should focus on the following four aspects:

- Building the title as a brand.

- Developing a relationship with potential strategic partners and other stakeholders.

- Collaborating with those brands which will share the title's core values.

- Having a strong online and social media identity.

Working around these core strategies will ensure that PR tactics focus on those aspects that need the most publicity in order to succeed.

# What your distributor needs

The run up to launching a new title on the news-stands is a busy time for the publisher and newly appointed distributor. According to COMAG, a distributor needs up to 17 weeks to prepare prior to the launch issue going on sale. Therefore a publisher must be prepared before approaching a distributor.

Once a distributor has agreed to take on a new publication the next 17 weeks working towards the launch will require the action shown in Table 11.1.

To ensure that a distributor is able to get media buyers' attention in order to secure the best retail outlets, the company will need evidence that this title will be a success. This will entail thorough research in the early stages, as discussed in previous chapters. Potential sales targets should have been set after deciding how big the first issue's print run will be. The latter will of course depend on the budget.

Target market and segment must be clearly defined. Potential saturation should have been considered too. A publisher must indicate the market gap that a new title is aiming to cover. If the market is already saturated it is unlikely that a retail buyer would be persuaded to take on the magazine.

## Table 11.1

| Week | Publisher's action | Distributor's responsibility |
|------|-------------------|------------------------------|
| 17 | Produce a pilot issue, plus product information such as: target market, frequency, cover price, editorial position, sales objectives and promotional activity to support the launch. | Agree proposed launch quantity. |
| 16 | None. | Start pitching title to retail and wholesalers. |
| 12 | If appropriate supply pilot issues for USA sell-in. | Begin presentations to wholesale and commence export sell-in where appropriate. |
| 3 | Advise printers of confirmed print run. | Confirm print order. |
|  |  | Issue trade press release. |

According to a guide by magazine distributor, COMAG: 'A magazine needs to have some retail promotional support to provide it with additional visibility during the launch period. Examples of these include a preferred shelf position, a guaranteed number of facings, a specially mounted acrylic unit or "shelftalker" – a long narrow card positioned under the magazine display' (COMAG, 2013).

COMAG estimates that to be effective when reaching mass audiences the cost of such in-store promotions should equate to around £5 spent to every copy sold. But this was peanuts compared with the financial muscle put behind *Glamour*. However, this figure depends on the market a publisher is trying to reach and the type of magazine. For example with more niche titles, promotion on a smaller scale can still be as effective as mass publicity.

Other considerations the distributor will need to know prior to the launch include:

- Budgets set aside for in-store promotions.

- Whether the magazine is time sensitive.

- What the publisher has planned in terms of PR campaign tactics to promote the launch.

In the early stages not every publisher appoints a distributor unless planning to launch immediately on the news-stands. However, if taking on a distributor, make sure that you keep the communication lines open. Ask for regular detailed feedback from the buyers and act on it. Always negotiate promotional costs and fees.

# Planning a campaign

The objective of any magazine launch is to generate as much publicity as possible. Likely readers need to be told about the new magazine, as do potential advertising clients and reciprocal partners. However, it is crucial to plan the launch carefully. While it takes around six months from concept to launch, campaign planning should begin three months prior to the magazine's debut.

Creating a timeline with a three-month plan to the launch should be the first job. Once this has been done then promotional activities can be mapped out. Timings are crucial. Use the table compiled in Table 11.2 as a starting point.

**Table 11.2**

| Month 1 | • Scrutinize the content of the launch issue for promotion ideas. |
|---|---|
| | • Research related target groups both as potential readers and advertisers. |
| | • Look for sponsorship opportunities. |
| **Month 2** | • Develop launch tactics. |
| | • Present a pilot issue and target circulation to potential advertisers. |
| | • Contact all interested parties such as potential reciprocal partners. |
| | • Liaise with distributors for in-store promotions. |
| **Month 3** | • Implement launch strategy. |
| | • Gain the maximum publicity. |
| | • Incorporate social media tactics. |

Effectively, publicity should generate a buzz. Keep in mind its purpose is to raise the magazine's profile before the launch. How will you promote your title? The key points to focus on should be:

- **Budget** – a marketing budget should represent approximately 20 per cent to 25 per cent of your overall launch costs.

- **Launch issue** – ensure this provides an opportunity for publicity such as a high-profile competition or a well-known columnist or guest editor.

- **Effective publicity** – generate as much publicity as possible through advertising campaigns with reciprocal partners, in-store promotions, social media promotions and, if appropriate (depending your magazine), a launch party.

- **Adverts** – see if you can exchange adverts with non-competitive, independent magazines. For example with *Writer's Forum* we had a reciprocal deal with *Saga Magazine*. Also if you have other magazines in your stable do include a house advert promoting the new title.

- **Follow-ups** – a campaign shouldn't end with the launch issue, there needs to be the same momentum with next two issues.

Do look at potential threats and weaknesses in the campaign as well as the opportunities. Identifying as many flaws as possible will protect you against potential disaster, which in publishing means high losses. Include opportunities for free publicity or reciprocal deals for the launch issue such as:

- **Sponsorship through advertising of related events/trade fairs** – are there any special events that coincide with your launch date? For example if launching a new wedding magazine, then a national bridal fair would be an ideal opportunity to reach your public – both in term so potential readers and advertising clients.

- **Reciprocal deals** – offer event organizers a free cover advert in return for a stand and a mention on all their promotional literature.

- **Groups** – if the title is aimed at a special interest sector, be it hobbies or business, there are likely to be national and local groups, as well as related courses. All are potential readers and advertisers therefore must be contacted. Offer their members/students an exclusive deal.

- **Other opportunities** – often you can get virtually free publicity just by turning up at events related to your genre and handing out free copies of the magazine. Permission is usually granted by the organizers.

Time spent researching a campaign for the launch will be worth the effort. It may also benefit a publisher to team up with final year undergraduates or Masters students who are looking for an opportunity to work on a live brief.

To be effective, marketing needs to be ongoing. Ensure publicity is generated with every issue.

# A new launch model

Launched in 2011 *Mollie Makes*, the craft magazine from Future, is a prime example of a very modern launch. Instead of focusing on the print issue, the launch team first built up online content and secured a healthy following.

This strategy secured *Mollie Makes* as an online resource for crafters and those who want to create a homemade home, before launching the more traditional editorial model. In addition Future used social media to engage the audience, thus creating a sense of community. With an average age of 37 and 50 per cent of readers under 35 (as reported in inPublishing) *Mollie Makes* filled a gap in the market. Previously, similar titles had targeted an older audience, but with TV programmes such as *Kirstie's Homemade Homes* craft has become cool. It now appeals to a much younger audience, eager to save money and create something original.

The magazine and its unusual launch strategy worked because of two factors. First, at the time of this turnaround there wasn't a craft magazine that targeted the new age make-do-and-mend audience. Secondly, by creating a sense of community with online forums, how-to videos and social media input, *Mollie Makes* became a primary resource for its intended target market.

When the print edition finally launched it was big on style and mirrored the website, with scrapbook-style layouts featuring line drawings. Its easy to follow project instructions further enamoured the growing readership. Future has created a strong, sustainable brand across all of the *Mollie Makes* extensions.

Its success can be measured in terms of circulation. According to its last BRAD entry *Mollie Makes* has an average monthly circulation of nearly 50,000 with 10,000 being digital editions. Its Facebook page has more than 44,000 Likes and the Twitter account has 23,361 followers. According to InPublishing the title also set a new record for Future's subscriptions, achieving 3,000 subscribers before the second issue went on sale (Morgan, 2012).

Its digital editions are also doing well. So why has the digital edition succeeded alongside print? Well, perhaps there are many would-be crafters (like me) who find it difficult to understand written instructions. But with a tablet or website comes the possibility of visual demonstrations in the form of how-to videos to back up the instructions on the page. But more than this it is about a sense of finding likeminded people who share ideas and being a part of the conversation magazines now aspire to create.

Thus *Mollie Makes* is a good example of a new launch model. It maximizes technology to create that all-important sense of community. The lesson here is that it pays to engage your readers first online before investing in a print issue. It is certainly a safe strategy.

## CASE STUDY – *MIDCENTURY*

It was a gap in the market and a love of 1950s' and 1960s' furniture that prompted Tabitha Teuma to start her own magazine. Launched in the spring of 2011 *MidCentury*, a biannual publication, followed the traditional route of the starting with the print issue before developing an app and website. Here Tabitha shares her story:

Biannual publication *MidCentury* (www.midcenturymagazine.co.uk) came about through my interest in 1950s' and 1960s' furniture and architecture. I was looking to start my own magazine and I could see that, despite several US titles, there was no UK publication covering the subject. I wanted to create a quality magazine for people like myself – the content needed to strike a balance between specialist and coffee table.

I found a design agency with a personal interest in the subject, who agreed to design the first issue for a minimal fee, and the website was built for us by a friend. The print was paid for by advertising revenue: I promised to drop a significant portion of the print run through letter boxes in ABC1 1950s' and 1960s' homes in London and by giving out copies of the first issue at London's biggest mid-century furniture show. This event also functioned as our launch.

From here, the business evolved organically. Subscriptions grew as I increased my social media activity and the magazine appeared at other vintage fairs, and started a bimonthly e-newsletter to retain contact with our readership between publications. I found a distributor and it became clear that the magazine was best placed in specialist design stores. The hope was that we could convert a core group of buyers into subscribers with each issue.

There are no shortcuts to distribution and it remains one of the most time-consuming facets of the project.

For issue 02, we hired an external agency to sell our advertising, to allow me the time to focus on editorial and marketing. We commissioned a digital edition and app from a specialist company to coincide with issue 03, sold on Apple iTunes.

Issue 04 saw an end to the ABC1 drop. By now we no longer needed this as a bargaining tool for advertisers. We also decided to double the page count – it was clear that the biannual model was here to stay and it needed to be chunkier. The cover price was increased accordingly.

I started the business on a modest scale, without the need for a bank loan, and two years on, it's gathered a momentum of its own. Setting up a magazine has been a steep learning curve for me, but as my expertise grows and as I'm able to invest more time into it, I hope that *MidCentury* will become the go-to title for design aficionados all over the country.

Since its debut *MidCentury* has survived that crucial post-launch period and is thriving. Proving the right idea can be successful despite a minuscule budget and a recession. Currently undergoing a rebrand, *MidCentury* now has a combined print and digital circulation of 5,000. There is also full catalogue of back issues available as digital editions to reinforce this title's value as a collectable. While social media growth is slow – *MidCentury* has 2,054 followers on Twitter and 1,044 Likes on Facebook – a few well-chosen promotional tactics will no doubt enhance growth.

# Summary

No doubt this is the most exciting and stressful part of the journey to take a magazine from concept to publication. It will vigorously test your product and any flaws will not only be exposed, but magnified. But this should not dishearten a new publisher or editor. I have yet to meet an editor who doesn't cringe at that first issue.

A brand takes time to build, as does a team. Make the launch issue as strong as possible, then aim to improve each issue by 10 per cent – you will be amazed by the difference such small tweaks can make over a year when the magazine begins to mature.

What is the key to a successful launch? Set clear objectives, then work out the priorities from these. Overall the aim is to build a sustainable readership and achieve high advertising revenue targets. It is these two things that determine whether a magazine succeeds or fails. Therefore the core objectives need to focus on where to find both of these stakeholders – and how to attract them.

Budget is also a consideration. Try to secure as much free publicity as possible through reciprocal deals with likeminded partners, which share your brand's values. In fact you should look to build strategic partnerships as soon as possible. Do watch spending. Any investment in promotion needs to be carefully monitored to ensure that it is successful. Set one rule: that every promotional outlay – in terms of actual cost or sponsorship – results in a revenue opportunity, be it through copy sales or advertising space. And above all be passionate about your magazine.

# INDUSTRY INPUT

**Figure 11.1** *Jane Toft*

**Jane Toft, Editor-in-Chief of *Mollie Makes*, reveals the story behind the launch of one of Future's fastest growing titles.**

*Mollie Makes evolved: as publishers of traditional crafts magazines we were becoming increasingly aware of the emergence of a new type of crafter, younger and trendier. Helped by increasing use of social media and blogs to share ideas. They were crafting socially in pubs and cafes. There was a certain aesthetic evolving that marked out the new crafters, from typography used to the way a project was photographed. We knew there was no magazine available for these girls.*

*To test the viability of our concept, initial research focused on several factors. First was the marketplace for handmade goods. Searches here revealed that there had been an upsurge in the rise of craft cafes and workshops – 7.2 million people belong to craft groups who believed making things by hand is an investment. TV coverage such as Kirstie's Homemade Home series have inspired individuality, promoting an 'I could make that' attitude. As a result the high street has embraced a vintage/retro trend and many women are now up-cycling clothes, soft furnishings and furniture.*

*Next we looked at the market context and found that the sewing magazine market showed a growth of 15 per cent nationally in the sewing and knitting segment, and has grown, currently worth £5.9 million per year. As a genre sewing offers a wide market. It can be divided into two sectors, home décor sewing – step-by-step instructions to produce accessories for the home or gifts, and dressmaking – involving following exact paper patterns, high skill level.*

*Finally we considered retailer growth. Research revealed that Liberty was planning to expand their haberdashery department, while sales of John Lewis' own-brand sewing machines were up 24 per cent year-on-year. Added to that, HobbyCraft's profit was up by 67 per cent year-on-year and its sales up by 11 per cent.*

*These findings supported our rationale that there was an opportunity to fill the gap within the sewing magazine market for a home and fashion accessories title.*

*When deciding how the issue should look in terms of size and format we had gathered together various clothes brochures, books and direct mail, which had the aesthetic we were after. All of them were printed on matt paper. So it was a definite requirement to fit in to the look. Pagination was set at the standard 100 pages that our existing craft titles use, while the cover price again was the standard £4.99.*

*Unlike many magazines, Mollie Makes was first launched online as we established a blog initially before launch, to grow our audience so we hit the ground running with the print edition. We also set up Facebook and Twitter before the print magazine launched, again to grow an audience to raise awareness of the print product.*

*This strategy meant that when the magazine launched we had a group of brand champions who were more than willing to blog about us and recommend our mag. When we finally launched, the magazine broke Future Publishing's subscription record in the first few months. The first issue of Mollie Makes sold out and copies were fetching up to £60 on eBay so we knew that the magazine was going to be a huge success.*

*Prior to the launch our trade marketing team put together a strong presentation, which won space in WHSmith and all major supermarkets. Key elements of the launch marketing plan included:*

- *Print and online promotion across Future brands which totalled:*
  - *257,000 print readership.*
  - *70,000 unique online users.*
  - *30,000 craft newsletter database.*

*We also put a sampler (pilot issue) on the digital magazine shop Zinio and created a word-of-mouth buzz across fabric craft blogs, in addition to a very active blogging community. There was also a social media campaign to raise awareness and build loyalty. Third-party promotion with lifestyle magazines and the national press, while the PR campaign focused on driving awareness among key industry and mainstream audiences.*

*The most effect promotion tactic with Mollie Makes was to build our online audience prior to launch. With the digital edition there was a softer launch. We ran in-mag adverts for the digital versions but the most crucial factor was developing our presence on Apple Newsstand. We created a free container app – effectively a bookshelf for people to download their digital editions of Mollie Makes into. We were featured on the front page, which really helped our digital subs sales on iPad.*

*What lessons did I learn from the launch? Don't forget about the media. If I were to do it again I would ensure more PR via mainstream websites such as the Guardian, also place more quirky stories with PR to gain coverage in regional and national press.*

*My advice to an inexperienced publisher who wanted to launch a new title would be to have a very strong vision of the product. Ensure there is a gap in the market and a genuine need for the product – do your research. But above all believe in what you are doing and communicate that passionately. There will be many people along the way who will tell you it can't be done!*

*Lastly network, both in person and online to get you and your product talked about – and loved.*

## ACTION PLAN

Develop a launch campaign for your new magazine. This should include at least three of the following tactics:

- A launch party or participation in an associated event.

- Social media campaign.

- In-store promotions organized by your distributor such as PoS and shelf positioning.

- Reciprocal advertising deals.

- Sponsorship opportunities.

- Competitions co-organized with reciprocal partners.

Don't forget that the overall cost must be included in your total budget and appear in your financial summaries.

# 12

# Conclusion

**B**y the time you reach this part of the book your concept should have evolved sufficiently to decide if it is a viable prospect. At this point I would urge you to go back and read the industry input section at the end of every chapter. Our contributors have a wealth of experience – learn from it.

In the same way no two people who have witnessed an event will record exactly the same version, each of our contributors have taken different lessons from their involvement with new launches. No doubt your experience will also be unique.

Whether you are developing a concept for a final major project (as part of a degree or Masters programme), have a good idea you want to start up from home, or have the backing of a multinational publishing company – take ownership of it and be passionate. A new launch requires utter dedication. Yes, it will be more work than you imagined. But it also needs passion, a sound business plan, and money to get started. A good idea is one thing, developing it into a successful magazine is quite another.

If you are short on start-up funds take heart in Tabitha's story in Chapter 11. She launched *MidCentury* from her kitchen table. Two years later it has survived to become an established and respected specialist magazine, proving that even with limited resources a new title can succeed.

Determination is half the battle. As John Jenkins, my former publisher and editor of this book, says: 'There is always a solution to every problem – you just need to think of it in time.'

John has written a summary below of his top ten essentials for starting up a new title. It's the sort of stuff most people won't tell you about.

## John Jenkins – what experience taught me

No matter how much research you complete, or how experienced you are nothing fully equips you to set forth as a publisher. It's a little like training to be a Royal Marine commando. Scaling cliffs in the dark and exercises with live ammunition are nothing compared with the reality of facing an enemy determined to kill you. Most small publishers who have gone it alone have bought much of their experience.

Many have admitted that if they had known the amount of work and stress involved in becoming successful they would not have had the guts to try.

You might be a genius wearing an editorial hat, a wizard with new technology and an economist of Keynesian talent but you need to be adept at many trades and a master of six or seven.

Here are the ten essentials you need to know.

## 1. *A people person*

Top of the list must be handling people. Can you inspire them to share your dream? Can you choose a partner as keen and willing as you to bring a dream to reality?

Unless you have a partner you can trust you will never have a holiday or a moment's real peace when you are away from the task.

It is so easy to appoint directors and investors but absurdly difficult to get rid of them if they do not work out. Try to initiate a trial period. If the chemistry does not work end the association amicably. Divorce is a doddle compared to getting rid of a co-director. If you cannot trust a man or woman with a handshake, a 32-page legal contract is not going to solve any problems.

Similarly, if you strike gold in your choice of personnel introduce incentive rewards.

In the first two perilous years of my first launch we could not afford a staff Christmas party. But in a few months the picture had changed – so we had a festive lunch complete with turkey and Christmas pudding in July. The effect on morale was enormous.

You are also going to have to face some disappointments and setbacks. Key personnel will want to leave if offered a better job. Mistakes in recruiting will be difficult to solve.

This is where a partner is invaluable. When we launched Choice Publications, John Kemp and I fell naturally into the good cop bad cop routine, rather like one of those formulaic TV crime series. Although we occasionally had our disagreements it was always in private.

We agreed, for example, that if a disgruntled member of staff resigned or threatened to resign it would be accepted immediately. If a rapprochement was needed that would happen a few days later when emotions had cooled. If we needed to replace somebody we would wait until we had a better recruit to put in their place.

In a small operation involve all your staff in planning meetings. Some of our best ideas came from an annual weekend away with two brainstorming sessions as well as lunch and dinner to which husbands, wives, partners and girlfriends were invited.

If you tell your advertising manager's wife that her husband is a great guy who does a tough job superbly well it has the same effect as a bonus.

## 2. *A super salesman*

Can you sell? For once you put your own name on the door you have to be your own most dedicated salesman. What will help you in this respect is a firm conviction that you believe in your idea. Here are a few of the things a publisher must be able to sell:

- Your big idea.
- Advertising in tough market.
- Subscriptions.
- A job to an A-plus candidate.

But above all you must be able to accurately assess any situation. The secret? Knowing when to negotiate and when to stand firm.

## 3. *Cash is king*

Most advertising agencies are sympathetic to small businesses and in their heyday J. Walter Thompson and Collett Dickenson Pearce & Partners (CDP) taught me much on how to deal with agencies. But not all are so high-minded and you can find yourself waiting three or four months to be paid.

Nothing is more galling than to be running a successful business and yet be short of cash. If your terms of settlement are 'within 30 days of publication' then insist on it.

If an agency is dilatory about paying up then it is equivalent to theft. They are using your money to run their business. Most have been paid money in advance by their clients – so why should you wait?

If they threaten that you 'will never get another advertisement from us' record the conversation and pass it on to their client.

## 4. *Business angels*

Most business angels work on the basis of one investment becoming successful for every five they make. Some do better. Some do worse. The term comes from the theatre where there have been some spectacular returns and equally spectacular losses. If you had been one of the original investors in *The Mousetrap* you would have been living in luxury for years.

Any investor will want to know how much of your own money is going into the project. This is called hurt money. If he loses he wants to ensure that you share the pain. Thus you have an additional incentive to succeed.

They always expect your estimates of success to be overrated and just like bank managers they will add 10 per cent to your cost and drop your estimated income by another 10 per cent. Have your explanations ready, back them up with good research and figures. Don't forget a contingency sum.

They may well take your publishing credentials as excellent but what about the financial management? This is where a solid firm of accountants, who have prepared the figures, are worth their weight in gold.

What are your future financial plans? Are you going to build up the title and sell it to realise a healthy profit? Perhaps you are looking for a merger? Or do you see it as the foundation of an ongoing profitable publishing company?

A business angel or venture capitalist will want to know your exit strategy.

## 5. *Production*

A new publication cannot afford to make mistakes. The *Daily Mail* overseas edition published in Madrid ran the same page twice in one edition and the ill-fated *European* newspaper once published the previous week's sports results in its paper.

These mistakes could not have happened when page proofs were stuck up around an office or checked by a machine minder at the printer. Do not consider that because an idea has been around for years it is out of date and worthless compared with what appears on your computer screen.

Those who saw *The Devil Wears Prada* will have noticed that 'the book' was a bible. It had every page, editorial and advertising stuck into an old fashioned dummy and perused nightly by the editor-devil herself.

If this character drew on some of the habits of American *Vogue's* editor, Anna Wintour, I'm not surprised. Her father, Charlie Wintour, I knew as one of Beaverbrook's top newspaper editors and no fool.

## 6. *Do it in style*

Content is everything. I know that this is anathema to designers and others but the only magazine in recent years to add circulation regularly is *Private Eye*, the British satirical title. It pays no attention to design at all, is published on rubbish paper and sells purely on content.

Obviously, a lifestyle or fashion title cannot ignore the accoutrements of good paper and elegant design but fundamentally it is the words that matter.

Buy and deliver the best content you possibly can – for without that you have nothing. In fact buying the best writers can save you hours in editing. And why spend hours making up a style-book when *The Times*, the *Guardian* and *Economist* have theirs available for everybody?

## 7. *The core business*

It is so easy – particularly with peripheral activities gaining ground every year – to take your eye off the core business and work at the peripherals. Beware of this pitfall.

*Readers' Digest* was once a byword for excellence and then it discovered mass marketing. How the profits rolled in. But they ignored the title at the centre. It fell behind current requirements and did not evolve. Slowly the engine that provided the impetus for mass marketing faded as the circulation declined.

If you have a peripheral idea which is difficult to exploit remember the words of that great military philosopher, Clausewitz: 'Reinforce your strengths and abandon your weak positions'.

## 8. *Dismal Jimmies*

When you first announce your idea to start a magazine most people will tell you that it will fail. And each one will have a different reason. *The market is overcrowded . . . nobody reads magazines these days . . . we are in a financial depression . . . it will cost too much . . . it has been tried before.*

Such was the advice handed out to Frankel and Fraser who launched *Car Magazine* into an overcrowded market. They had a simple formula. They just aimed to make it the best magazine in the market. They succeeded.

Another title to defy the critics was *Slimming Magazine* launched by husband and wife team Audrey and Tom Eyton. They did not have a chance according to the dismal Jimmies. After all, every newspaper and every woman's magazine ran slimming articles so why would a woman pick up a magazine, which was tantamount to admitting she was fat?

*Car* and *Slimming* made millions for these brave entrepreneurs.

## 9. *Circulation*

If there is one area, which leads to frustration and bad temper it is circulation. Like banking in the modern world it has moved away from experienced operators and handwritten report sheets to computerized programs with boxes to tick. Do not imagine for one moment that you can leave this safely to your distribution company – even if you have paid for special display space.

If you are in a strange town go into every newsagent you can find and look for your magazine. Is it supposed to be on show? If not, why not? Has the newsagent heard of it? Have the staff in WHSmith?

A selection of stock replies:

- We don't stock it.

- There's no call for it here.

- It has not arrived this week.

- It is due out next week.

- They're on strike.

- Is it a hobbies magazine?

- Have you looked under puzzles?

I have heard all these replies and learned that there is no point in throttling the shop assistant. They are often badly paid and poorly trained. Just log the time, date and venue then pass the information to your circulation manager or distributor.

And if they do not react, change them.

I remember Tom Eyton scanning his distributor's sales report in the early days of *Slimming Magazine*. He was in a fury. The sale was 125,000 – a record. 'But it's not a big enough record to justify the effort and money we have put in,' he explained and promptly fired the distributor. He was right.

My first distributor for *Choice* fully backed my initial print order of 70,000 and promised that he would get the title out all over the country.

Some 10 months later I learned by accident that 30,000 copies never made it out of his warehouse. After five years hard work that circulation went up to a genuine 85,000 with 60,000 on subscription. By then we had had three different distributors.

Always remember that printers, distributors and retailers will support you when you are spending money on promotion because it's not their money at risk.

Try to peg your returns at a maximum of 15 per cent.

## 10.  *Contracts and printers*

When you ask printers to quote for a magazine bear in mind that they love this kind of work. It is regular and they can program their machines accordingly.

Make sure that each printer receives the same specification and add a rider that any quotation that deviates from the requirements will be disqualified. If you ask 12 to quote, throw away the three most expensive and the cheapest three. The dearest are probably pretty near capacity and will not want you unless there is a fat profit. The bottom three are probably desperate for work and will shove the price up at the first opportunity.

Check the ones in the middle. Go to the works. See what they are printing. Make sure they are specialists in magazine production. Ask to follow the copy through from reception to delivery. Have they got their own binding line? How many inserts can they handle? What reciprocal arrangements do they have with another printer in the event of a breakdown or fire? What are their terms for settlement? Do they have their own transport or do they use contractors? Will you supply the paper or will they?

If you accept their quotation you will be presented with 'their standard terms of contract', printed on the reverse of the quotation in type so small and faint it will be impossible to read without a magnifying glass.

Enlarge it and read it aloud before you sign anything. Amend it to include your standard terms of contract, the most important of which may well be that no deviation in price will be accepted by you unless you agree it in writing in advance.

## Magazines in 2020

It seemed fitting to end this book by considering the future. How do you see magazines evolving by 2020? Planning for the future is a must if you want your magazine to be sustainable in the long term. Therefore you must have a vision of how you expect the title to involve in the next five or ten years.

Below some of the contributors to this book have chosen to share their vision for magazines in 2020.

**Gill Hudson**, former Editor of *Reader's Digest*, says print will still have a future:

What will magazines be like in 2020? I don't have a clue. The pace of change is so exponential that most of us don't know what magazines will be like this time next year, let alone in a few years' time.

We're in the middle of a new Industrial Revolution, but the big difference this time is that change isn't a process of linear progressions, but one in which everything is firing off in every direction, making often unforeseeable connections, and spawning yet more change in the process. We need to stop looking for 'the answer' in an iPad or a smartphone in the hope that, having found it, life will get back to normal. Change is the new norm, and we have to learn to live with it.

Print still has a future but it is a limited one, and the days of sending your magazine off to the printer and saying 'That's another one finished!' are long gone. We are now in a never-ending dialogue with readers, and there is no finish. The future will be about targeted content, with a magazine just one possible incarnation of it rather than being at the heart of that content.

My concern is that behavioural analytics will become all powerful – everything will be tracked and measured half to death across every platform. Useful, indeed, but we need to make sure that great creative ideas don't get suffocated in the process. Nearly all the great pioneering magazine brands have that indefinable spark at their hearts that just won't sit still to be measured and calibrated.

**Bill Dunn**, Editor-in-Chief at Redwood, sees a future for high-end magazines:

Did people throw out their radios when TV came along? Did people throw out their vinyl when CDs became popular? Er, yes, they did. And in most cases, they made a huge blunder – because whenever a new medium for dispensing information is produced, it never negates the merits of the previous one. I still buy vinyl because I enjoy the warm sound it produces on my Rega turntable and Naim amp. Life without Radio 6 Music and Radio 4 would be much poorer. And I still love magazines.

The smell (largely glue, apparently), the way the paper takes the ink. That luxury is not available to the digital customer. Sure I can see the benefits of digital – I'm happier reading an airport blockbuster on a Kindle than hauling round a brick of 400 porous, poor quality pages. But I'm talking luxury. Weekly, throwaway mags morph quite happily on to a screen, but luxury content needs a luxury format – one that you'll want lying round your house, one you want to keep. So magazines will get more luxurious – thicker, fatter and more indulgent than ever.

A few years back, everyone wanted an app. Now people are getting more savvy. If you're producing content, you just have to work out what content fits which channels.

Magazines provide a quick access, shareable platform that people engage with totally without the temptation to flick between Facebook and Twitter and email. Our working and leisure hours are dominated by screens, so it's nice to give ourselves a holiday. If I'm not still reading magazines by 2020 I'll eat my *Carl's Cars* collection. Now there was a magazine . . .

**David Mascord**, independent editorial training consultant and university lecturer, thinks print-on-demand could be the answer:

There's no doubt that print is in decline in the magazine industry. But predictions of its imminent demise may be premature.

Some titles have already chosen to abandon print for two simple reasons. One, their audience has moved online. Two, the cost of print, paper and distribution no longer makes economic sense.

We know that online products work best for niche audiences and communities. But that doesn't mean it's the only answer in every sector. Some specialist markets will still demand print – perhaps because their readers prefer it. And because it's still the most effective means of delivering what the audience wants.

Audience preferences will vary, so why not print just for those who want it? A viable group of readers may be willing to pay a premium price to satisfy their print habit. In the near future some titles will publish limited print-run editions for subscribers who've already paid up-front. Or publishers will offer print on-demand for individual magazine issues – for the right price.

Frequencies will change. Publishing monthly, fortnightly or weekly no longer makes sense for some titles. The decision on how often to publish was linked to advertising trends and reading habits that have changed with the growth of multi-platform and multimedia. Some print titles will become bimonthlies or quarterlies. And brands will produce more one-shots published to exploit specific interests or to coincide with key events in the readers' calendar.

Of course few, if any, publishers now solely produce magazines. They're coming up with creative ways of delivering content in an environment that now encompasses print and digital. In 2020, for those publishers for whom it makes sense, print will continue to be a small but vital part of the mix: a niche product served up by publishers who know how to serve niches well.

**Fiona Forman**, Chief Sub-Editor at *Full House! Magazine*, predicts a decline in print, but rise of the freesheet:

Magazines have been hit hard by the recession. The men's market in particular has suffered, with just a handful of men's lifestyle titles left.

Women's weekly titles – an overcrowded sector – are also in decline. The competition is fierce and overheads high due to weekly print runs plus the volume of staff needed.

Strong, well-established luxury women's monthly titles like *Elle, Vogue* and *InStyle* are likely to survive the downturn. Aimed at middle class readers who can still afford to spend money on luxuries like magazines, they will undoubtedly survive into 2020. Although they will probably continue to expand their digital presence as an increasing numbers of readers prefer to read instant free news and features online.

There is likely to be an increase in freesheets by 2020. *Time Out*'s recent decision to make the publication free in September 2012 has paid off, giving a huge boost to their readership by increasing it six-fold to 300,000 readers a week. No doubt massively increasing advertising revenues, too. Free titles, *Stylist* and *ShortList* are also doing well in the weekly sector, and have a strong online presence too.

By 2020 I think there will be a decline in print, although it won't die out completely. Women's monthlies, special-interest titles and TV listings magazines like *Radio Times* and *What's On TV* are almost certainly going to weather the storm. More brands will be online-only, and we can probably expect more paid-for online content as well as digital subscriptions.

**Ian Betteridge**, Digital Content Strategist at Redwood, sees digital bringing in more revenue, but feels the current model won't work in the long term:

Initially much of the industry will seek to 'go digital' by simply replicating their print products using platforms like the iPad, giving readers the convenience of reading in an electronic format (and coincidentally getting rid of those pesky print costs). There will be a place for this – but it won't be the saviour of magazines as some think. Advertisers aren't convinced that ads in tablet magazines are worth the same amount of money as those in print, and readers don't see why they should pay the same for 'bits' as they do for 'atoms' if there's no extra content.

This will force publishers to be more inventive, so I expect the straight 'print replica' to die out fairly quickly in favour of something that's more than just a copy of an existing format.

And, at some point before 2020, the majority of magazines will get more revenue from digital activities rather than print. Note the use of the word 'activities', rather than 'editions': while most magazines will continue to have an episodic publishing model where new issues are put out weekly, monthly, or quarterly it will be the content and events which happen between these episodes which brings in the money.

That activity might include social engagement, through content sharing or even creating unique content driven by readers on social platforms. It might be live events, which have always been a staple for some, but which will assume more importance as advertising revenues diminish.

Print will become more of a statement about the magazine's brand rather than the biggest revenue generator. It will be the exemplar of what the brand means, who it's for: a luxurious digest which starts the conversation with readers, but isn't the end of it.

**Margi Conklin**, Editor-in-Chief of *Page Six Magazine*, predicts publishers will start to create a luxury multimedia experience:

Magazines in 2020 won't just be a series of articles and pictures printed out and bound together. Magazines will be an experience. When you say the name of a magazine, it will conjure up an entire brand, one that includes a TV show, online videos, a Twitter feed, a website, a line of products, a collection of events, and, yes, a series of articles and pictures printed out and bound together.

Traditional print magazines, if they're bolstered by a thriving multimedia experience, won't need to kowtow to the competitive scrum of the newsstand if loyal subscribers are already getting the brand delivered to their TVs, mobiles and computer screens. Some magazines will avoid the newsstand altogether. Wouldn't it be better to get your magazine from a concierge hand-delivering it straight to your front door? All part of the experience.

Magazine editors of the future will seek a way around the old sales model. They won't expect readers to find their product lying on a newsstand, surrounded by 100 others preening for attention. They will find the reader and create a connection. They won't think solely about storytelling, but focus on serving a reader best within the context of their brand. In the future, print magazines will survive but traditional circulation will cease to have meaning.

Forget how many 'readers' you have. The new question is this: How many people are you touching with the magazine experience – and how deeply immersed are they?

**Jess Arthur**, recent MA graduate and freelance journalist sees subscribers getting more free content:

The future of print magazines is not bleak despite being in the digital information age. All those years in the time of Web 2.0 online news was free and available but journalists and publications have realised the value of this copy and have changed ways.

An increasing number of online content is not free because more and more publications are introducing paywalls and pay-per-article initiatives. This gives a similar value to articles written online to articles printed. This is mainly in the news industry but I think magazines will take the same route.

Print publications need to be multi-platform with websites, blogs and social media. Online copy needs to be fresh but the content needs to compliment each other. Possibly magazine subscriptions will give readers free access to more content online. Social media is the tool that binds all the platforms together.

Magazine readers are loyal and they like print publications because the stories and writing feel like they have been worked on carefully and thoroughly. Print will not be phased out if the industry modernizes and keeps up-to-date with the digital world.

**Stuart Nissen,** Group Production Editor at Reed Business Information, feels there is a lot more work to be done on the publishing model:

Too many people enjoy reading print for it to die any time soon, however, it will never be the cash cow that it once was. The costs of print production and distribution combined with changing advertiser expectations will push up the price point for print magazines and many existing publications will decline and disappear over the next 20 years. Consumer lifestyle and leisure magazines read for pleasure thrive as retail add-on sales and are likely to have a longer life than most; trade magazines read for information are in the most precarious position.

Circulation will continue to decline on print products as digital natives become the majority in the UK and readers choose other sources of information. However, circulation has already been seen to rise on some magazines that have gone digital because of the global nature of internet-based distribution and the removal of print production costs, enabling reallocation of resources to creating quality content.

Margins have narrowed, but there is a market for publications with lean but expert editorial teams who put digital and online first and are primed to phase out print as reader needs evolve. As the large corporate publishers diversify into data services and consolidate around their flagship publications, companies that are willing to accept a smaller percentage profit and temper expectations of year-on-year growth will take over many trade and niche publications.

Authority is key to survival in a digital publishing environment. Readers will keep returning to trusted sources of information. If the publisher provides something of value, the reader will pay.

There is no room in the market for companies that use weak content as a coat hanger for advertising. Advertisers will increasingly demand metrics on open rates and click-throughs and adjust their spending accordingly. The few remaining free advertorial-based trade magazines will be dead by 2020 unless they become more honest about what they are doing and reposition themselves as digital product catalogues.

Currently digital magazines are essentially replicas of print magazines with multimedia bolted on. I expect a new format to emerge by 2020 that will make better use of the capabilities of the digital environment. Publications will likely be smaller in terms of pagination, but far larger in terms of the amount of content they provide. The divisions between broadcast media, publishing and websites will blur, with more multimedia incorporated in digital magazines and hyperlinks breaking the linear journey through a publication as readers follow information trails outside the container of the magazine format. An edition may also continue to grow after publication, with user-generated content, comments and feeds from social media dynamically populating areas of the magazine.

Magazines have always been aggregators of content, but this will become more overt, with links to stories in past publications, sister websites and third-party sources. The fact that the editor has chosen and vetted a source will have value to readers. A key lesson for editors will be: 'write what you know best, link to the rest'. Editors will also need to decide whether the written word is the best format for the content. For example, video may be best for 'how to' articles, while slideshows and info-box pop-ups allow the inclusion of far more content on a page and give the reader more control over what they choose to read.

The elephant in the room for all publishers is whether the magazine format still makes sense in a digital environment. A cleverly designed email with short summaries linking to online content will make more sense for some, while tablet-sized pages are a nuisance to read on mobile phones. I have no doubt that there will remain a demand for content edited, packaged and delivered to a defined readership daily, weekly or monthly, but something radical is going happen to page format and the positioning of advertising. When someone gets it right, we will all follow.

**Tim Danton**, Editorial Director and Deputy MD of Dennis Technology predicts magazines will be of a much higher quality:

Magazines face huge challenges over the coming decade, but challenge doesn't equate to a remorseless slide into the abyss. What we will see is further consolidation: sectors that used to support a dozen magazines will concentrate down to a hard core three or four. And those magazines are likely to get smaller, perhaps while the paper pushes up in quality to take advantage of print's tactile advantage over a screen.

We'll also see new titles, sectors and business models. In the past year Dennis Publishing has launched a premium magazine called *Cyclist*, on beautiful paper with beautiful photography, and it isn't designed to sell 80,000 copies per issue. It's there to hit its niche, to provide its target readers with a superb, immersive read they can't get online – or even on a tablet. And in doing so, it pinpoints a lucrative set of cyclists – the kind who buy £5,000 bikes – that advertisers would otherwise struggle to talk to.

I suspect we'll also see a move away from giving content away for free online. Some brands will move to that most trendy of things known as a freemium model: where you can consume a certain amount of articles online for free per month, but if you're a repeat visitor then you'll be forced to pay.

Other brands have already stopped putting their articles online. If you want to benefit from the research, time and skill of their journalists, you have to pay for it. If you don't believe they will, take note of *Web User*: it adopted this approach in 2011 and posted an ABC increase in 2013. And that's a technology magazine!

So yes, there are challenges. Yes, there will be some magazines that don't survive the cut. But by 2020 I predict we'll actually see, overall, higher quality magazines on the news-stand than we do today.

**Mike Goldsmith,** Editor-in-Chief of digital editions at Future Plc acknowledges technology has a big part to play, but thinks that content will always be king.

The future of publishing, as any quick Google search will tell you, is a subjective one. Book publishers selling direct to readers, authors not bothering with publishers, editors commissioning for channels not even invented yet, social media making the whole thing redundant as we're too busy keeping up with our friends to worry about anyone else.

My opinion? Honestly, no idea – but surely that applies to anyone and everyone else as, however insightful, all the above are purely guestimates based on the now. Current technologies, commercial models and marketing tactics inherently shape every Google result you click upon. The truth about iPads and Kickstarter and SEO and everything else the internet spews at you is that it changes constantly – so anything you read around the future of publishing can change. Sorry.

Then there's the other thing that changes, effortlessly evolving and adapting to whatever edge is bleeding at the time. The audience. Always thirsty for more, whether it's moving or still. Surely that hunger for opinion (whether it's shared and acted on or socially shared and mocked) is going to play a massive part in ensuring what future publishing has, whatever flavour it may take.

My five cents? I'll let Google deal with how Flipboard lets anyone make magazines (actually, it doesn't) and suggest two things. First, as well as laser-targeted content recommendation and the subsequent cookie-cut ads, I believe there will always be a place for surprise – that something new you only take a chance (whether on reading or purchasing based upon) on because of a trusted brand or byline. Secondly, the role of the retailer and our relationship with them is changing thanks to content.

Myself, I buy records from an online retailer based on editorial written by employees of the shop. That editorial is passionate, knowledgeable yet inherently biased as it's written by someone who wants me to buy something from them. But when you're an audience who wants to be sold to (me) and you've clicked on a niche retail site something not available in many other places (them), a little bit of enthusiasm goes a long way – especially if it comes with a streaming sound clip to let you make your own mind up. Is this the brave new hope that is content marketing? Don't care, as long as it's good and relevant – which I understand is the trick.

Trust in a brand or writer. Specialist content. Global audience. Retail interest. Willing audience of consumers. . . All this still sounds an awful lot like a magazine or website to me – but hey, don't trust me. I'm stuck in the present. With a lot of records.

# Summary

It seems all our contributors are in agreement – print is likely to survive, though perhaps not in its existing format. Nothing stands still, not in nature or life. When the future comes it brings change. Those who embrace it thrive, while those who fear it often fall victim to the old adage that it is better to do nothing.

When planning for your publication's future, keep an eagle eye on competitors, look at technological developments and adapt accordingly. Change for the sake of it is not good, but continual evolvement is – a well thought through development plan will make it sustainable and may be even take a new title into the next decade.

# Contributors

**B**elow are the biographies of all those who have taken time out of their busy lives to contribute to this book. They have carefully answered my in-depth questionnaires, responding with a wealth of knowledge and experience.

**Jessica Arthur** has contributed to the research of the Glossary and Resources pages. An MA Public Relations graduate from Southampton Solent University, Jessica is currently freelancing. Her experience includes stints on magazines such as *Good Housekeeping* and local newspapers.

**Ian Betteridge** is Digital Content Strategist at Redwood, one of the world's leading content marketing agencies. He has been a journalist since 1995, and is a former editor of *MacUser* magazine. In addition, he has freelanced for many publishing companies including Ziff Davis, EMAP, IDG and Future, contributing to a wide range of technology and business titles.

**Margi Conklin** is Editor-in-Chief of *Page Six Magazine*, a glossy insert in the New York Post. She first took the reins in July 2007, launching the title as a weekly publication before re-establishing it as a thrice-yearly title in February 2009. In addition to her magazine role, Margi is also Managing Editor of Features for the *New York Post*. Before arriving at *Page Six Magazine*, Margi was Executive Editor of *Harper's Bazaar*. An American, she spent most of her early career at British glossy monthlies in senior positions including Editor of *New Woman*, Deputy Editor of *In Style*, Deputy Editor and Acting Editor of *ELLE*, and Editor of *Celebrity Looks*. Margi holds a BSJ degree from the Medill School of Journalism at Northwestern University.

**Sara Cremer**, the CEO of Redwood Publishing and a visiting professor at Southampton Solent University, has more than 20 years experience in publishing. Her previous posts include chair of the ETCC (Education and Training Consultancy Committee), a part of the PTC (Periodical Training Council), editor of *Eve* and *New Woman* both global publications, as well as editorial roles in prominent titles such as *Men's Health*.

**Tim Danton** is the Editorial Director and Deputy MD of Dennis Technology. After leaving university in the middle of the 1993 recession, his professional life started at John Lewis on the shopfloor and he soon began writing for the in-house magazine. He went on to edit the Watford branch's magazine for over three years before joining *PC Pro* in 1999 as reviews writer, working up the ranks to become editor in 2004. He became editorial director of Dennis Publishing's Technology division in 2007, before becoming deputy MD of the division in 2011.

**Katy Dunn** is a writer and editor. Her background is in art and design journalism – she was deputy editor of *Grand Designs Magazine* and culture and architecture magazine, *Blueprint*. These days she writes about interiors, food, literature and the outdoors for a range of consumer and customer titles including *Sunday Times Style*, the *Guardian* and *Grand Designs Magazine* and is editor of *The Clarion*, a local magazine in the Chilterns.

**Bill Dunn**, now Editor-in-Chief at Redwood Publishing, has worked for some of the biggest names in publishing including John Brown, Dennis Publishing, Condé Nast and The National Magazine Company.

**Fiona Forman** graduated from Southampton Solent University in 2008 and is now Chief Sub-Editor at *Full House!* a weekly women's real-life magazine. Her experience includes three years as a feature writer and sub-editor at Oxygen 10 publishing working on a portfolio of women's lifestyle magazines. Fiona also spent 18 months working as a freelance sub-editor on publications such as *Glamour, InStyle, Company, She, Brides, Harper's Bazaar, Fabulous, Closer, More!, Prima, Time Out, Olive* and *Total Film*. During this time she also worked on customer titles for Net-a-Porter, Waitrose, Superdrug and Westfield.

**Mike Goldsmith**, Editor-in-Chief of digital editions, is editorial lead for delivering Future's specialist content and brands onto tablet devices. He headed the company's 2011 transition of its print brands to iPad, successfully bringing 65 titles to Newsstand for launch. Mike has spoken about digital publishing at a variety of conferences including the Publishing Expo, Specialist Media Show, Creative Week, news:rewired and digital summits organized by the PPA, Association of Online Publishers and Advertising Photographers of America. He was recently shortlisted for the Digital Editorial Individual in the 2012 AOP Digital Publishing Awards and Outstanding Team Leadership in the PPA Digital Publishing Awards 2012.

While at Future, Mike has been Editor-in-Chief of http://musicradar.com/ for which he was shortlisted for British Society of Magazine Editors (BSME) Website Editor of the Year (2009). In his two years on *MusicRadar*, he grew traffic from 100,000 to 800,000 monthly uniques and from 800,000 to more than 5.5 million monthly page views.

**Steve Hill** is a Senior Lecturer in journalism at Southampton Solent University. He has worked in technology and business journalism for more than 15 years and has written for *The Independent, Sunday Express, New Statesman* and *New Media Age* among many other print and online publications. He has also appeared as a pundit on the BBC News Channels, Sky News, ITN and numerous radio outlets. During the late 1990s and early 2000, he reported extensively on the dotcom boom and bust as senior editor at *Internet Magazine* then owned by EMAP.

**Gill Hudson** a multi-award-winning editor of a wide range of titles, including *Maxim, Company, New Woman*, and *Radio Times*. She has recently retired from her post as Editor-In-Chief of *Reader's Digest*, for which she won editor of the year award in 2011. Gill is also chair of the PPA's editorial training committee.

**Hazel Isaacs**, Business Development Director at COMAG, has worked at COMAG in news-stand distribution for over 25 years. In that time, Hazel has been involved in the marketing and distribution of hundreds of new and existing magazines, ranging from specialist titles with a niche audience to mass market products.

**Wendy Kearns** has worked in advertising sales for more than 30 years. After starting a *Devon Life* she went on to form The Space Agency, which now sells space for many magazines including national titles such as: *Vegetarian Living, Writers' Forum* and *The Self Publishing Magazine*.

**Patrick Knight** was appointed Strategic Development Director of MagazineCloner in 2012 having worked for the company since its launch in early 2010. With experience in all aspects of the business, Patrick has overseen the astonishing growth of the digital publishing start-up in the last three years with responsibility for the development of the technology which sits on all major platforms; Apple, Android, Amazon, Windows 8, Blackberry Playbook and online. Other highlights have included the growth of the Pocketmags brand and the launch of more than 1,900 branded magazine apps from publishers including Immediate Media, Key Publishing, Edisport Italia and Axel Springer España.

**David Mascord** is an independent editorial training consultant and university lecturer in journalism. He has worked as a journalist for business and consumer magazine titles across print and digital formats and is a former director of two award-winning journalism training companies. David has run training for magazine publishers include IPC Media (part of Time Warner), Reed Business Information (RBI) and the UK Professional Publishers' Association.

**Martyn Moore** was a journalist and editor at Emap/Bauer for more than 20 years. He started as a staff writer at *Practical Photography* magazine and then went on to edit *Bike, Photo Answers, Practical Photography, Max Power, Internet Magazine, Classic Cars, Practical Classics* and *Fleet News*. He now runs a film production business.

**Stuart Nissen** is Group Production Editor at Reed Business Information. As a Chief Sub-Editor his magazines have won several PPA awards and he has won the RBI award for editorial excellence twice. He was part of the team that designed RBI's standard editorial workflow and has been at the forefront of the transition to multi-platform editorial production desks.

**Mark Payton**, Editorial Director of Haymarket Consumer Media, has over 25 years' experience in specialist consumer magazines and websites. He works in markets as diverse as sport, motoring, technology and finance.

**James Pembroke**, Publisher of *The Oldie* (James Pembroke Publishing), owns a stable of more many titles including *Cycle, Odyssey* and *languages today* as well as national membership organizations and blue chip clients across a range of sectors. He has amassed more than 30 years experience in the publishing industry.

**Kate Pettifer** has worked in consumer publishing for over 15 years on titles such as *House Beautiful* and *Eve*, where she was chief sub. A world of travel writing, editing and subbing beckoned and Kate now freelances. Currently she is now travel editor at *Reader's Digest* UK and contributing editor for Smith Hotels.

**Jessica Strawser** is Chief Editor of *Writer's Digest* magazine. In her 12-year career in publishing, she has served as an editor with North Light Books, Emmis Books, Memory Makers Books and *Personal Journaling* magazine. During her career she has dabbled in marketing and public relations, and has worked as a freelance writer, editor and writing instructor. She lives in Cincinnati, Ohio, and can be found on Twitter @jessicastrawser and on the There Are No Rules blog at WritersDigest.com.

**Tabitha Teuma**, Editor and founder of *MidCentury* magazine, trained as a Paintings Conservator. She developed an interest in publishing in 2009, when she took on the two-year editorship of specialist journal *The Picture Restorer*. She founded *MidCentury* in 2011, working from her flat in the evenings and at weekends, and now also devotes two days a week to the project.

**Jane Toft**, Editor-in-Chief of *Mollie Makes* and *The Simple Things*, has more than 25 years' experience in magazine publishing, working with many major publishing houses in the UK. Her experience includes being part of the small editorial team that started Future Publishing in the 1980s. Experienced in launching titles, Jane was launch Art Director of Needlecraft Future's first craft magazine and was part of the original team for *Mollie Makes*. Other posts including a stint as Senior Designer at women's magazine *Candis*, and freelance Art Editor across Future's craft portfolio.

# Glossary

The magazine industry is constantly changing, but the terminology stays mostly the same with a few terms added with each advance. Below is an A to Z list of terms included throughout the chapters in this book.

All these are common industry terms that you will hear in offices around the world and are essential knowledge for anyone who wants to set up their own magazine.

This glossary also includes some general terms for your reference. Not all of these will have been mentioned in the text as they are deemed to be dated and therefore may not now be used in all editorial offices.

**ABC** Audit Bureau of Circulation, the industry body for media measurement. Manages standards that reflect industry needs, offers an audit service and services for media owners to report their brand performance.

**Advertorials** are adverts written in the style of a feature that provide information on a product or service. These must be labelled as such with the headings 'Promotion', 'Advertorial' or 'Advertiser's Announcement' usually appearing at the top of the page.

**Alignment** justification of the text, such as centre aligned, left aligned, right aligned or justified (aligns with the left and right margins).

**Apps** also known as application software, are downloadable apps for smart phones or tablets. Numerous magazines apps are available to allow readers quick and easy access to digital or online versions of articles, competitions, products or services.

**Assistant editor** looks after the whole magazine and assists the editor. They are responsible for generally overseeing the production of the magazine including articles and layout. But duties and status can vary from publisher to publisher.

**Back issues** previous issues of the publication, which can be useful for inspiration and referencing purposes.

**Barcodes** a Universal Product Code, also known as a barcode needed for all retails magazine sales. They help to track publications and data.

**Biannual** a publication published twice a year. These usually have a higher cost price or subscription rate.

**Biweekly** a magazine published every two weeks.

**Bleed marks** artwork such as a full-page advert or photo that bleeds off the page. The bleed marks are used to ensure that when the magazine is trimmed in the printing process that there isn't a white line around the edge of the pages.

**Business Angels** an informal investor, usually an affluent individual who provides capital for a business start-up often in exchange for convertible debt or ownership equity.

**Byline** the writer's name (and sometimes their position) is included in the article, either in a stand-alone box or written into the stand-first or above the piece.

**B2B** aka business to business is a term used to describe a business or trade magazine.

**Caption** a title or explanation for a picture. It can be underneath the image, alongside it or on top.

**Circulation** a publication's total net paid subscriptions and single copies brought. Subscriptions can include online.

**Classified adverts** these are small text or boxed out adverts on a dedicated page(s) usually near the end of a publication.

**Column** vertical division of text used in magazine page layouts.

**Columnist** a writer who contributes to a publication in a series and they usually write comment or opinion pieces.

**CMYK** Cyan Magenta Yellow and Black are colour formats that printers use when printing magazines.

**Contributing editor** someone who regularly contributes to the choice of articles or ideas in a particular issue of the publication. Usually this is a celebrity or well-known personality whose name is likely to attract readers.

**Consumer magazines** leisure interest publications aimed at a particular interest, for example cycling. The publication will feature information and entertainment tailored to this interest.

**Convergence** specifically linking the publication and content to other mediums such as radio, TV or a website.

**Copy tasting** deciding which freelance features plus news stories will be in the edition and a decision will be made about where it should be used and in what form.

**Cover lines** major article information on the front cover, which focuses on the top features and information in that issue.

**Covers** front cover (FC), inside front cover (IFC), inside back cover (IBC) and outside back cover (OBC). IFC, IBC and OBC are usually full-page adverts.

**Creative director** leads the advertising and design teams. They are responsible for the outcome of the design including photo shoots.

**Crop** cutting the size of an image or photograph. But beware as cropping can change the meaning of an image as well as enhance it.

**Deck** refers to how many lines the headline or sub-heading is, such as one or two decks.

**Digital edition** the online version of the publication, usually a website but could also refer to the app edition.

**Direct mail lists** a list of a publication's subscribers including their postal or email addresses, or a database to target potential readers.

**Distribution** refers to how a magazine is distributed. For example publications are usually distributed via retail outlets, door-to-door, subscription or target outlets.

**Drop cap** the first letter of a word at the start of an article, which is set to drop below the baseline by two, three or even five lines. The exact drop is determined by the house-style.

**Editor** the person in charge of preparing the content for publication. An editor may have overall responsibility or responsibility for a specific area. See also Assistant editor, Contributing editor, Editor-in-Chief, Features editor, Picture editor for some commonly used descriptions for specific types of editorial responsibility. As the industry adapts to working on content presented across many different platforms the titles and scope of editorial roles changes to suit the publisher's current needs.

**Editorial calendar** a plan of content usually for 12 months in advance, which should be broken down into story ideas, published content and content production. It is beneficial to have a paper and an electronic copy.

**Editor-in-Chief** oversees one or more publications, from authorizing the final drafts to heading up the staff and departments. Also represents the magazine at events and may develop reciprocal partnerships.

**EPoS** electronic point of sale: see PoS.

**Extended media list (EML)** a research technique which presents titles initially in groups of six, so that the respondent can decide which groups of six include titles that they have read and discard the rest.

**Features editor** oversees the features team and is responsible for checking that each issue is full of appropriate and interesting entertainment articles. Also helps with proofreading, generating ideas and delegating work.

**Flat plan** a plan of the complete issue detailing the content and advertising that will go on each page. A template is usually set up in Adobe InDesign and is updated throughout the production cycle.

**Freelance** a journalist or feature writer who is self-employed and works either from home or may do shift work at a publication.

**Ghostwriter** a writer who produces copy for someone else and does not get a byline or acknowledgement.

**Going to press** the date an issue is sent to the printers. Also known as the press date.

**Gutter** the white, folded centre area of a magazine or the space between columns.

**Haptics** non-verbal communication involving touch, so it is the look and feel of a magazine. However, this term can also be used to describe the title's basic production details such as number of pages, page size and the paper it is printed on.

**ISSN** International Standard Serial Number is a code that identifies a single publication and must be obtained before a barcode can be purchased.

**Leading** used for InDesign or Quark, this refers to the space between the lines of text, measured from the bottom of one line to the top of the line underneath. This setting will be dictated in the House Style.

**Masthead** title of the magazine and is usually placed along the top of the front cover and sometimes through the inside pages.

**Media kit** a promotional pack for potential advertisers containing information on the publication, its circulation and readership, plus advertising rates and copy deadlines.

**NUJ** National Union of Journalists, an independent trade union that campaigns for media freedom and rights of journalists. They help freelancers, permanent staff and photographers.

**Pen profile** this is a profile of your average reader. Information includes gender, age, household and marital status, education, employment, income, hobbies, aspirations and fears.

**PESTLE** (**P**olitical, **E**conomic, **S**ociological, **T**echnological, **L**egal, **E**nvironmental) this is an analysis of a company's environmental influences with the purpose of using this information to guide strategic decision-making particularly when writing a business plan. The assumption being that if the company is able to assess its current environment and predict potential changes, it will be better placed than its competitors to respond to changes.

**Picture editor** sources and sets out the images for articles or text taking into account the budget and the target audience. Also arranges photo shoots.

**Pitching** an email or letter selling a feature idea to the commissioning editor. Pitches are brief and usually not longer than three paragraphs. Some publications provide pitching guides.

**PoS** Point of sale is a display unit found near or around the checkout containing merchandise, in this case magazines. It provides a good advertising opportunity particularly for promoting new or relaunched magazines.

**Print run** the number of magazine copies printed each issue. This usually increases once a title has become established.

**Pseudonym** a name used to disguise a writer's identity. Freelancers often use pseudonyms if they do not want other publications to know that they have written for a rival title.

**PTC** Periodicals Training Council, part of the PPA. Enhances performance of people in the industry by improving the quality of training, encouraging new talent and giving guidance on best practice.

**PPA** now known as the Professional Publishers Association, but it used to be called the Periodical Publishers' Association. It promotes the industry, protects members through lobbying activities and offers advice as well as an opportunity to network.

**Press day** when PR agencies or in-house PR teams host a day where journalists can test and review new products.

**Press release** promotional material usually compiled by a public relations department of a company. Usually relates to a product or event, but can be summaries of news stories.

**Public Relations (PR)** a sector of industry that manages the flow and channels of communication between a company and the public, this can be in-house or an agency. Often supplies publications with information.

**Pull quote** quote from an article or interview that has been 'pulled out' and made larger to attract readers to the article. Often termed 'drop in' quote.

**Rate card** contains details of readership demographics, online and print advertising rates plus deadlines for advertising copy: see also Media kit.

**Rejig** moving inside pages to change the content flow.

**Running story** one that is developing, which could lead to further stories and will need updating and monitoring.

**Run of paper (RoP)** refers to the placement of an advert or advertorial, meaning it can be placed anywhere in the publication.

**SEO** Search Engine Optimization is the visibility of a web page in a search engine's results. The earlier or higher a web page features in the results, usually the more traffic it will get.

**Sidebars** aka page furniture is information relating to the article that is placed in a separate box or panel on the page.

**Social media** social networking sites where people can interact and share information. These include Facebook, Pinterest and Twitter. Magazines can use these to share content to increase readership, gauge public opinion and communicate directly with readers.

**Stand-first** appears after the headline and summarizes an article. Usually no more than 40 words, it is a lead into the feature.

**Strapline** a phrase used on the cover to sell/promote a magazine.

**Style guide** sets out the editorial rules and layout guidelines for the publication. The layout guide is referred to as the house-style. The latter determines the fonts, type-sizes, page layouts and decides on alternative spellings.

**Sub-editor** or Copy Editor. Improves and corrects spellings, grammar, format and style of text.

**Sub-heading** headings/titles that break up the main body of text. Sub-headings make it easier for readers to breakdown the information, particularly in lengthy features.

**SWOT Analysis** (**S**trengths, **W**eaknesses, **O**pportunities, **T**hreats) can uncover opportunities that the business owner is able to exploit. Understanding the weaknesses of a business is essential, while identifying threats allows the business owner to prepare in advance.

**Tagline** text explaining the headline and summarising the content in a sentence.

**Taster** text that promotes or signposts features in a magazine.

**Tracking** the space between each letter in copy and will be set in the house-style.

**Trademark** this is a name, symbol, figure, letter, word, or mark adopted and used by a manufacturer or merchant, or in this case the publisher to distinguish a product (magazine).

**UGC** User Generated Content produced by readers or the general public. Magazines (print, digital and online) or newsfeeds will sometimes use UGC to get witness accounts or 'everyday' perspectives.

**USP (unique selling point)** in terms of magazines is a description of why a magazine stands out from the competition; it should also succinctly summarize its best attributes.

**Vox pop** are interviews with members of the public to obtain their opinion. They are usually bite-size no more than 20 words.

# Resources

**ABC (Audit Bureau of Circulations)** authenticates circulation figures offering an audit and compliance service to check that data and processes meet industry agreed standards. Visit: www.abc.org.uk

**Adobe** is a manufacturer of software packages used to design and layout magazine pages, then turn them into print-ready pages, digital or online content. These include InDesign, Photoshop and Acrobat. Visit: www.adobe.com

**American Society of Media Photographers** find media photographers in the US. Visit: www.asmp.org

**Alliance for Audited Media (US)** is the audit bureau for media circulations. Visit: www.auditedmedia.com

**Alliance for Audited Media (Canada)** is the audit bureau for circulations. Visit www.magazinescanada.ca

**APA (American Press Association)** is an advocate for national and international news, freedom of the press and open government. Visit: www.americanpressassociation.com

**APC (Australian Press Council)** promote good standards and practice and freedom of expression. Visit: www.presscouncil.org.au/about

**AOP (Association of Online Publishers, UK)** is an industry body that represents publishers and broadcasters in the UK, who create quality digital be it for newspapers, magazines, TV, radio or online. Visit: www.ukaop.org.uk

**AOP (Association of Online Publishers, US)** is an industry body that represents publishers and broadcasters in America, who create quality digital be it for newspapers, magazines, TV, radio or online. Visit: www.online-publishers.org

**ASJA (American Society of Journalists and Authors)** is an organization for freelance writers. Visit: www.asja.org

**Australian College of Journalism** provides online learning and training for journalists. Visit: www.acj.edu.au

**Australian Commercial and Media Photographers** online resources for finding a photographer and acts as a voice for photographers. Visit: www.acmp.com.au

**Australian Health and Safety** find government advice and obligations for employers on workplace health and safety. Visit www.australia.gov.au/topics/health-and-safety

**Australian Securities and Investment Commission** contributes to Australia's economic reputation and wellbeing by ensuring that Australia's financial markets are fair and transparent, supported by confident and informed investors and consumers. Visit: www.asic.gov.au

**ASTW (The Australian Society of Travel Writers)** founded in 1975 and incorporated in 2011, it is a not-for-profit organization, dedicated to promoting ethical and honest travel, and the unbiased reporting of it. Visit: www.astw.org.au

**AWG (The Australian Writers' Guild)** is the professional association for Australian performance writers including film, television, theatre, radio and digital media. Established by a group of radio writers in 1962, the Guild has been representing the professional interests of Australian performance writers for more than half a century. Visit: www.awg.com.au

**Barclays Bank** has a great guide to help you write a successful business plan. Visit: www.barclays.co.uk

**Blogger** is a Google blogging tool, which works well for creative blogs. Visit: www.blogger.com

**Barcodes** PPA offer advice and they recommend GS1 UK for getting a barcode. Visit: www.gs1uk.org and www.simplybarcodes.net in the US.

**BRAD** set up a free listing to increase a publication's profile among advertisers. Visit: www.bradinsight.com

**British Guild of Travel Writers** a professional body that represents travel writers, photographers and broadcasters. Visit: www.bgtw.org

**Business Angels** will put you in touch with potential investors. Visit: www. angelsden.com

**Business Link, UK** now provides information on starting up and running a business in the UK. Visit: www.gov.uk/browse/business

**Business plans** a video guide on how to write a business plan can be found on Gov.UK. Visit: www.gov.uk/write-business-plan

**Business plan templates** are available from Microsoft. Visit: http://office. microsoft.com/en-gb/templates/results.aspx?qu=business%20plan&CTT=1

**Canadian Association of Journalists** a professional body for journalists providing information including news, events and code of conduct. Visit: www. caj.ca

**Canada Business Network** provides advice on all aspects of starting a business in Canada. Visit: www.canadabusiness.ca/eng/page/2856

**Canada Periodical Fund** provides funding and support for Canadians setting up printed, as well as online magazines. Visit: www.pch.gc.ca/ eng/1267303755421

**Canada Revenue Agency** provides information on business tax and fees. Visit: www.cra-arc.gc.ca

**Chartered Institute of Journalists** the oldest professional body in the world with useful resources and information. Visit: www.cioj.co.uk

**COMAG** a distribution company owned by The National Magazine Company and Condé Nast Publications. Visit: www.comag.co.uk

**Companies House** Where you can register a new business and company name. Visit: www.companieshouse.gov.uk

**Content Marketing Institute** offers practical advice on how to use social media, alongside a publication. Visit: www.contentmarketinginstitute. com/2013/01/strengthen-social-media-channels/

**Department of Labor** for health and safety advice in workplace for employers and employees in the United States. Visit: www.dol.gov/dol/topic/safety-health

**eHow Money** how to set advertising rates for a publications, for more guidance. Visit: www.ehow.com/how_7566066_set-advertising-rates-magazine.html

**Facebook** social media site where a group for readers can be created. Readers' opinions, surveys and links to online content can then be shared. Visit: www.facebook.com

**Forum of Private Business** provides tips on hiring freelancers, health and safety and making a profit. Visit: www.fpb.org

**Google Calendar** get a free online calendar so you keep track of the whole team's appointments and whereabouts. Visit: www.google.com/calendar

**Gov.UK** government guide to starting your own business. Visit: www.gov.uk/starting-up-a-business/start-with-an-idea

**Guardian Media** online news and comment on changes in the media, which also available in print the paper edition is published every Monday. Visit: www.guardian.co.uk/media

**HG.org (Global Legal Resources)** provides advice on US media law. Visit: www.hg.org/media.html

**Health and Safety Executive** has advice on how to look after your business and employees. Visit: www.hse.gov.uk/business

**Hold the Front Page** a good news website with events and resources for journalists. Visit: www.holdthefrontpage.co.uk

**HMRC (HM Revenue & Customs)** offers advice on setting up a new business and tax guidelines in the UK. Visit: www.hmrc.gov.uk/startingup/

**ICFJ (International Centre for Journalists)** offers worldwide training for journalists with online resources. Visit: www.icfj.org

**inPublishing** a UK publishing website with news, events and information services on publications. Visit: www.inpublishing.co.uk

**International Finance Corporation** information for starting a business in the US. Visit: www.doingbusiness.org/data/exploreeconomies/united-states/starting-a-business

**Intellectual Property Office, UK** find advice on protecting your content. Visit: www.ipo.gov.uk

**IRS Tax** has information and guidance on tax for businesses in the US. Visit: www.irs.gov/Businesses

**IRS Starting a Business** a US Government guide to starting a business. Visit: www.irs.gov/Businesses/Small-Businesses-&-Self-Employed/Starting-a-Business

**ISSN numbers** an ISSN assignment is free to request. Visit: www.issn.org

**Issuu** a free online publishing tool for material, including magazines, catalogues and newspapers. Visit: www.issuu.com

**Journalism.co.uk** is an online resource with news, events, guides and details training conferences. Visit: www.journalism.co.uk

**Journalism Education Association of Australia** an industry body for journalism teachers. Visit: www.jeaa.org.au

**Mag+** is based upon an InDesign plugin and made for creating tablet and smartphone apps without the need for programming skills. Perfect for consumer, corporate and enterprise apps. Visit: www.magplus.com

**Magazine Publisher** has a guide to starting up a magazine and for information. Visit: www.magazinepublisher.com/startup.html

**Media in Canada** news and events that are going on the Canadian media. Visit: www.mediaincanada.com

**McNae's** a guide to essential laws for journalists in the UK used in the National Council of Training for Journalist's law syllabus. Visit: www.mcnaes.com

**Media Week** news and events print publications, online, video and radio. Visit: www.mediaweek.co.uk

**MPA** (The Association of Magazine Media) is an industry association for multi-platform magazines in the US. Visit: www.magazine.org

**NCTJ (National Council for Training of Journalists in the UK)** delivers and accredits training schemes for journalists in the UK. Established in 1951, it is dedicated to providing a world-class education and training system that develops current and future journalists for the demands of a fast-changing multimedia industry. Visit: www.nctj.com

**NRS** The National Readership Survey has a wealth of data on magazine readerships. Visit: www.nrs.co.uk

**NUJ (National Union of Journalists)** an active, campaigning organization seeking to improve the pay and conditions of members and working to protect and promote media freedom, professionalism and ethical standards in all media. Visit www.nuj.org.uk

**Online Journalism Review, US** provides information focusing on the future of digital journalism from the University of Southern California. Visit: www.ojr.org

**PPA (Professional Publishers Association)** promotes the magazine industry and represents more than 200 companies in the UK, covering everything from consumer magazine publishers to business-to-business data and information providers and smaller independents. Visit: www.ppa.co.uk

**Pocketmags** digital newsstand where you can download publications off the internet for your laptop, iPad or smart phone. Visit: www.pocketmags.com

**PA (Press Association)** is a UK national news agency. Visit: www.pressassociation.com

**Press Gazette** a resource for industry news, events and resources. Visit: www.pressgazette.co.uk

**Reporters Committee** a non-profit association that provides journalists in the US with free legal advice. Visit: www.rcfp.org

**SATW (Society of American Travel Writers)** promotes responsible journalism and provides support and development for members. Visit: www.satw.org

**Society of Editors** works to protect the freedom of the media on behalf of the public interest. Visit www.societyofeditors.co.uk

**Society of Professional Journalists** provides professional development and journalism advocacy for members in the US. Visit: ww.spj.org

**The Australian Media** has a comprehensive coverage of Australia's media news and events. Visit: www.theaustralian.com.au/media

**The British Press Photographers Association** find freelance professional photographers. Visit: www.thebppa.com

**The Magazine Production Company** business that works with designing, producing and printing magazines in the UK. Visit: www.magazineproduction.com

**TrustMedia** is a Reuters training programme. Visit: www.trust.org/trustmedia/journalism-training

**Tumblr** a creative online blogging tool for images, and video. Visit: www.tumblr.com

**Twitter** social media site where you can keep up-to-date with journalists, news and events. It can also be used as a tool for sharing content on. Visit: www.twitter.com

**UNESCO (United Nations Educational, Scientific and Cultural Organization)** includes the UN's Code of Ethics and Standards for journalists. Visit: www.unesco.org/new/en/communication-and-information/

**US Copyright Office** provides impartial leadership and expert advice on copyright law and policy to Congress, federal agencies, the courts, and the general public. Visit: www.copyright.gov

**US Small Business Administration** provides guidance and advice on setting up a small business and a listing of available resources. Visit: www.sba.gov/content/follow-these-steps-starting-business

**Warners Group** a UK publishing company that also deals with magazine distribution and subscriptions. Visit: www.warnersgroup.co.uk

**Web Domains** set up a website, buy domain names and hosting. For the UK visit: www.123-reg.co.uk, in the US: www.domain.com and www.domain.ca for Canada.

**WordPress** set up a free professional looking blog. Also sells professional templates, hosting and domains names. Visit: www.wordpress.com

**Writers Guild** a union that supports writers across media and campaign for best possible pay and conditions. Visit: www.writersguild.org.uk

**WGAW (Writers Guild of America West)** is a union of writers who write the content for television shows, movies, news programs, documentaries, animation, and Internet and mobile phones (new media) that keep audiences constantly entertained and informed. Visit: www.wga.org

**Yudu** a multi-platform publishing website. Visit: www.yudu.com

# Bibliography

## Texts

Barrow, P. 2001. *The Best-Laid Business Plans*. London: Virgin Publishing Ltd.

COMAG. 2013. Your Guide to The Newstrade. PDF.

Hill, S. and Lashmar, P. 2013. Online Journalism: Principles and Practice. London: Sage.

'The Radio Times Promise'. 2012. *Radio Times*, p.143, issue 25–31.

Von Clausewitz, C. 1993. *On War*. New Edition. London: Everyman.

## Online sources

Apple. 2012. 'Apple Reports Third Quarter Results (2012)'. *Apple Press Info*, 24 July. Accessed 9/5/2013. http://www.apple.com/pr/library/2012/07/24Apple-Reports-Third-Quarter-Results.html

Baker, R. 2010. 'Cosmo extends brand in free student title.' *Marketing Week*, 5 Aug. Accessed 14/4/2013. http://www.marketingweek.co.uk/cosmo-extends-brand-into-free-student-title/3016730.article

Barrie, G. 2011. News:rewired Conference.

Batten, N. 2012. 'IPC to ramp up Apple Newsstand presence'. *Media Week*, 18 June. Accessed 9/5/2012. http://www.mediaweek.co.uk/news/1136818/

Batten, N. 2012. 'Stylist reaps record £1m ad revenues in September'. *Media Week*, 4 Oct. Accessed 14/4/2013. http://www.mediaweek.co.uk/news/1153459/

The-Beauty-Pages.Com. 'Media Kit PDF'. Accessed 25/3/2013. http://www.the-beauty-pages.com/Media.pdf

Blakes Marketing. 1998. *Magazines as Brands: Branding Solutions for Tomorrow's Publisher*. PDF. Accessed 27/5/2012. http://www.brandlabuk.com/Branding%20for%20Tomorrow%27s%20Publisher.pdf

BRAD. 2013. Accessed 8/2012 http://www.bradinsight.com

Candis Magazine. 2013. 'The Candis story so far'. Accessed 18/4/2013. http://www.candis.co.uk/about-us/the-candis-story-so-far/

Candis Magazine. 2013. Media Pack. Accessed 20/4/2013. http://www.candis.co.uk/media/download/id-media-pack-download.pdf

Chunn, L. 2013. 'Digital publishing is changing magazines, just don't call it "content" '. *The Media Briefing*, 17 Mar. Accessed 2/4/2013. http://www.themediabriefing.com/article/2013-03-17/louise-chunn-digital-magazines?utm_source=newsletter&utm_medium=email&utm_campaign=mobile

Cook, J. 2013. 'The Behavionomics of Paywalls.' *The European Magazine*, 31 Jan. Accessed 17/3/2013. http://www.theeuropean-magazine.com/953-cook-jonathan/954-online-paywalls#

Darby, I. 2004. 'Conde Nast sets date for Easy Living launch'. *Campaign*, 24 Sep. Accessed 20/4/2013. http://www.campaignlive.co.uk/news/223264/

Delicious Magazine. 2013. 'Online advertising opportunities.' Accessed 17/3/13. http://www.deliciousmagazine.co.uk/articles/online-advertising-opportunities

Easy Living Magazine. Media Kit. Accessed 20/4/13. http://digital-assets.condenast.co.uk.s3.amazonaws.com/static/condenast/EL-media-pack-2013vg.pdf

Entrepreneur.Com. 2012. 'Unique Selling Proposition: USP'. Accessed 23/04/2013. http://www.entrepreneur.com/encyclopedia/unique-selling-proposition-usp

Farey-Jones, D. 2012. 'Future's T3 claims 17,682 tablet circulation.' *Media Week*, 17 Aug. Accessed 17/3/2012. http://www.mediaweek.co.uk/news/1146089/Futures-T3-claims-17682-tablet-circulation/

Freelance UK. 2013. 'Why You Need A Business Plan.' Accessed 8/3/2013. http://www.freelanceuk.com/become/need_business_plan.shtml

Future Plc. 2012. 'T3 Delivers Best Ever Circulation Across Print and Digital Platforms'. Accessed 26/3/2013. http://www.futureplc.com/2012/02/16/t3-delivers-best-ever-circulation-across-print-and-digital-platforms/

Greenstreet, R. 2010. 'Q&A: Felix Dennis'. *The Guardian*, 8 May. Accessed 25/5/2013. http://www.guardian.co.uk/lifeandstyle/2010/may/08/felix-dennis-interview

Halifax Market Watch. 2013. 'Future Overview'. Accessed 27/3/2013. https://www.halifaxmarketwatch.co.uk/security.cgi?username=&ac=&csi=14123&record_search=1&search_phrase=FUTURE%20PLC

Hearst Magazines UK. 2013. 'Cosmo on Campus'. Accessed 14/4/2013. http://www.hearst.co.uk/Cosmopolitan/5-magazine.htm

HM Revenue and Customs. 2013. 'Pensions Schemes – Automatic Enrolment'. Accessed 7/8/2013. http://www.hmrc.gov.uk/pensionschemes/index.htm

Immediate.co.uk. 2013. 'Delicious Magazine.' Accessed 17/3/2013. http://www.immediate.co.uk/advertising/magazines/delicious._.html

Issuu. 2013. 'About'. Accessed 19/4/2013. http://issuu.com/about

Kelsey, L. 2012. 'Helen Gurley Brown: the Cosmo Girl who changed the world'. *Telegraph*, 14 Aug. Accessed 30/5/2013. http://www.telegraph.co.uk/culture/9475071/Helen-Gurley-Brown-the-Cosmo-Girl-who-changed-the-world.html

London Freelance. 2013. 'Feelance Fees Guide.' Accessed 26/4/2013. http://www.londonfreelance.org/feesguide/index.php

Mag+. 2013. 'Features & Price'. Accessed 27/4/2013. http://www.magplus.com/features-price/

Magazines Canada. 2013. 'Grants and Subsidies'. Accessed 26/4/2013. https://www.magazinescanada.ca/resources/grants_subsidies

Market Research Society. 2010. 'Code of Conduct'. Accessed 7/8/2012. http://www.mrs.org.uk/standards/code_of_conduct/

Marshall, S. 2003. 'Glamour – the big launch of a little magazine.' *InPublishing*, Nov/Dev 2003. Accessed 27/1/2013. http://www.inpublishing.co.uk/kb/articles/glamour_the_big_launch_of_a_little_magazine.aspx

Marshall, S. 2012. 'mm#12 Apple Newsstand advice from Future Publishing and Dennis Publishing' *Journalism.co.uk,* 25 Sep. Accessed 26/3/2013. http://blogs.journalism.co.uk/2012/09/25/mms12-apple-newsstand-advice-from-future-publishing-and-dennis-publishing/

McAthy, R. 2010. 'New figures suggest continued growth for US magazine advertising'. *Journalism.co.uk,* 12 Oct. Accessed 9/11/2012. http://blogs.journalism.co.uk/tag/publishers-information-bureau/

Mollie Makes, Facebook. Accessed 5/5/2013. https://www.facebook.com/MollieMakes

Mollie Makes, Twitter. Accessed 5/5/2013. https://twitter.com/MollieMakes

Morgan, C. 2012. 'Media Pioneer: Mollie Makes'. *InPublishing.* Accessed 28/4/2013. http://www.inpublishing.co.uk/kb/print/media_pioneer_mollie_makes.aspx

Mortensen, D. 2012. 'Making digital journalism sustainable'. News:rewired Conference.

National Readership Survey. 2013. 'Readership.' Accessed 9/5/2013. http://www.nrs.co.uk/readership/

National Readership Survey. 2013. 'Social Grade – Definitions and Discriminatory Power'. Accessed 26/4/2013. http://www.nrs.co.uk/lifestyle-data/

O'Reilly, L. 2011. 'Glamour rolls out doughnuts and dresses to mark 10th anniversary'., 2 Mar. Accessed 17/3/2013. http://www.marketingweek.co.uk/glamour-rolls-out-doughnuts-and-dresses-to-mark-10th-anniversary/3024038.article

PPA. 2013. Combined Circulation Chart. Accessed 9/5/2013. http://www.ppa.co.uk/marketing/abc/abc-digital-hub-page-july-december-12/~/media/PPANew/PPA%20Marketing/Research/ABC%20July%20December%202012/Combined%20Circulation%20Chart%20-February%202013.ashx

The Pensions Regulator. 2013. 'Employers'. Accessed 26/4/2013. http://www.thepensionsregulator.gov.uk/employers.aspx

Press Gazette. 2008. *So You Want To Be A Journalist?* PDF training supplement.

'Future closes two more gaming mags'. 2012. *Press Gazette,* 14 November. Accessed 26/4/2012. http://www.pressgazette.co.uk/future-closes-two-more-uk-gaming-mags

Princeton.Edu. 2013. 'Cosmopolitan (magazine)'. Accessed 30/5/2013. http://www.princeton.edu/~achaney/tmve/wiki100k/docs/Cosmopolitan_%28magazine%29.html

Ponsford, D. 2012. 'Full breakdown of magazine sales for first half of 2012'. *Press Gazette,* 16 Aug. Accessed 30/12/2012. http://www.pressgazette.co.uk/node/49860

Romenesko, J. 2010. 'Reader's Digest exhibit recalls the magazine's heyday'. *New York Times,* 22 Feb. Accessed 3/5/2013. http://www.poynter.org/latest-news/mediawire/100975/readers-digest-exhibit-recalls-the-magazines-heyday/

Turvill, W. 2012. 'New look for Easy Living in print and online'. *Press Gazette,* 1 Feb. Accessed 20/4/2012 http://www.pressgazette.co.uk/node/48662

The Vegan Society. 2013. 'Key Facts'. Accessed 23/04/2013. http://www.vegansociety.com/media/key-facts.aspx

Wilkerson, B. 2009. 'Age Concern England to close Heyday'. *Marketing Magazine,* 9 Feb. Accessed 26/4/2013. http://www.marketingmagazine.co.uk/news/879630/Age-Concern-England-close-Heyday/

# Index